UNSEASONABLE

UNSEASONABLE

CLIMATE CHANGE
IN GLOBAL LITERATURES

SARAH DIMICK

Columbia University Press   *New York*

Columbia University Press
Publishers Since 1893
New York   Chichester, West Sussex

Copyright © 2024 Columbia University Press
All rights reserved

Library of Congress Cataloging-in-Publication Data
Names: Dimick, Sarah, author.
Title: Unseasonable : climate change in global literatures / Sarah Dimick.
Description: New York : Columbia University Press, 2024. | Includes bibliographical references and index.
Identifiers: LCCN 2024022408 (print) | LCCN 2024022409 (ebook) | ISBN 9780231209243 (hardback) | ISBN 9780231209250 (trade paperback) | ISBN 9780231557849 (ebook)
Subjects: LCSH: Climatic changes in literature. | Seasons in literature. | Ecocriticism.
Classification: LCC PN56.C612 D56 2024 (print) | LCC PN56.C612 (ebook) | DDC 809.9336—dc23/eng/20240606

Cover design: Chang Jae Lee
Cover image: Saeed Khan/AFP © Getty Images

Climates are shaped by what we have read of them.

—DEREK WALCOTT

CONTENTS

Introduction: Climate Arrhythmias 1

PHENOLOGICAL LITERATURE AND MEDIA

1 Phenological Writing and the Composite Year 31

2 Repeat Photography During the Great Acceleration 67

UNSEASONABLE NOVELS

3 Urban Phenology and Monsoon Realism 99

4 Climate Fiction and the Unprecedented 129

RHYTHM AND ENVIRONMENTAL PRACTICE

5 Occasional Poetry in Stressed Times 163

6. Keeping Time 199

Epilogue: More Habits Than Dreams 229

Acknowledgments 235
Notes 239
Bibliography 273
Index 297

UNSEASONABLE

INTRODUCTION
Climate Arrhythmias

Better to forget what once was normal, the way season followed season, with a temperate charm only the poets appreciated," the writer Zadie Smith mused back in 2014. That April, when her essay "Elegy for a Country's Seasons" appeared in the *New York Review of Books*, it voiced the nascent suspicion that climate change was altering the cadences of seasonal time. There it was, that gnawing sense that habitats are pulsing offbeat—those tomatoes on the fire escape that withered after just a flower or two, those bats that emerged from the underpass during that strange warm spell last winter—there they were, linked to climate change in print.

"We always knew we could do a great deal of damage to this planet," Smith admits, "but even the most hubristic among us had not imagined we would ever be able to fundamentally change its rhythms." Now, as the world warms and environmental time becomes disordered—as pollen clouds the air weeks earlier, chafing breath; as monsoons grow erratic and city pipes run dry; as the migrations of birds and insects disconnect from the moments of ripeness that sustain them—climate change produces what I call "climate arrhythmias": environmental pulses experienced as disturbingly premature or delayed, pronounced or absent. By climate arrhythmias,

I mean times that are off, seasonal cadences gone haywire, temporal misalignments that fray connections and threaten survival. I mean experiences that strike us as unseasonable.

Climate arrhythmias can diminish beauty, touching even communities that remain sheltered as the world heats. Smith recounts wandering "into an Italian garden in early July, with its owner, a woman in her eighties, and upon seeing the scorched yellow earth and withered roses," hearing the elderly woman's confession: "*in all my years I've never seen anything like it.*" Backyard roses wilting at peak season are a small aesthetic deprivation, perhaps—as Smith admits—not "worth mentioning." And yet, those brown-edged and brittle petals remain an "intimate loss," a broken relation between an elderly gardener and her vines. I am interested in climate arrhythmias' capacity to reverberate even within the realms of what Lisa Sun-Hee Park and David Naguib Pellow call "environmental privilege," unsettling and occasionally galvanizing those who might otherwise remain unmoved.[1] Thinking about how wrenched time throbs in pastoral scenes and within the nature writing associated with these landscapes is to track how climate change bruises time even for the globe's affluent and powerful.

But as climate arrhythmias wither backyard roses, they also endanger the people exposed to the harshest or most disjointed beats of this overheated world. Rhythm may be an aesthetic force, a compelling and beautiful pulse, but it is also a condition of continuance—a steady heartbeat and the regular surge of sap sustain myriad lives. Rhythms determine what flourishes and what perishes. In places subjected to poverty, especially in communities bearing the brunt of colonialism and racial capitalism, climate arrhythmias exacerbate precarity. Smith, who began her life in a London housing project and grew up as part of the city's diasporic Caribbean community, is well aware that in Jamaica, "the ever more frequent tropical depressions, storms, hurricanes, droughts, and landslides, do not fall, for Jamaicans, in the category of ontological argument." Instead, for those across the globe without access to air conditioning, the prolonged pulse of a heat wave can produce heart palpitations and emergency room bills. For those lacking reliable transportation, an accentuated fire season becomes a matter of life and death. "The weather has changed, is changing," Smith writes, and "livelihoods and actual lives... are being lost." Climate arrhythmias are most pronounced for people left out to dry—by states, corporations, and hardened histories—and in this sense, the unseasonable generates and aggravates climate injustices. Arrhythmias threaten survival.

By arrhythmia, I mean an achingly absent rhythm, the *want* of a known pulse. Climate arrhythmias occur in relation to the loss of familiar environmental rhythms. They are times and timings that feel unanticipated—they are only detectable, by definition, in relation to a previously established cadence. Here for instance, is Smith, intimating that seasonal rhythms persist in the memories of her environmentally privileged neighbors, even as the weather grows subtly irregular:

> What "used to be" is painful to remember. Forcing the spike of an unlit firework into the cold, dry ground. Admiring the frost on the holly berries, en route to school. Taking a long, restorative walk on Boxing Day in the winter glare. Whole football pitches crunching underfoot. A bit of sun on Pancake Day; a little more for the Grand National. Chilly April showers, Wimbledon warmth. July weddings that could trust in fine weather. The distinct possibility of a Glastonbury sunburn. At least, we say to each other, at least August is still reliably ablaze—in Cornwall if not at carnival.

As Smith's pastoral elegy progresses through the year, moving from fall towards the height of summer, it chronicles the entwined environmental and social pulses that continue like a ghostly metronome beneath the unpredictability of England's anthropogenic seasons. Expectations do not change as quickly as environmental time alters, and the pull of the climate's previous forms persists.

"Every country," Smith suggests, "has its own version of this local sadness," each place and community its own precarious beats. Beyond the strategic pastoralism of Smith's elegy, bent rhythms turn grave. In northern Iraq, Harriet Rix, a landmine detonation expert, describes how flares from nearby oil wells coat the bark of Lalish's oak trees with soot, darkening the branches that hold stork nests each March. Despite threats of drones and airstrikes, which rise and fall in rhythm with the mist, Rix reports that Kurds still "harvest acorns, normally in the last week of October.... This year the harvest was late, in the third week of November, and there were few acorns, perhaps because of the drought or the late spring."[2] And in Quilinco, Guatemala, where *canículas*—dry spells—linger, the seed bank director Esvin Rocael López explains that no one knows when to plant maize. For years, April seedings were followed by rain, but the pulse of precipitation has gone awry. "If the rains don't come at a predictable time, how do you know?" López asks. "These crops are for survival. If there aren't crops, people leave."[3] As homes in the Guatemalan highlands empty, those that remain speak of their *vecinos fantasmas,* their ghost neighbors.

Literature reinforces bygone rhythms in collective memory even as environmental pulses grow untimely. "The dream of a White Christmas" in England, Smith notes wryly, "is only a collective Dickensian illusion," a climate expectation produced by a canonical story written during the Little Ice Age rather than by average snowfall in the contemporary era. Similarly, Derek Walcott recalls that reading English literature on St. Lucia in the West Indies cemented the rhythms of a foreign climate in his mind: the snow and daffodils "were real, more real than the heat and the oleander, perhaps, because they lived on the page, in imagination, and therefore in memory. There is a memory of imagination in literature which has nothing to do with actual experience."[4] The literature we are immersed in, Walcott suggests, impacts which pulses of environmental time are enforced within us. And as seasonal rhythms across the globe begin to break down, literature can conserve past cadences, serving as a temporal baseline from which change is assessed. A. E. Stallings, who translated Hesiod's *Works and Days* from Ancient Greek to English, recalls that the poem is "studded with phenological observations ... spring sailing must wait until the topmost leaf on a fig tree is the size of a crow's foot.... it's summertime when the golden thistle blooms and the cicada starts singing." With these indicators seared into her memory, she now notes bloomings along Greece's Saronic Gulf, but "not as Hesiod did—to map out the cycles of time—but to notice what is changing, what is off, where we might be headed."[5] The literary heightens her sensitivity to arrhythmias.

PHENOLOGY

As the study of environmental events that pulse according to seasonal and climatic conditions, phenology is concerned with the recursivity of environmental time. When do fireflies reappear, glittering in that empty lot next to the auto shop? Are they flickering there in the crabgrass earlier or later than last year? And have the frogs that devour them emerged yet? Are they croaking just beyond the chain-link fence? Phenology tracks seasons of growth and rest, newness and ripeness, sound and silence, convergences and departures, thirst and wetness, closures and openings. To date, definitions of phenology place it squarely within the sciences, delimiting it in dictionaries and textbooks as "the field of science concerned with cyclic and seasonal natural phenomena."[6] These definitions are usually followed by examples of nonhuman phenological events: bird nestings, bud openings, animal migrations, insect hatchings, and hibernations. Succinctly, phenology is "the biological expression of climatology,"[7] but in practice, the field also encompasses nonbiological seasonal occurrences like fires or the thawing of lake ice. It is the study of environmental pulses and temporal patternings.

Conducting phenological research involves its own dedicated repetitions: in northeastern Puerto Rico, Marcela Zalamea and Grizelle González placed baskets at designated sites throughout the Luquillo Experimental Forest, returning every two weeks for the next year to gather the leaves that drifted down into them, thereby charting peak periods in the forest's leaf fall.[8] On the island of Ponza in the Mediterranean Sea, scientists used mist nets to monitor when birds migrated from their African wintering grounds to southern Europe, tracking their spring arrivals for eighteen years.[9] In Ghana, the ecologist Bismark Ofosu-Bamfo, a member of the African Phenology Network, examines a sandpaper tree every day on his way to work, watching for the straw-colored fruit bats that arrive as it fruits. The tree, he reports, follows a regular subannual rhythm: it buds and sheds its leaves every few months, its branches bare in September of 2021, January of 2022, and July of 2022.[10]

During these unseasonable times, phenology is undergoing a renaissance as a science. According to tallies by the historian of science R. Ashton Macfarlane, the Web of Science database returned only 841 results for "phenology" between 1900 and 1989, and then 27,118 results between 1990 and 2019. As Macfarlane argues, "this upsurge of attention tracked with increased recognition of phenology's use as a biological indicator of anthropogenic climate change."[11] In a warming and unstable world, observing when algae appears on the water each year is not a matter of rote accounting but, instead, a means of perceiving and appraising disruption. Phenology is a crisis science. For the same reason, the gravitational weight of this book hews towards the late twentieth and early twenty-first centuries. When its chapters delve into documents and narratives drafted earlier—prior to the groundswell of public concern about anthropogenic climate change—they do so to ask how anthropogenic climate change has altered the interpretation of these earlier literatures in the present.

Thus far, as Michelle Bastian and Rowan Bayliss Hawitt confirm in a thorough survey, phenology has "been largely neglected in the environmental humanities."[12] But as concerns about anthropogenic change reenergize phenology and the climate histories associated with it, knowledge is increasingly derived from sources more often handled by humanists, including archived manuscripts, poems, and oil paintings. In 2021, Kyoto's cherry blossoms peaked earlier than they had in the past 1,200 years—a record determined through dates extracted from imperial court diaries and Japanese chronicles.[13] Similarly, a team of American phenologists, led by Caitlin McDonough MacKenzie, studied a journal kept by a hunting guide in northern Maine during the mid-twentieth century, gleaning the dates of bird migrations from its pages. Comparing these dates to their contemporary observations, they determined that species including the chestnut-sided warbler and white-crowned sparrow now arrive earlier than they did in decades past.[14] Phenologists have also begun working with herbariums—collections of dried plants. At the University of Cape Town and Rhodes University in South Africa, campus herbaria established that *pelargonium* plants advanced their blooming date by nearly two weeks between 1901–2009.[15] Moving from archives to art museums, a paper published in *Atmospheric Chemistry and Physics* measured the red to green ratio of oil paintings by Gustav Klimt, Edgar Degas, J. M. W. Turner, and others to reconstruct the "atmospheric conditions at the time of the creation of the work of art."[16] I find it heartening that environmental scientists are delving into archives, frequenting museums, and poring over literary texts, and I want to see these interdisciplinary efforts expand and deepen. The arts and humanities have so much to offer during temporal uncertainty.

That said, approaching writing and art as though they are warehouses of data, documents from which dates and information can be extracted and sterilized, can be risky. To offer an extreme example: a team of phenologists, focused on the Guanzhong region of China, mined seasonal descriptions from Tang and Song Dynasty poetry to reconstruct the region's climate between 618 and 1279 CE. This was a challenging task, the researchers noted, because metaphor, personification, and other rhetorical devices make it "difficult to extract clear phenophases from poems." Forging ahead, they converted a line of poetry composed by Quan Deyu on April 19, 790 CE—"peonies occupy the spring breeze with their fragrance alone"—to a phenological occurrence, logging it as the "full-flowering date of *Paeonia suffruticosa*." In this way, the phenologists argue, once poems have been "scientifically processed," they can "be leveraged as a data source for reconstructing past climatic changes."[17] But lines of poetry by Su Shih that initially seem to describe phenological events—"a few branches of peach blossoms beyond the bamboo, / as the spring river warms, the ducks are the first to notice"—turn out to be part of an ekphrastic poem, a description of a landscape painting by the monk Hui-ch'ung.[18] Poetic logics resist scientific processing.

It is worth asking what is lost when poems are scientifically processed, when paintings and photographs are converted to tables of data, when phrasings from manuscripts and journals are stripped down to the calendar dates contained within them. There is something depleting or evacuative about these kinds of projects, and in the residue that they leave behind other questions lie dormant. What draws attention? What holds it? How can phenology be practiced to clarify the temporalities of injustice? In attending to the unseasonable, how can we remain tender to what is at stake?

Unlike other branches of environmental studies, phenology has yet to grapple with its connections to histories of dispossession and the inequities of the present. Perhaps the most radical claim of this book is that literary phenology expands the purview of phenology as a field, allowing it to intersect with social and political life, and thereby engage with issues of climate injustice. Rather than tracking seasonal temperature changes or bloomings in isolation from the human lives that intersect with these patterns, writers and artists portray the complex interweaving of phenological rhythms and the ethics of inhabiting those rhythms alongside others. For instance, in Harlem on January 1, 2019, the writer Emily Raboteau began her own climate observations. Rather than monitoring ice cover on the Hudson River or repeatedly observing the thornless honey locust trees in Harlem, Raboteau returned again and again to a question. During 2019—over dinners with friends and family, in the basement of Our Savior's Atonement, on her social media accounts—she asked how people experience "the effects of the crisis in their bodies and local habitats."[19] These conversations were both situated—they took place over Goldfish crackers on the sidelines of her children's T-ball practices—and undeniably global in scope—she asked about climate change during her forays as a travel writer and through her international online networks. Acknowledging that her question could be startling, she persisted: "I would break climate silence as a woman of color, as a mother raising black children in a global city, as a professor at a public university . . . I listened to their answers. I noted the echoes."[20] Raboteau then transcribed the conversations solicited by this question, explaining: "My approach . . . is just to record what I'm hearing," to offer a running "narrative testimony" over the course of the year.[21] Raboteau's methodology may be qualitative rather than quantitative, but it shares the disciplined daily routine and intellectual preoccupation of conventional phenological projects. It seeks to cultivate what Min Hyoung Song calls "everyday attention," developing a practice to "work through the difficulty of self-consciously contemplating a fact like climate change."[22] Raboteau's study is also, like scientific phenological projects, interested in tangible and perceptible patterns in local habitats. It riffs on the idea of environmental field work, if the field is understood as ongoing conversations between friends and neighbors, and not a footpath along a pond.

Rather than scrawling her findings in a journal or field notebook, Raboteau first filed them as Twitter posts. Like phenological entries in a case study, each of Raboteau's observations for 2019 is therefore timestamped, her year-long project of documenting climate change "as it's being lived in real time," structured as a temporal log or record.[23] In the chapters ahead, many writers approach environmental observation and literary craft as entwined practices, and Raboteau initially planned to compile her posts into "a poetic book-length essay/elegy," possibly "making it a Decalogue, actually, running for ten years." Instead, her 2019 Twitter thread transformed into a piece titled "This Is How We Live Now: A Year's Diary of Reckoning with Climate Anxiety, Conversation by Conversation," published in 2020 in *The Cut*.[24]

Raboteau's essay is a forceful reminder that phenological change can be detected socially as well as scientifically, that her qualitative observations in Harlem capture a variety of seasonal arrhythmias. On Thursday, April 18, she records:

> Carolyn warned me at the breakfast table, where I picked up my grapefruit spoon, that I may have to get used to an inhaler to be able to breathe in spring going forward, as the pollen count continues to rise with the warming world. My wheezing concerned her, and when she brought me to urgent care, a sign at the

check-in desk advised, DON'T ASK US FOR ANTIBIOTICS. Valerie, the doctor who nebulized me with albuterol, explained that patients were overusing antibiotics in the longer tick season for fear of Lyme.[25]

And on Thursday, October 31, she describes generational shifts in seasonal custom: "'It's because of global warming,' said Geronimo, dressed as a wizard, when his father recalled having to wear a winter coat over Halloween costumes during his own New York City childhood. The jack-o'-lanterns were decaying. It was 71 degrees when we walked to the parade."[26] In Raboteau's brief vignettes, observers track inhaler usage, jack-o'-lantern life cycles, increasing strain on the sewage system during floods, and overflowing hospitals during heat waves. Pollen, ripeness, water levels, and temperature—quintessential subjects of phenological studies—remain invisible in Raboteau's work only if a reader's phenological biases towards the rural and the nonhuman obscures their presence.

Because Raboteau's observations are beautifully anthropocentric, gauging the changing climate via conversations and community experience, her record is more attuned to seasonal injustices than phenological records that attend solely to the nonhuman. Seasonal injustices are the pronounced impact of climate arrhythmias on the poor, people of color, people with disabilities, and others disproportionately exposed to the changing climate. For instance, on July 4, at a Black-owned business in Philadelphia, she discusses climate change with a man named Charlie. He tells Raboteau that he can sense "our seasons are changing" because his children are now unable to inhabit their classrooms during the last weeks of the spring semester. "His girls' public school had closed early this year," Raboteau writes, "because its sweltering classrooms lacked air-conditioning to manage the heat wave."[27] The closure of the doors on this public school is a climate arrhythmia, an annual pulse shifted

12 ⁊ INTRODUCTION

by a warming world. If the bare heads of dandelions next to the school—already flowered, seeded, carried off by wind—are a phenological indicator, then so too are the closed school doors and the question of seasonal access to education. Observations like this, that reveal the heavier toll of seasonal arrhythmias on those uninsulated by environmental privilege, are producing what Rob Emmett calls an "emerging phenology of survival," a tracking of pulses as strategy for holding on in a changed world.[28]

FORM AND ENVIRONMENTAL PROSODY

Rhythms enliven literary works as well as environments, and the accumulated insights of literary scholarship—how rhythms cohere, combine, move, and lapse—are increasingly vital for those of us thinking toward collective survival in unseasonable times. A rhythm is a patterned pulse or perennial cadence, an arrangement of durations and intensities that sustains itself over the course of time.[29] Here, as I use it, rhythm is habitual not in the sense of being conformist or formulaic or normative, but rather as a temporality that supports a habitat. Rhythms are patterns that generate a habitable world. "Each living thing remakes the world through seasonal pulses of growth," Anna Lowenhaupt Tsing writes, these rhythms collectively "making landscapes."[30] These lively, habitable rhythms are the ones that interest me: they are signals of continuation and endurance against the tremendous odds of the climate crisis.

Seasons are rhythms in relationship. Thinking alongside Tsing, who understands rhythms as timings that invite connection, I refer to "the gathering of these rhythms, as they result from worldmaking projects, human and not human" as seasonal form.[31] Form is—following Elaine Gan's line of thought—a matter of mutuality, "not things that just happen to occur simultaneously" but instead "coordinations [that] emerge historically, from relations that sediment, recur, endure, echo, extinguish, and lie dormant.... a specific attunement unfolds and recurs."[32] Within environmental literary criticism, form is articulated as inherently relational, echoing conversations unfolding around seasonality in anthropology, biology, and other fields. Devin Griffiths posits ecological form as "a sequence of events that happen at the interface between multiple things." Participating in the work that Nathan Hensley and Philip Steer term "ecological formalism," a reconsideration of literary structures in relation to ongoing and intensifying environmental concerns, I emphasize the temporality of form in this book. I demonstrate how rhythm transects climate science and literary formalism.[33]

The stakes of this connection between literary and environmental rhythms are high: as the globe heats and arrhythmias sever seasonal connections, literary rhythms fray. "Cultures," Mike Hulme writes, "bear the imprint of the weather in which they exist and to which they respond. As with trees or human bodies, cultures too are weathering; indeed, they cannot avoid being weathered in some way or other."[34] This relationship between culture and climate is reciprocal—if cultures bear the imprint of climate, climate also bears the imprint of culture. Just as climate change is gauged by carbon dioxide records, sea level rise, and temperature charts, it can also be gauged through art and literature. I argue that climate rhythms and arrhythmias are encoded in literary form.

To my mind, the crucial thing about form is its ability to generate anticipation, its capacity to shape projections of the future, the way it acclimates those immersed within it—plants, people, insects, and other lives—to ongoing patterns or pulses. Rhythm, perhaps, is the form exerting the strongest anticipatory force. The literary critic Paul Fussell describes it as "that pattern which works on the reader," a sequence which "prove[s] itself upon the pulses of readers."[35] The rhetorician Kenneth Burke concurs, noting that rhythm "very distinctly sets up and gratifies a constancy of expectations; the reader 'comes to rely' upon the rhythmic design after sufficient 'coördinates of direction' have been received ... the regularity of the design establishes conditions of response in the body, and the continuance of the design becomes an 'obedience' to these same conditions."[36] Rhythms—manifesting in poetry, in narrative structure, in photographic practices—tend toward continuance. As rhythms are internalized and absorbed, they generate a yearning for their pulses, a desire for perpetuation of the form. They influence how those living within them—whether readers of a text or inhabitants of an environment—perceive the future.

But when a rhythm ceases or suddenly accelerates, when it weakens or strains, it produces the sensation of arrhythmia. A discrepancy emerges between an established pattern and a pulse that goes haywire. Rhythms are not unyielding and can sustain a degree of variation without collapsing. A wet year or two can swell local rhythms of precipitation, adding an accent or emphasis to the pulse, but when "a beloved pear tree, half-drowned, loses its grip on the earth and falls over," as in Smith's elegy, a rhythm is pushed past the point of variation and into disruption. In the early twenty-first century, as discrepancies between established climate rhythms and fluctuating pulses increase, we exist in "shadowtime," a "parallel timescale that follows one around throughout day to day experience of regular time."[37] Coined by the Bureau of Linguistical Reality, a participatory dictionary that solicits neologisms to articulate "what people are feeling and experiencing as our world changes as climate change accelerates," shadowtime encapsulates the cleaving of the climate's pulses from the rhythmic designs to which we acclimated. Living within it, there is an "acute consciousness of the possibility that the near future will be drastically different than the present."

These rapidly shifting environmental rhythms demand more of literary prosody. Although prosody—as the 1993 *Princeton Encyclopedia* of *Poetry and Poetics* notes—is usually considered "a desiccated subject," climate change infuses it with an alarming urgency.[38] To outfit prosody to address the unseasonable—to track literary rhythms as the globe heats—two alterations are necessary. First, environmental prosody must be more capacious than a four-season model. Detailed and rigorous studies, especially Haruo Shirane's *Japan and the Culture of the Four Seasons*, elucidate literary cultures that cultivate a four-part seasonal aesthetic. But as Caribbean writers document across myriad speeches and essays, a four-season rhythm, particularly when universalized from European or American literature, is tinged with cultural imperialism. Describing the English poetry assigned in Caribbean classrooms, Kamau Brathwaite notes that while "the models are all there for the falling of the snow," the syllables necessary to depict "the force of the hurricanes that take place every year" are lacking:

> The pentameter remained, and it carries with it a certain kind of experience, which is not the experience of a hurricane. The hurricane does not roar in pentameter. And that's the problem: how do you get a rhythm that approximates the natural experience, the environmental experience. We have been trying to break out of the entire pentametric model in the Caribbean and to move into a system that more closely and intimately approaches our own experience.[39]

Although seasonality is ubiquitous, its rhythms clearly vary with geography. The chapters ahead move from the temperate pulses of the northern United States to the monsoonal rhythms that recur across West Africa and much of Asia. They reflect on the rhythms of tropical Australia, where thousands of desert frogs burrow underground for months or years, waiting for rain before they emerge, and how they differ from the seasonality of Arctic reindeer, whose eyes change color as daylight extends and contracts near the pole. Each chapter attempts to approximate the environmental experience of a distinct and situated geography, tracking how climate rhythms and arrhythmias register across various environments and cultures. In attending to these variations in environmental rhythms, *Unseasonable* works to dilute the cultural imperialism of seasonal pentameter.

Secondly, prosody must be capable of reading across the literary and environmental. After all, as Caroline Levine cautions, "form has never belonged only to the discourse of aesthetics. It does not originate in the aesthetic, and the arts cannot lay claim to either the longest or most far-reaching history of the term."[40] I argue for a prosody that is not restricted to pentameter nor the methodological parochialism of close readings unwilling to venture off the page. I advocate for a prosody capable of reading rhythms in poems, cityscapes, scientific records, and photographic studies, a scansion capable of detecting arrhythmia across a variety of texts, media, and habitats. But even more crucially within an era of accelerating climate change, I work to theorize connections *between* environmental stress and rhythmic stress, between climate tensions and literary tensions, between unprecedented timings in both habitats and literatures. Climate urgencies shape the literary, and contemporary prosody must address the accents and emphases generated by wildfires and wreckage, as well as identify iambic feet. Formalism and prosody have to extend into the world if they hope to bring their insights to bear on the altered times we now struggle to read.

PROXIMITIES

In the chapters that follow, I use the term *global* rather than *world* or *planet* for two reasons. First, scientific and popular discourse about the climate crisis already inclines toward the global: *global warming*, *global climate change*. Part of my use of the term is practical, an effort to speak to disciplines and publics more accustomed to these terminologies. But just as importantly, scholars and writers committed to analyzing entrenched disparities and injustices currently distinguish between the Global North and the Global South, between those that accrued—and are accruing—wealth and power through colonization and racial capitalism and those who are weathering life within and organizing to upend these structures. As Anil Agarwal and Sunita Narain argue, global warming "is indeed a global phenomenon in effect—all of us will suffer," but it is "caused by the willful overconsumption of a few."[41] When I use the term "global," I use it in this sense, with an awareness that reading across geographies and positionalities requires vigilant attention to uneven—yet intertwined—histories and futures. The global has always been a fraught scale, one that showcases violent disparities more often than coalitions.

Entreaties for environmental humanities scholarship extending beyond national borders are now longstanding, and this project is buoyed by forerunners demonstrating its possibilities. In 2008, Ursula Heise challenged literary critics to shift from a "sense of place" to a "sense of planet," identifying stories and images capable of engaging "with steadily increasing patterns of global connectivity."[42] Pondering this task via temporality, the chapters ahead move between "seasonality" and "climate," the former profoundly localized and the latter often spoken of in global terms. In this book, the global is not a matter of total literary coverage—I make no claims to a geographically comprehensive account—but rather a lens of literary analysis. I take inspiration from Karen Thornber's insistence that accelerating environmental degradation requires assessing "how literatures from multiple sites treat shared phenomena found in one form or another across the world."[43] To my mind, Thornber's methodology becomes ever more vital as climate change wreaks universal, but highly variegated, havoc on the globe's seasonalities and the literatures associated with them. This kind of literary analysis entails "seeing one place always as imbricated with another," as Jennifer Wenzel advises in her 2020 book *The Disposition of Nature: Environmental Crisis and World Literature*.[44] Achieving this imbricated outlook in relation to climate literature requires tracing the arrhythmias manifesting in one environment back to emissions originating an ocean away. It necessitates a postcolonial awareness—in Elizabeth DeLoughrey, Jill Didur, and Anthony Carrigan's words—of "how the history of globalization and imperialism is integral to understanding contemporary environmental issues."[45]

Toward this end, scholarship on literature and climate change has a particular responsibility to acknowledge what Wenzel calls the "political ecology of literature."[46] Intimacies between the arts and carbon-heavy corporations are threaded throughout *Unseasonable*—the Arctic Coal Company, the Dutch East India Company, the Mahindra Group, the Koch Foundation, and others—appear in the chapters ahead. The profits of fossil fuel companies and associated multinational industries underwrite literary preservation and publishing, an unsettling reminder that manuscripts and texts are entangled in emissions. But occasionally, the literary pushes back on patronage and power. In the penultimate chapter, spoken word poets from the Pacific Islands, Southeast Asia, and their diasporas balk at the United Nations' efforts to tokenize their work, crafting poetry that inflects institutional proceedings on emission pathways.

As arrhythmias multiply, throwing environmental time out of joint, distances can fracture, bringing disparate places into startling proximity. In these moments, climate change produces affinities across vast geographies, affinities that are often formed by the deep grooves of capitalism and colonial power but can also exceed these gouges in unexpected ways. Raboteau describes these proximities as "echoes," pointing out the "rhyme between the rising sandstorms and the dying mangroves, hemispheres apart."⁴⁷ For instance, over a shared dinner, her friend argues that New York City has "more in common . . . with the effective stresses of low-lying small-island coastal regions such as the Maldives, the Seychelles, Cape Verde, Malaysia, Hong Kong, and the Caribbean than with a place like Champaign, Illinois." But he is quickly interrupted by someone else at the table: "I'm from Champaign! . . . It's in a flood plain too!" And another moment of unforeseen resonance: Raboteau's friend, Salar, writes from Tehran to tell her about the watermelon vendor walking through the neighborhood of Yaftabad, where overirrigation and ongoing drought have caused "ruptures in water pipes, walls, and roads." As Salar describes the watermelon vendor's call, he notes that people in Yaftabad now fear "the collapse of shoddier buildings." When Raboteau tells her friend Catherine that the ground beneath Tehran's airport is giving way in the midst of such aridity, Catherine, who has flown in from San Francisco to attend a literary reading, exclaims: "Our airport's sinking too!" I call this a proximity, a shorthand for the growing porosity between Tehran and San Francisco, a term for these utterly incommensurable yet cognate experiences of unstable ground. While the emphasis should always be on incommensurability, these new resonances matter insofar as they indicate how the choreography of the climate crisis unfolds across a global stage.

The project of climate justice has long been stymied—by fossil fuel corporations and national governments, but also by an intransigent "ethic of proximity." As Heise notes, global solidarities disintegrate because environmental thought associates "spatial closeness, cognitive understanding, emotional attachment, and an ethic of responsibility."⁴⁸ Communities care for, and feel responsible for, the people and habitats that are nearest to them. Distance seems to dilute connections to each other. For Rob Nixon, this impasse forms a key challenge of achieving transnational environmental justice: "How, indeed, are we to act ethically toward human and biotic communities that lie beyond our sensory ken?"[49] As climate change forges new translocal proximities, connecting the streets of Tehran to the sinking runways of SFO, it becomes ever more imperative that people—particularly environmentally privileged residents of the Global North—learn to enfold distant neighborhoods within the realm of their proximal ethics. *Our ground is sinking too*: proximities hold out the possibility of recognizing a shared, if severely uneven, catastrophe. These proximities of the changing climate are painful, particularly when they are forged through historical and ongoing inequalities, but recognizing how the faraway flows into home, and how home flows into the faraway, remains a central task in the overheated decades to come.

UNSEASONABLE LITERATURE AND CRITICISM

Until recently, the seasons have been a stale subject in literary criticism, languishing in the type of books now sold at estate sales or gathering dust in the off-site storage facilities of academic libraries. The idea of seasonal criticism conjures Northrop Frye, who blithely associated spring with the romance; summer with comedies, idylls, and pastoral literature; autumn with tragedies and elegies; and winter with satire.[50] In 1957, Frye declared in *The Anatomy of Criticism* that "rhythm, or recurrent movement, is deeply founded on the natural cycle, and everything in nature that we think of as having some analogy with works of art, like the flower or the bird's song, grows out of a profound synchronization between an organism and the rhythms of its environment, especially that of the solar year."[51] Despite Frye's fascination with rhythm—his interest in rhythm as a temporal form manifesting across both literature and ecologies—his conception of literary seasonality was never more than symbolic and it faded with time.

The first wave of ecocriticism, which launched just before the turn of the twenty-first century, reignited interest in literary seasonality and textual manifestations of environmental time. In *The Environmental Imagination,* published in 1995, Lawrence Buell strengthens Frye's observation that seasons are an "organizing principle" in literature, their rhythms often generating the momentum of a text.[52] Analyzing seasonality in a corpus of books comprising much of the initial canon of American nature writing—*Walden, My First Summer in the Sierras, Pilgrim at Tinker Creek*—Buell notes that when seasonality is employed as a literary form, the seasons "as both a plastic mental construct and an environmental imperative" tend to "counter, not further, the vision of a chancy indeterminate universe."[53] Literary seasonality, he implies, resists crisis or disorder, functioning as a structure of assurance. Despite Buell's efforts, and perhaps because of its association with nature writing, seasonal literature acquired a reputation of environmental sentimentality, a literature of white settler America that kept the concerns of the world at arm's length. As ecocriticism and the environmental humanities turned their focus to questions of environmental justice and expanded beyond the confines of American literature, transnational or justice-oriented analyses of seasonal literature largely failed to transpire.

As concerns over anthropogenic climate change spike, literary critics are revitalizing theories of seasonality and textual production. In a literary history of the four seasons, Tess Somervell notes that during the medieval period, genres held strong seasonal associations: "In Northern Europe, for example, the dark nights of winter became associated with the ghost story; in Japan, only mild spring and autumn were deemed fit subjects for high court poetry. In France and Italy, and later England . . . spring's aphrodisiacal effects made it the season of choice for romance and love lyric."[54] Working with British blank-verse poetry written between 1667 and 1807, Tobias Menely explicates the relationship between energy and literary genre, arguing that James Thomson's poem *The Seasons*—written just after the peak of the Little Ice Age—is "marked by an acute awareness of seasonal uncertainty and climatic extremity."[55] Weaving through fragments of Sappho's verse, Anne-Lise François ponders "time without season" to confront "the existential crisis of having been ejected from the (more) normal rhythms of diurnal, circadian, and seasonal time."[56] In these projects, as in the pages ahead, literature serves as a touchstone during climatic turbulence.

Meanwhile, other scholars and thinkers, especially within Indigenous and Black feminist studies, emphasize that the unseasonable is not an unfamiliar experience for communities who have weathered racialized violence and displacements. The climate writer Mary Annaïse Heglar argues, "I'll grant that we've never seen an existential threat to *all* of humankind before. It's true that the planet itself has never become hostile to our collective existence. But history is littered with targeted—but no less deadly —existential threats for specific populations. For 400 years and counting, the United States itself has been an existential threat to Black people."[57] Heglar's insight recalls an archaic use of the verb "to season": slave traders referred to the period of enslaved people's adjustment to the unfamiliar climates of the Americas as "seasoning." In a resonant but culturally and historically distinct account, Kyle Whyte, a Potawatomi scholar-activist, notes that Indigenous peoples have "deep collective histories of having to be well-organized to adapt to environmental change," particularly as forcible displacements like the Trail of Tears separated Indigenous communities from their seasonal knowledge.[58] "Talking about climate change is an exercise in telling time," Whyte insists. But rather than clocking atmospheric changes in linear time, Whyte tracks changes through what he calls kinship time, in which "time is told through kinship relationships that entangle climate change with responsibility." [59]

As climate change intensifies, a wave of what I call unseasonable literature is reinvigorating the topic of literary seasonality, granting it fresh resonance and import. As public awareness of anthropogenic climate change increased near the turn of the twenty-first century, literature entered a period that Lynn Keller helpfully designates as "self-conscious," a period in which disrupted seasonality within texts is explicitly understood as the result of concentrating greenhouse gases.[60] This wave of unseasonable literature is not restricted to American and European writing—it reverberates through a variety of seasonal schema. "August was the month for dust storms, not January," a character recounts in a short story by the Zambian writer Mbozi Haimbe. "But here we were, dust instead of rain right in the middle of the wet season."[61] Or, in the Waanyi novelist Alexis Wright's *The Swan Book,* discussed in depth in chapter 4, the narrative voice describes how Australia's seasons are scrambled both by the cultural imperialism of a four-season model and by climate catastrophes: "Mother Nature? Hah! Who knows how many hearts she could rip out? She never got tired of it. Who knows where on earth you would find your heart again? People on the road called her the Mother Catastrophe of flood, fire, drought, and blizzard. These were the four seasons, which she threw around the world whenever she liked."[62] Meanwhile, in Japan, the poet Namiko Yamamoto responds to the sense that climate change has disrupted the *Saijiki*—the "year-time almanac" of seasonal referents traditionally included in haiku. Yamamoto now employs the haiku form to indicate seasonal dissonance:

> Spring in the mind
> if not actually
> in the air[63]

And in Callum Angus's *A Natural History of Transition*, featured in chapter 6, two characters mourn the final migration of geese above Massachusetts, popping a bottle of champagne to commemorate the moment when "the last signs of seasons are fleeing us . . . saluting a birdless state, toasting the last of them with big gulps, their final squawks teetering out as they head away from this unseasonable heat."[64] In unseasonable writing, the temporal ruptures of anthropogenic climate change are not cast into the future, not anticipated nor foreshadowed. They are self-consciously detailed, already unfolding.

Within the literature of this period, Evie Shockley's poem "weather or not," included in a section of her 2017 collection *Semiautomatic* titled "o the times," exemplifies the complete reversal of seasonality's function in the literary. In unseasonable literature, seasonality furthers a vision of unstable times: "time was on its side, its upside down. it was a new error."[65] The mistiming and disorientation that suffuse Shockley's poem are grounded in the phenological: "meanwhile, in the temper-temper zone, the birds were back and I hadn't slept—had it been a night or a season?" But this sleeplessness—the unrest produced by shifting environmental rhythms—is linked to global political unrest by the close of the poem: "there's been an arab spring, but it was winter all summer in america." Unseasonable literature points to climate change's imbrications in social and political life, often on a transnational scale. It is edgy and sharp, shattering rather than sentimental. It reflects on gender and ongoing colonialism and racial capitalism in unseasonable eras, pulling the concerns of the world towards it.

Unseasonable enters these emergent conversations via three pairs of chapters. The first pair focuses on phenological literature and media, detailing the interchanges between tables of phenological data, nature writing, and photographic projects. Chapter 1, which delves into phenological records and charts kept by the American writers Henry David Thoreau and Aldo Leopold—as well as the frequently overlooked ecologist Sara Elizabeth Jones—pursues a form I call the composite year. As a template for the seasonal occurrences, temperature shifts, and weather patterns anticipated in a given place over the course of twelve months, the composite year inflects both U.S. nature writing and phenological study. I argue that these two fields evolved together, primarily as a response to settler ignorance regarding the climate rhythms of stolen lands. Moreover, as twenty-first-century phenologists now mine Thoreau and Leopold's literary journals and writings for baseline data, their findings attract publicity due to the literary renown of these authors. Insofar as an association with the literary canon increases media attention to seasonal change, phenological knowledge remains tethered to the canon's limited purview and politics.

Crosscurrents between photography and phenological research take center stage in chapter 2, which traces longstanding efforts to visualize seasonal variations in glacial regions through repeat photography, time-lapse film, and long-exposure shots. Analyzing the photographic practices of both artists and scientists—including Christina Seely, Isla Myers-Smith, Alison Beamish, and Mary Caswell Stoddard—this chapter advances an argument about temporal optics. By turning away from the temporalities of deep time and the dominant discourse of the Anthropocene, it suggests that seasonal timescales bring the visceral experiences of an overheated world into focus, including hunger and disorientation across glacial habitats. Throughout, colonialism and militarism direct camera angles: a set of historical photographs taken by the Royal Canadian Mounted Police during their occupation of Herschel Island, and another set taken by the U.S. Navy during a search for oil in the National Petroleum Reserve-Alaska, are replicated as climate scientists now assess vegetation spread in the warming subarctic. Visions of the climatic future are literally reproductions of colonial and military history.

From here, *Unseasonable* turns to prose from India and Australia, tracking the affordances and limitations of seasonal realism during climatic disruption. Chapter 3 opens with an account of phenological observation and writing along the Bay of Bengal, where the fisher S. Palayam and the writer Nityanand Jayaraman gauge seasons through currents, winds, and the shifting patterns of plastic litter along the beach. Moving through classical Tamil poetry's seasonal motifs and Amitav Ghosh's arguments about the impossibility of realist literature in a climatically altered world, this chapter centers on Ashokamitran's novella *Water* and the disrupted seasonal rhythms of the monsoon. As Ashokamitran's characters struggle to collect water in Chennai during the 1969 drought, they model urban phenological practices, observing dry pipes, empty wells, and the lines of plastic buckets near neighborhood pumps. Attending to the rhythms that shape realist narratives like *Water* can train readers to identify climate arrhythmias, not solely through spectacular occurrences, but also within ordinary routines.

Rather than thinking of "average" or "composite" seasonality, chapter 4 posits the unprecedented season—the season that surpasses all records and baselines—by reading Alexis Wright's novel *The Swan Book* in light of the devastating 2019–2020 Australian bushfire season. The arrhythmias portrayed in this novel—prolonged hibernations and jarred migrations—result from both global warming and the enforcement of European seasonal rubrics under settler colonialism. The chapter builds to a theorization of climate fiction: as geophysical and historical precedents go up in flames, literature becomes the baseline by which expectations are set. Readers turn to works like *The Swan Book* for precedent during unimaginable times. This effort to understand or navigate a changed world via fictional touchstones is the pattern that makes climate fiction coherent as a genre.

INTRODUCTION ⚭ 27

The final two chapters are concerned with literary and environmental praxis. Chapter 5 returns to the idea that literature produces and amplifies climate knowledge. As spoken word poets from the Pacific Islands, Southeast Asia, and their diasporas performed at the United Nations Climate Summit in 2015, their accounts of extreme storm seasons demonstrated the need for frontline testimonies alongside graphs of rising carbon dioxide levels. Formally, this chapter reoutfits scholarship on the occasional poem—a category of verse crafted to be timely and opportune—for an era of climate activism. It highlights the deft poetic maneuvers of environmentally and politically subjugated poets tasked with representing their communities at intergovernmental summits. At these summits, the fraught status of the global is especially pronounced. Most crucially, I read the stresses of these poetic performances—their deliberate crescendos, intensities, and volume—in relation to environmental stress, tracking how intensified storm seasons impact prosody. The arrhythmias of unexpected extremity move from a storm to a poem.

Moving from the global stages of the UN to the alleys and boulevards of Ontario and Michigan, chapter 6 asks what is required to keep time in an increasingly arrhythmic world. A constellation of works centered on the seasonal practice of maple sugaring—including Leanne Betasamosake Simpson's "Plight," Amanda Strong's film *Biidaaban (The Dawn Comes)*, Callum Angus's *A Natural History of Transition*, and news reports of the Detroit police threatening a sugarbush in 2022—convey the challenges of maintaining seasonal practices in anthropogenic times. These stories and accounts of sap collection entwine Indigenous futurisms, trans literature, and the anti-capitalist stirrings of the early twenty-first century. As climate change, economic precarity, and police violence threaten communities undertaking spring tapping, the continuation of seasonal practices becomes a necessary politics of repetition. And adaptation—from a story to a film or from a livable climate to an overheated one—must be undertaken with extreme care.

"A season is hard to move, but not impossible," Angus notes in his reflection on maple sap and trans life—an essay featured in chapter 6. "At its heart, a season is a story told to predict the movement of a year.... Now, in the throes of climate change, the story of seasons is being revised.... We face the challenge of telling a new story: the story of a larger season, one more confusing and less straightforward, with significant changes already affecting everyone around the globe, a new season of suffering and adaptation and altered ranges and resilience which, if we listen closely, can tell us something new about ourselves."[66] So we turn now to the stories and literature ahead—

PHENOLOGICAL LITERATURE AND MEDIA

1

PHENOLOGICAL WRITING AND THE COMPOSITE YEAR

Visiting the Morgan Library in New York City late in the winter of 1945, the phenologist Sara Elizabeth Jones examined Henry David Thoreau's charts of seasonal occurrences.[1] Sifting through these century-old records, she settled on two charts as representative samples of Thoreau's phenological work and acquired photostat reproductions. "I am sending them on for you to see," she wrote to her colleague, the ecologist and writer Aldo Leopold. "They were the most legible of the lot and while I can read the one titled 'Earliest Flowering of Flowers' without too much trouble... the one concerned with general phenomena of May takes more concentration—I think they will be a big help when I start checking over the journals. The titles under May are interesting enough: sunsets red, high winds, frost kills plants, fog, heavy dew, meadow fragrance, peculiar fragrance in air, plant my melons!"[2] Thoreau's meticulous phenological records were of particular interest to Jones. In collaboration with Leopold, she was compiling her own phenological record, encompassing a decade of observed blooming times, migratory arrivals, and ice melt in southern Wisconsin. Through this record, Jones and Leopold hoped to clarify the landscape's seasonal rhythms, or—as they phrased it—the "datable events in that cycle of beginnings and ceasings which we call a year."[3]

Fully immersed in her own phenological work, Jones recognized Thoreau's attention to subtle seasonal change as a commitment to measuring and articulating the pulses of environmental time.

This chapter, which details the conjoined histories of phenology and American nature writing, centers on a form that I call the composite year. The composite year is calculated or composed by layering the seasonal occurrences and weather patterns of previous years upon each other, crafting an annual template for a given place. As a form, the composite year is employed across scientific and literary projects: phenologists amass years of data to calculate typical dates for events like the first frost, while nature writers often condense years of experience in a particular setting into a narrative that unfolds over the course of a single annual round.[4] Although the composite year—in both its scientific and literary renditions—is a form of historical accretion, past seasons sedimenting upon each other, it structures expectations of the future. People with strong relationships to a place, especially those with multigenerational knowledge or those attending to an environment over the course of decades, find that the accumulating years solidify into an archetype that influences their sense of seasonal time. As the baseline of climatic expectations—the standard against which climate arrhythmias are gauged—the composite year is a necessary precondition for identifying and articulating seasonal disruption. Analyzing the methodologies of phenological practice and American nature writing can expose how the composite year crystallizes and reveal how deeply it is engrained in cultural imaginaries.

Treating the composite year as both a scientific and literary form, I focus on the work of Henry David Thoreau and Aldo Leopold before turning to contemporary adaptations of the form. In one sense, Thoreau and Leopold's presence in this chapter has surprisingly little to do with their literary prestige—as the authors of *Walden* and *A Sand County Almanac* respectively, Thoreau and Leopold are cemented in the canon of American nature writing—but is, instead, due to their sustained phenological practices. Both Thoreau and Leopold spent the last decades of their lives observing and recording phenological events: ice-out dates or the appearance of pollen on quaking aspens. Many environmental writers are attuned to seasonality, but Thoreau and Leopold are notable insofar as they systematically recorded their observations, producing extensive phenological records alongside their literary writing. In my scholarship, I hold no particular allegiance to literary canons—there are abundant and ethically vital reasons to move beyond enshrined works and writers—but as authors who were also phenological recordkeepers, Thoreau and Leopold remain especially useful case studies in the coevolution of phenology and American nature writing.

Indeed, to the degree that I write Sara Elizabeth Jones back into phenology's literary history, this chapter endeavors to put a small crack in the canon of American environmental literature.[5] Readers and researchers are accorded less space in literary history than authors, and while Jones wrote neither *Walden* nor *A Sand County Almanac*, she is nonetheless a key figure in the lineage of phenological writing. Her careful study of *Walden* and her archival research on Thoreau's phenological practices link two benchmark works of American nature writing, definitively connecting Leopold's interest in environmental time to Thoreau's. Jones's omission from literary history is mirrored by her omission from scientific history: the phenological article she coauthored with Leopold in 1947 is too often attributed solely to him.[6] As Sara Grossman demonstrates, fields that rely on repetitious observation to generate data—like phenology—are rife with the erasure of women's labor; even the contributions of professionally accredited white women like Jones are too often elided in climate science.[7] Prior to 2019, the Leopold Papers at the University of Wisconsin-Madison archives contained only half of Jones and Leopold's correspondence regarding their research and publication, making it difficult to ascertain the degree of Jones's contributions. In the process of my research, I began my own correspondence with Jones's daughter, Barbara Frey, who heroically dug through boxes of family memorabilia and uncovered the missing letters, pages of handwriting that lay dormant for seven decades.[8] Those letters inform the story told here, bringing Jones's labor at the intersection of literature and phenology into focus.

And yet, what follows also attests to the pervasive power of canonization: this chapter exposes how the literary canon impacts knowledge far beyond the literary, influencing the selection of scientific data sets and the circulation of climate knowledge. Put more provocatively, I argue that contemporary American phenology, particularly within public discourse, is yoked to the cultural currency of the literary canon. Handwritten logs detailing the annual dispersal of horsetail spores and the blooming of bloodroot are more likely to be retained and archived if they are penned by canonical writers: literary prestige influences which pieces of paper are cherished and which are discarded. Writerly fame determines which logs are celebrated and which logs remain—in attics, on floppy disks, in diaries—unnoticed. Unsurprisingly, as twenty-first-century phenologists began searching for past records to establish baseline temporal measurements, they landed on observations taken by Thoreau and Leopold. Not only were Thoreau and Leopold's records preserved, cataloged, and well-known within literary and historical circles, but they added a degree of general interest appeal to any new research associated with them. As phenologists resume observations near Walden Pond and in southeastern Wisconsin, their findings attract publicity generated by Thoreau and Leopold's literary fame. Unlike the majority of contemporary phenological papers, which rarely circulate beyond their scientific subfields, publications based on Thoreau's observations have been picked up by media outlets including the *New York Times*, *The Guardian*, NBC, the *Boston Globe*, the *Los Angeles*

Times, and *Slate*. Work based on Leopold and Jones's observations has been featured on *NPR*, *Wisconsin Public Radio*, and *PBS Wisconsin*. The literary canon now functions as a vehicle for the popularization and circulation of climate science, which means that climate science is tethered to the canon's purview and politics.

Now, as phenologists return to Walden Pond and the Leopold Shack, they track the degree to which the rise in global temperature has altered the annual rhythms that once captured the attention of Thoreau, Jones, and Leopold. For instance, the biologist Richard Primack notes that Thoreau's *Journal* records the average flowering date for the forty-three most common plant species in Concord, MA as May 16. In notes kept by Concord naturalists at the close of the nineteenth century, this same group of plants flowered just a few days earlier, around May 12. By the early twenty-first century, as Primack and members of his lab resumed phenological observations in the Concord area, these same flowers blossomed on May 8. And in 2012, as the global temperature spiked, Primack observed these plants blooming on April 20.[9] Similarly, while Jones and Leopold recorded the mean flowering date of twenty-three native plant species in Wisconsin as May 7, a team of phenologists working in the same area in 2012 recorded the mean flowering date for this same set of plants as April 13.[10] These studies document a rapid shift in temporal ecology: under the pressure of accumulating greenhouse gases, established seasonal rhythms are moving toward new intervals.

Turning now to read Thoreau's and Leopold's literary writing in tandem with the phenological records that they initiated, I show how American nature writing and phenological science are conjoined fields. I detail the projects undertaken by Thoreau, Jones, and Leopold, articulating the settler aspirations and agendas that inflected them. And crucially, I begin the process of assessing how the canon of American nature writing—a collection of texts penned primarily by well-connected, white men—continues to affect the scope of phenological knowledge. Throughout this chapter, I argue that climate change is now disrupting the composite year. As high volumes of carbon dioxide and other greenhouse gases are emitted in the U.S.—where this chapter is set—and seasonality shifts, a literary form is jarred. In this period of accelerating climate change, the composite year serves as a gauge against which the contours of future years are measured; its disruption registers the unseasonable in contemporary environmental writing.

TEMPORAL ATTENTIONS

The observational charts that Jones examined in the Morgan Library on that wintry day in 1945 originated a century prior. In 1845, just before concentrations of carbon dioxide began to rise, Henry David Thoreau "went to the woods because [he] wished to live deliberately, to front only the essential facts of life."[11] This famous literary declaration originated as a statement about his desire to attend more carefully to phenological events and environmental data. Thoreau referred to annually recurring events as *phenomena*, a term that shares an etymological root with *phenology* and features prominently in the first draft of *Walden*'s manifesto: "I wish to meet the facts of life—the vital facts, which were the phenomena or actuality the Gods meant to show us,—face to face, And so I came down here. Life! Who knows what it is—what it does?"[12] His craving for natural phenomena solidified into a recognizable phenological practice by mid-November of 1850, when Thoreau began consistently dating the field notes in his *Journal*.[13] These time stamps reflect his increasingly methodological—one might say obsessive—approach to environmental observation. On his daily walks through the outskirts of Concord, Thoreau was striving for temporal precision:

I soon found myself observing when plants first blossomed and leafed, and I followed it up early and late, far and near, several years in succession, running to different sides of the town and into the neighboring towns, often between twenty and thirty miles in a day. I often visited a particular plant four or five miles distant, half a dozen times within a fortnight, that I might know exactly when it opened, besides attending to a great many others in different directions and some of them equally distant, at the same time. At the same time I had an eye for birds and whatever else might offer.[14]

In addition to the blossoming and leafing of plants, Thoreau observed the date each year that farmers sent cows "up country," the date each winter that he first observed children skating on the pond, the date that he abandoned his greatcoat and donned thinner clothes each spring, and the date that the weather allowed him to sit "with open window."[15] In Stephanie LeMenager's elegant phrasing, Thoreau observed "at which points in time and space human and nonhuman lives . . . might habitually touch one another," developing a phenological practice that integrated the seasonal rhythms of human activity with the rhythms of nonhuman phenomena.[16] These rhythms did not follow an invariable annual meter—they did not occur on precisely the same date each year—and yet, they were rhythmic insofar as they produced anticipated temporal patterns. "This is the case in this place every year," Thoreau notes as he describes a peculiar ice formation on the river, "and no doubt this same phenomenon occurred annually at this point on the river a thousand years before America was discovered. This regularity and permanence make these phenomena more interesting to me."[17] His eagerness to understand the pulses of the landscape prior to colonization exposes a paucity of long-term knowledge. Thoreau's phenological study was an effort to compensate for environmental memory that he—like other American settlers—did not possess.

As a settler phenologist, Thoreau spent the last decade of his life making observations and producing charts. If his vocation was a surveyor of land, his avocation might best be described as a "surveyor of time."[18] Both pursuits were enmeshed in colonial settlement: Sara Grossman documents how longitudinal climate surveys in the nineteenth-century United States "grew out of land surveying, which furthered Indigenous land theft."[19] Thoreau certainly believed that the contours of seasons, like the contours of a place, could be mapped and delineated. "Methinks the season culminated about the middle of this month," he notes in the summer of 1854, "having as it were attained the ridge of the summer—commenced to descend the long slope toward winter—the afternoon & down hill of the year."[20] Relying on the field notes contained in his *Journal*, Thoreau compiled the documents that Jones would pore over in the Morgan a century later. He first produced month-by-month lists of fruit ripening, migratory bird arrivals, insect activity, and leafing of trees and shrubs.[21] Using these lists as reference points, he then sketched massive tables illustrating the general phenomena of each month. Listing phenomena down the left side of each page, he created rows, and then listing the years across the top of the page, he produced columns. In the resulting boxes, Thoreau entered a number—indicating the day of the month the phenomena occurred—and sometimes included a brief explanatory note. The form of his phenological charts gestures toward the composite year. As Kristen Case notes, Thoreau's charts allow a reader to "conceive of the seasons as a palimpsest within which every April is overlaid on top of every other April, giving our experience of temporality a kind of depth."[22]

Phenological activity is marked by its own periodicities, phases in which whole neighborhoods sally forth as seasonal observers. In the 1850s, the Smithsonian Institution distributed a circular titled

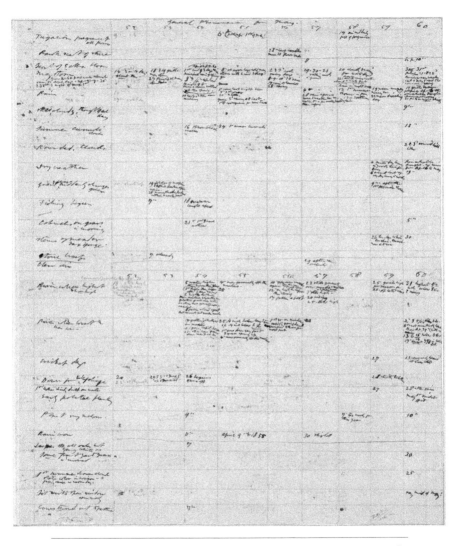

FIGURE 1.1 General phenomena for May, Manuscript 610. Courtesy of the Morgan Library and Museum, New York.

"Registry of Periodical Phenomena," inviting readers to observe and report on "the first appearance of leaves and flowers of plants; the dates of appearance and disappearance of migratory or hybernating animals, as mammals, birds, reptiles, fishes, insects, &c.; the times of nesting of birds, of moulting and litterring of mammals, of utterance of characteristic cries among reptiles and insects, and anything else which may be deemed noteworthy." The plants that Thoreau began observing regularly bear a "striking resemblance" to the plants listed in the Smithsonian's circular, suggesting that his phenological study was partially prompted by the Smithsonian's project.[23] Phenology blossomed into a national pastime, a trend that Thoreau beheld with wry humor in 1852: "This is my year of observation, & I fancy that my friends are also more devoted to outward observation than ever before—as if it were an epidemic."[24]

Indeed, this national pastime was indicative of colonial blight: the Smithsonian's call for phenological data divulged a widespread seasonal ignorance among settlers living on stolen land. The particular information sought also suggests that this data was required to augment the country's commerce and increase its agricultural profits. In addition to reports on "animal and vegetable life," the Smithsonian requested observations of "general phenomena of climate," including the breaking up of ice on bays, the rise and fall of water in interior rivers, and the growing periods of "important annual staples." This phenological knowledge would prove crucial for military activity and economic expansions of the U.S. government. In this sense, phenology was fundamental to ongoing colonial settlement.

But for Thoreau, phenological observation was not a means of maximizing the nation's agricultural production or obtaining commercially useful statistics. Instead, Thoreau practiced phenology as a method of temporal attunement, a way to "improve the nick of time."[25] As Daegan Miller observes, "*improve* was one of Thoreau's favorite verbs, but he meant something very different from . . . the agricultural improvers. . . . for him *improvement* meant living rather than getting one. It meant being present, aware of the birdsongs, the taste of the river, the character of the breeze; it meant being alive and sensitive to one's surroundings."[26] Although Thoreau's phenological studies emerged from—and always should be contextualized in relation to—U.S. settler science, his obstinate refusal to produce economically or politically useful information suggests an important divergence from the temporal conquest underway. Without absolving Thoreau's phenology of its deep entanglements in colonial science, his approach poses the question of whether phenology can be practiced by settlers in order to cherish a place rather than control it.

This history returns us to Sara Elizabeth Jones as she examines Thoreau's charts in the Morgan Library's reading room in the winter of 1945. While completing her PhD in Zoology at the University of Wisconsin-Madison, Jones established her own phenological practice: for a span of two years, from 1944 to 1945, she documented plant life in the university's arboretum. Just as Thoreau's observations date from the onset of the American Industrial Revolution, her phenological records coincide with the spike in global temperature and disruption of large-scale earth systems known as the Great Acceleration. Aldo Leopold was also assembling a record during these years: "For a decade," Leopold explains in *A Sand County Almanac*, "I have kept, for pastime, a record of the wild plant species first in bloom."[27] He finds that "every week from April to September there are, on average, ten wild plants coming into first bloom. In June as many as a dozen species may burst their buds on a single day. No man can heed all of these anniversaries; no man can ignore all of them."[28] Combining their data, Jones and Leopold assembled a detailed log of 328 environmental rhythms observed in southern Wisconsin, including the dates that pollen first appeared on skunk cabbage and the dates that ring-necked pheasants began their first "fall cackling and crowing."[29]

In order to track as many of Wisconsin's "anniversaries" as possible, Jones and Leopold supplemented their own observations with data from the U.S. Weather Bureau, unpublished records maintained by a local ornithological club, and notes from ecologists and friends in Leopold's vast correspondence network. For example, a man named Joe Alexander sent Leopold a hand-drawn chart recording the annual commencement of tree cricket chirping between 1921 and 1945, explaining, "they tune up at dark, then gradually fall into a synchronized pulsation until all in a wide area are on the same 'beat.'"[30] An observer identified in their study only as "Mrs. Arthur Koehler" donated nine years of her birding notes.[31] The hand-scrawled charts and lists supplied by friends and colleagues underscore how many people maintain phenological records, how rarely these records are published or preserved, and how association with a renowned figure can determine whether or not phenological observations survive. These records also demonstrate how easily phenological labor and knowledge—certainly Ethelyn Koehler's, but also Estella Leopold's and even Jones's—fade, attributed in contemporary media solely to Aldo Leopold. His celebrity as the author of *A Sand County Almanac* often overshadows the coauthorship of his phenological record, the idea of a single literary author eclipsing the convention of multiauthored scientific work.

As Jones and Leopold exchanged letters regarding their phenological publication, Jones also initiated a discussion about Henry David Thoreau. Responding to her interest—"I'm pleased that you are really getting into Thoreau"—Leopold mailed Jones an article from *The Atlantic Monthly* arguing that "if Thoreau was a scientist in any field, it was ecology, though he preceded the term."[32] Jones sent him a copy of *Walden*. "While I had read *Walden* a couple of times before this summer," she confided in September of 1946, "discovering Thoreau in the true sense of the word has been one of the most thrilling experiences I have known."[33] Jones's letters during this file phenology

TREE CRICKET — ŒCANTHUS NIVEUS — GRYLLIDÆ

"CHIRPING" RECORD

YEAR	DATE	REMARKS	PLACE
1921	July 21	Strong	915 Spaight St.
1922	" 22	"	"
1923	" 20	"	"
1924	" 21	Moderate	"
1925	" 26	Strong	2241 Rugby Row
1926	" 20	"	"
1927	" 24	"	"
1928	" 21	Light	"
1929	" 23	Strong	"
1930	" 22	"	"
1931	" 21	"	"
1932	" 21	"	"
1933	" 20	Moderate	"
1934	" 22	"	"
1935	" 20	Strong	"
1936	" 21	"	"
1937	" 22	"	"
1938	" 21	"	"
1939	" 21	"	"
1940	" 21	Light	"

(OVER)

FIGURE 1.2 Joe Alexander, "Tree Cricket Chirping Record." Courtesy of the Aldo Leopold Foundation and University of Wisconsin-Madison Archives.

period document her increasing understanding of Thoreau as a writer for whom observation and composition were linked practices. Her archival work at the Morgan also provides a crucial precedent for twenty-first-century phenological work engaged in historical comparison: Jones immediately ascertained the value of these earlier records. As she conveyed her interest in Thoreau's writing and observations to Leopold, her enthusiasm proved contagious. Although *Walden* and *A Sand County Almanac* are frequently compared as canonical works of U.S. nature writing, literary critics have tended to characterize Thoreau and Leopold's relationship as "a matter of affinity rather than influence."[34] The unpublished correspondence between Jones and Leopold, which documents Jones's deepening interest in Thoreau's writing and scientific inquiries, complicates this interpretation. Insofar as Jones imparted Thoreau's documentation of environmental rhythms to Leopold, Thoreau's influence on Leopold's literary writing should not be underestimated. Indeed, the strongest intellectual current running between these two writers is a preoccupation with the forms of seasonal time, a fascination that simultaneously drives their research and structures their literary productions.

CLOCKWORK AND THERMOMETERS

Before anthropogenic climate change prompted a reinvestigation of annual environmental cycles, phenology was employed as a means of intuiting the clockwork embedded in a landscape. Thoreau notes in his *Journal*, "I think it was the 16th of July when I first noticed [the blue vervain's flowers] . . . It is very pleasant to measure the progress of the season by this & similar clocks— So you get not the absolute time but the true time of the season."[35] Measuring time through blue vervain and other natural clocks, Thoreau begins to understand time as "relational," as emerging from the surrounding environment.[36] Phenological indicators—the blooming of the blue vervain or the closure of a window against the chill—allow Thoreau to locate himself temporally within the passage of the year. The landscape's clock ticks phenomenologically: warming or cooling air, shifting scents of foliage, the tenor and intensity of insect noise, and a host of other sensory data propel its hands around.

As a phenological observer, Thoreau finds that environmental time is influenced by climatic conditions. He notes that certain phenological rhythms are produced by humidity: the star fungi, he notes, "are hygrometers," opening in moist conditions and closing during dry spells.[37] Others, like the blossoming of the white saxifrage, are responses to "the increased light of the year."[38] However, many of the phenological rhythms that Thoreau studies are linked to temperature. Observing a patch of serviceberries in 1854, he records:

> I found an Amelanchier botryapium XX with its tender reddish green leaves *already* fluttering in the wind & stipules clothed with white silky hairs—& its blossom so far advanced that I thought it would open tomorrow— But a little farther there was another which did not rise above the rock but caught all the reflected heat which to my surprise was fully open— Yet a part which did rise above the rock was not open— What indicators of warmth. No thermometer could show it better.[39]

If blooming advances the season, shifting environmental time forward by a few degrees, then time is affected by temperature. Environmental time is a climatic mode of temporality. In *Walden*, this relationship between time and temperature is most easily discerned through observations of the pond. "Though I perceive no difference in the weather, [the pond] does," Thoreau writes. "Who would have suspected so large and cold and thick-skinned a thing to be so sensitive? Yet it has its law to which it thunders obedience when it should as surely as the buds expand in the spring."[40] In this sense, Walden Pond is not only the geographic location of Thoreau's experiment in deliberate living but also—like the blue vervain and the serviceberries—a seasonal gauge. Walden Pond, perhaps the central image of Thoreau's text, functions as an environmental timepiece: its unusual depth and lack of a through stream allow its freezing and melting to "indicate better than any water hereabouts the absolute progress of the season."[41] Its rhythms are regulated by the climate, its seasonality bound to temperature.

Despite nineteenth- and early twentieth-century phenologists' focus on ordinary, recurring events, the apprehension of these rhythms was often cast as a sublime experience, an act that allowed committed observers to take the "pulse of life."[42] Identifying environmental rhythms embedded in the landscape led to marvel at what Jones and Leopold called "that ultimate enigma, the land's inner workings."[43] As Thoreau thrusts a thermometer into an opening in the pond ice on March 6th, 1847, recording a temperature of 32°F, he is confirming the regularity of nature's rhythms. "In 1845, Walden was completely open on the 1st of April," he notes. "In '46, the 25th of March; in '47, the 8th of April; in '53, the 23rd of March; in '52, the 18th of April; in '53, the 23rd of March; in '54, about the 7th of April."[44] For Thoreau, this list of dates is infused with a sense of awe: the pond's responsiveness to cycles in temperature demonstrates its animation and vitality. "The earth is alive and covered with papillæ," he remarks in a passage of *Walden* that now rings as eerily prescient. "The largest pond is as sensitive to atmospheric changes as the globule of mercury in its tube."[45] Thoreau's ebullience while observing the melting pond ice stands in marked contrast to contemporary anxieties over premature melt: as twenty-first-century phenologists note, Walden Pond nearly failed to freeze in

2012. Ice formed on January 19th of that year, but ice-out was recorded on January 29th, only ten days later.[46] However, in *Walden* and the *Journal*, the environment's sensitivity signals its cohesion, not its vulnerability. Phenology was a practice associated with awe, not apprehension.

PHENOLOGICAL WRITING

Thoreau's and Leopold's literary works are clearly linked to their phenological practices: as they studied the land's phenological rhythms, they also began to arrange their prose according to seasonal progression. The progressive drafts of *Walden* document how Thoreau incorporated his phenological data to strengthen his descriptive prose. Between the initial draft of *Walden*, composed between 1846 and 1847, and the book's publication in 1854, the phenological precision within Thoreau's text increases. For instance, in his initial draft, Thoreau mentions sand cherries and sumac growing near his house at Walden Pond, observing that the sumac berries turn red "in the fall." Revising this paragraph in 1852, he contextualizes the sand cherries within the year's annual cycle, noting that they produce flowers "near the end of May," and then increases the accuracy of his description of the sumac berries, replacing "in the fall" with "in August."[47] As Tristram Wolff argues, "Thoreau assumes that language is part of the landscape," and his increasing precision as an environmental observer translated into increasing precision as an environmental writer.[48]

Furthermore, while critics have frequently observed that *Walden* is structured around the seasonal cycle, it is worth noting that the seasons did not figure prominently in Thoreau's account of his years at Walden Pond until his fifth draft, written during late 1852 and early 1853.[49] Thoreau's use of seasonality as a narrative form, therefore, emerges during a period of particularly engaged phenological observation, suggesting his interest in environmental phenomena produced an aesthetic proclivity for seasonally-driven narratives. In the fifth draft, Thoreau expanded both the fall and winter sections of his text, transfiguring his prose into a full annual cycle. As Robert Sattelmeyer suggests, this new emphasis on the seasonal sequence transformed Thoreau's writing from a loose set of recollections and philosophies into a work with a discernible contour: "with the annual cycle developed and amplified, there exists for the first time a 'story' with a kind of plot.... Doubtless the addition of material about fall, winter, and the second spring contributes to verisimilitude and to a felt sense of the passage of a year. There is a satisfying structural coherence about this pattern as realized in the finished book, a kind of harmonic or tonic closure felt in arriving once more at spring."[50] Lawrence Buell's formative work on U.S. seasonal writing bolsters Sattelmeyer's analysis: Buell argues that the seasons provide a sense of momentum without generating suspense. They provide movement while maintaining order. Despite their continual revolutions, Buell suggests that aestheticized seasons, like those employed in *Walden*, "counter, not further the vision of a chancy, indeterminate universe. They are the elements that stand most clearly for structure rather than anarchy."[51]

In a similar fashion, literary histories tend to attribute Leopold's use of the almanac form to editorial pressures. Reviewing early drafts of Leopold's essays, various publishers complained of a lack of cohesion between his short vignettes. Clinton Simpson at Knopf remarked that the collection lacked a "clear and logical" structure.[52] Helen Clapesattle at the University of Minnesota Press described the essays as "pretty much a miscellany," noting that "the completed manuscript will have more chance of publication if it has some sort of pattern, rather than just being a loose collection of essays with little or no relation to each other."[53] In response to this request for greater formal cohesion, Leopold organized the first section of his manuscript into an almanac, "arranged seasonally" in order to cluster his literary sketches according to month.[54] Buell rightly describes this revision as "accommodationism," a response to "prodding by publishers and colleagues to make the book more accessible," but it is also clear that Leopold became increasingly invested in the almanac form over the course of his revisions.[55] In December of 1947, he wrote to William Sloane at Oxford University Press: "In looking these over myself I can see that those comprising part I, 'A Sauk County Almanac,' does not yet conform perfectly to the almanac idea. They were written before this particular arrangement was in my mind. In printing there should doubtless be some indication of month for each individual essay."[56] By this point in his composition process, the almanac was not a mere publishing conceit for Leopold, but a form he hoped to emphasize and fulfill.

Within existing accounts of Leopold's revision process, a key question remains unanswered: out of all the possible ways one might choose to unify a collection of essays, what drew Leopold to the almanac form? As Dennis Ribbens indicates, Leopold began conceiving of his text as a literary almanac sometime between 1944 and 1947, at the peak of his phenological research and writing.[57] As he searched for a greater sense of order and cohesion in his writing, it seems almost inevitable that he would choose to translate the "regular order" of his phenological observations into literary form. The annual rhythms of the landscape began to manifest in the shape of his book: Leopold was crafting phenological literature. He wrote to Charlie Schwartz, his illustrator, requesting that the small sketches interspersed throughout the text adhere to strict phenological realism: "the phenology paper is being sent you. This may give you some background for any sketches which are to pertain to certain dates in the region."[58] Most tellingly, Jones and Leopold's scientific study, "A Phenological Record for Sauk and Dane Counties," and *A Sand County Almanac* are conjoined texts: Leopold borrowed passages from the scientific manuscript to paste into his literary one. The opening paragraph of his literary almanac is a near textual replica of the opening paragraph of the scientific paper he coauthored with Jones: "Each year, after the midwinter blizzards, there comes a night of thaw. . . . one of the earliest datable events in that cycle of beginnings and ceasings which we call a year."[59] The direct confluence between these texts reveals the degree to which Leopold understood them as related publications, lending credence to the theory that Leopold's preference for the almanac form was the result of his absorption in phenological work.

Although Thoreau's and Leopold's phenological practices are rarely considered in relation to literary history, these writers approached phenology as an investigation into forms of seasonality in the northern United States.[60] If form, as Caroline Levine argues, is a concept extending far beyond the aesthetic, comprising "all shapes and configurations, all ordering principles, all patterns of repetition and difference," then seasonality is a prevalent form of environmental time.[61] The seasons are rhythmic configurations, phenological beats and accents that cohere into recognizable temporal patterns. Each year, as Thoreau and Leopold and Jones recorded the appearance of skunk cabbage blossoms, or the return of migrating geese, they were performing acts of scansion on the landscape—noting recurrences, crests, and cessations. As phenologists, they were fascinated by periodicity, a concept that Tobias Menely notes is "bound up with the enigmatic dialectics of duration and completion, repetition and rupture, that underlie our perception of time."[62] This work easily merged into the literary: "The seasons and all their changes are in me," Thoreau wrote in 1857, "I see not a dead eel or a floating snake, or a gull, but it rounds my life and is like a line or accent in its poem."[63] For Thoreau, as an American Transcendentalist, these rhythms were inherently meaningful, the order of the natural world corresponding to a higher spiritual order. Leopold and Jones inherited this Transcendental view of phenology, positing a link between environmental order and a sense of meaning. They write: "From the beginnings of history, people have searched for order and meaning in [phenological] events, but only a few have discovered that keeping records enhances the pleasure of the search, and also the chance of finding order and meaning. These few are called phenologists."[64] Their assertion is reminiscent of Cleanth Brooks's argument about literary form in *The Well-Wrought Urn*, published the same year as Jones and Leopold's phenological study. Brooks, who famously argued that "form is meaning," hypothesizes that a text's import is not derived solely from its content, but is, instead, partially generated by its form—by its patterns, orderings, and repetitions.[65] In phenology, as in literature, significance resides partially in form itself: order produces meaning.

My interest in form—much like the interest of nineteenth- and twentieth-century phenologists—stems from its ability to generate anticipation, its capacity to acclimate us to a pattern or beat. "A work has form," Kenneth Burke writes, "in so far as one part of it leads a reader to anticipate another part, to be gratified by the sequence."[66] For Burke, form is an unfolding pattern that "determines our expectation of its continuance."[67] Paul Fussell likewise emphasizes form's ability to shape expectation, defining it as "that pattern which works on the reader," a sequence which "prove[s] itself upon the pulses of readers."[68] Notably, Burke and Fussell both articulate form as a pattern that becomes internalized, seeping into readers and shaping their projections of the future. Lauren Berlant edges these discussions into the realm of affect, describing "an affective expectation of the experience of watching something unfold, whether that thing is in life or art."[69] When this expectation goes unfulfilled, when a form alters both substantially and suddenly—when plants that are expected to bloom on May 16 bloom instead on April 20—there is a profound sense of something amiss or "off" because our pulses have been acclimated to a particular course of unfolding. Heather Houser refers to this experience as discord, "an affect that takes shape when lived experience grates against preestablished expectations."[70] When a form alters, the sense of a predictable future is called into question—discord descends.

THE BELIEF IN A PERMANENT CLIMATE

In *Walden*, Thoreau proclaims that it is not necessary to "trouble ourselves to speculate how the human race may at last be destroyed. It would be easy to cut their threads at any time with a little sharper blast from the north. We go on dating from Cold Fridays and Great Snows; but a little colder Friday, or greater snow, would put a period to man's existence on the globe."[71] Writing at the close of the Little Ice Age, when prolonged or intense cold spells still raised specters of apocalypse in the public imaginary, Thoreau conceptualizes the climate as an agential force, capable of demolishing the human species through even subtle fluctuations. The climate chooses where to "put a period," thereby sentencing humanity. Agency resides in the thermometer's mercury, its rise and fall understood as a movement beyond the realm of human influence.

And yet, through his fine-grained study of Concord's phenological cycles and extensive reading in the field of climatology, Thoreau is ultimately persuaded that the climate is a reliable—if powerful— agent. "Every year men talk about the dry weather which has now begun as if it were something new and not to be expected," he complains in 1853.[72] Thoreau's years of phenological observation allow him to anticipate these seasonal rhythms, a practice that produces faith in environmental continuity. "Expectation," he explains, "may amount to prophecy." Thoreau often employs this form of prophecy—prophecy of reassurance and environmental stability—as a counterweight to apocalyptic visions. "Who could believe in the prophecies of Daniel or of Miller that the world would end this summer while one Milkweed with faith matured its seeds!" he exclaims.[73] Or later, "Is the world coming to an end?—Ask the chubs. As long as fishes spawn . . . we do not want redeemers."[74] In contrast to the linear model of time underwriting apocalyptic narratives, Thoreau's absorption in phenological rhythms predisposes him to a cyclical model of temporality: "as the planet in its orbit & around its axis—so do the seasons—so does time revolve."[75] Phenology, as Thoreau practiced it, was a science running counter to apocalypse.

As an avid reader in the field of climatology, Thoreau was well aware of nineteenth-century debates over the climate's relative permanence or malleability. Steeped in Charles Lyell's geology of "slow, gradual changes," he may have accepted the concept of climatic change over the course of deep time, but he was less persuaded that the climate could shift perceptibly within the timeframe of human history.[76] Toward the end of his life, he perused Lorin Blodget's *Climatology of the United States*, taking substantial notes on the chapter titled "Permanence of the Principal Conditions of Climate." While Blodget's chapter summarizes scientific arguments in favor of anthropogenic climate change, Thoreau's commonplace book—in which he transcribed passages of interest encountered during his reading—contains only quotations supporting the idea of a permanent climate. He records that there is "a strong array of independent proof that there has been no change in the climate of Europe within the historic period, and none in America since its settlement."[77] While interest should not be equated with endorsement, Thoreau's selected transcriptions suggest an inclination toward the idea of climatic permanence within the timeframe of human perception. "There is no French revolution in Nature," he notes in his *Journal*. "She is warmer or colder by a degree or two."[78]

Working nearly a century later, Jones and Leopold are well aware that temperatures have risen since the Little Ice Age. Comparing their own observations to observations kept at the Wisconsin College of Agriculture in the late nineteenth century, they reflect on "the coldness and lateness which prevailed during the early 1880's," concluding that earlier data "coincides with a cold period, and that in [our] paper with a warm period."[79] In their estimation, this shift may be indicative of deep time's regular pulses of warmth and chill, but their historical vantage point does not afford certainty: "whether these fluctuations are segments of a recurring cycle is another question which only time can answer," they declare.[80] While allowing for a degree of indeterminacy, Jones and Leopold, like Thoreau, are inclined to interpret climatic shifts as part of a stable geological cycle. A strangely warm spring did not yet produce a sense of phenological discord. Instead of alarming indications of formal breakdown, variations in biological rhythms were viewed as data to be incorporated into an overarching pattern. For instance, in an April 1948 letter to Jones, Leopold mentions an unusually early spring without invoking suspicions of formal breakdown: "I have been thinking of you recently and wish you were here to talk phenology. Jim Zimmerman and I swapped notes yesterday and find that April is nine days ahead of last year, which of course was very late. Pasque flowers started this week, and I can well remember your first expedition to see one."[81] The early spring registers simply as a peculiarity, the possibility of humanity altering environmental time itself still beyond the horizon of scientific understanding.

However, as Leopold tracked the blooming patterns of dogtooth violets and recorded March arrivals of woodcocks at his Wisconsin hunting shack, the clouds of the Dust Bowl and recent climatic devastation were likely not far from his mind. *A Sand County Almanac* is a literary work produced in the wake of "the dust-bowl drouths" of colonial agriculture. Just as Walden Pond is both the site and central image of *Walden*, a farm "skinned . . . of residual fertility" is both the site and central image of *A Sand County Almanac*.[82] It is not coincidental that Leopold began monitoring "the arteries of the land" there in 1935, recording their pulses.[83] Just a year before initiating restoration work in Sauk County, he issued a warning in *Parks and Recreation:* "The incredible engines wherewith we now hasten our world-conquest," he wrote, are "being used for ecological destruction on a scale almost geological in magnitude. In Wisconsin, for example, the northern half of the state has been rendered partially uninhabitable for the next two generations by man-made fire, while the southwestern quarter has been deteriorated for the next century by man-made erosion. . . . It has saddled us with a repair bill, the magnitude of which we are just beginning to appreciate."[84] His concerns about anthropogenic impact on the landscape foreshadow—to an uncanny degree—Naomi Oreskes's 2007 warning that "we have become geological agents . . . chang[ing] the chemistry of our atmosphere," or Dipesh Chakrabarty's 2009 assessment that "humans now wield a geological force."[85] Anthropogenic damage—on a regional if not yet a global scale—preoccupied Leopold and galvanized his phenological investigations.

THE COMPOSITE YEAR

As may be apparent by this point, the observational projects of Jones, Leopold, Thoreau and other early phenologists were predicated on the belief in "a natural order," a "deep structure to all vegetational patterns that could be ascertained by any diligent student."[86] As Thoreau suggests, the limited timescale of an individual's own observation may impede recognition of this natural order: "It takes us many years to find out that nature repeats herself annually. But how perfectly regular and calculable all her phenomena must appear to a mind that has observed her for a thousand years!"[87] Distilling centuries of phenological observations—smoothing the data—would reveal, Thoreau suggests, the composite year in Concord. Jones and Leopold, echoing Thoreau, acknowledge that this idea of a composite year is statistical or intellectual rather than material: "It is not to be assumed, of course, that the sequence of averages repeats itself exactly each year, and still less that the average sequence for our region is identical with that for other regions," they note. "Indeed, the whole concept of a series of average dates is in one sense an abstraction, for *it can never be found in toto* in the field. Nevertheless it exists, and it is an important characteristic of the flora and fauna."[88] They generated charts depicting these "average dates," even inventing a figure they called a "phenograph" to illustrate how "the character of a season can be expressed by a succession of deviations" from the average.[89] This project of discerning the composite year—of elucidating a "regular and calculable" seasonal order—galvanized nineteenth- and twentieth-century settler phenology.

Similarly, the idea of climate is premised on the concept of a composite year. Climate, as the Intergovernmental Panel on Climate Change notes, is "the average weather" in a place, often calculated over a period of thirty years or more.[90] This averaging of the annual weather is a process that can be done—as the IPCC suggests—statistically, but is more often done instinctively. The geographer Mike Hulme explains: "Beyond scientific analysis, climate may also be apprehended intuitively, as a tacit idea held in the human mind or in social memory of what the weather of a place 'should be' at a certain time of year."[91] And if the composite year is lodged in the mind or in social memory, then literature is partially responsible for

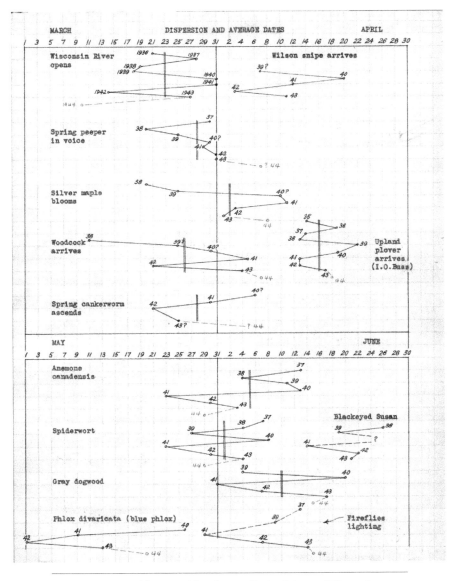

FIGURE 1.3 Aldo Leopold and Sara Elizabeth Jones, "Dispersion and Average Dates." Aldo Leopold Papers, Series 9/25/10-6, Box 8, Folder 3. Courtesy of the Aldo Leopold Foundation and University of Wisconsin-Madison Archives.

shaping its expected contours. In this sense, climate—the expectation of how the year will unfold in a given place—is inflected by the literary.

Literary texts with a phenological bent are paragons of the composite year, case studies in how this form coheres and functions.[92] While Thoreau chose a loose seasonal progression and Leopold employed a stricter almanac form, both writers structured their texts as composite years; Thoreau narrating his two-year residence at Walden Pond within a single seasonal cycle and Leopold condensing multiple years into a twelve-month time frame. Thoreau makes his methodology explicit: near the conclusion of "Spring," he moves from detailed phenological description into a statement of year-to-year equivalence: "On the third or fourth of May I saw a loon in the pond, and during the first week of the month I heard the whippoor-will, the brown-thrasher, the veery, the wood-pewee, the chewink, and other birds ... And so the seasons went rolling on into summer, as one rambles into higher and higher grass. Thus was my first year's life in the woods completed; and the second year was similar to it."[93] In that final phrase—"the second year was similar to it"—lies the crucial point: as a literary device, the composite year assumes a climatic average in which environmental rhythms from one year can be mapped onto any other. To write a composite narrative is to assume a climatic average, to trust that a year will unfold as anticipated, that established rhythms will proceed apace. The composite year that Jones, Leopold, and Thoreau infer as phenologists—their trust in a discernible pattern of repetition—is a precondition for the narrative form of phenological literature. Phenological writing of this kind—texts containing a heavy proportion of phenological description, combined with this formal condensation and compression of years—replicates, and contributes to, the production of a sense of climate.

"AS IF YOU COULD KILL TIME WITHOUT INJURING ETERNITY"

In 1995, as Buell reflected on Thoreau and Leopold's writing, he noted that "seasonal succession . . . has not (yet) been affected more than marginally" by human influence.[94] By 2014, however, scientists publishing on temporal ecology and phenological research had an entirely different understanding of how anthropogenic activity impacts seasonality and environmental time. While climate change has been most frequently measured and symbolized through increases in atmospheric carbon dioxide, Elizabeth Wolkovich and a team of scientists analyzing contemporary phenological data recently described climate change and contemporaneous environmental damage as "the effective manipulation of time by humans."[95] As rising global temperatures alter established phenological rhythms, they "fundamentally alter how organisms experience time."[96] And since warming registers temporally, it also registers aesthetically. The composite year is ruptured: each year is now understood as unprecedented and unpredictable, not easily condensed into an aggregate form.

Under the pressures of rising greenhouse gases, forms like the literary almanac—premised on the composite year—are already developing anachronisms. Etymologically, the word *almanac* is likely a derivation of the Arabic word for climate, *al-Munaakh*.[97] As prognostic publications detailing anticipated weather and phenological events, almanacs produced since the rise of the printing press have been compiled for fixed periods, most commonly a single annual round, but occasionally for ten or thirty years. Most of these utilitarian almanacs are print ephemera.[98] In contrast, the literary almanac—by which I mean literary prose employing a day-by-day or monthly calendar as an overt organizing apparatus—has been understood as more enduring, offering a profile of the year. Literary almanacs, often drafted by compressing multiple years of observations into a single year of prose, offer descriptive templates of the environmental rhythms that characterize a given place. For instance, in the "July" chapter of his almanac, Leopold describes the compass plant, or cut-leaf Silphium, "spangled with saucer-sized yellow blooms resembling sunflowers" that he notes commonly blooms on the fifteenth of the month.[99] However, phenologists resuming observations at the Leopold Shack between 1994 and 2004 note that the compass plant "would no longer find its place within the 'July' chapter" of Leopold's literary almanac because its average date of first bloom is now June 26.[100] Leopold's textual July no longer matches the month's manifestation on the material landscape. As climate and seasonality shift, the literary almanac, which hinges on enduring patterns of seasonal progression, becomes unmoored from its physical references, rendering it as ephemeral a form as its more utilitarian kin. To state this argument more forcefully, drastic climate change—anthropogenic times in which seasons no longer match what came before or what will come after—renders the literary almanac an impossibility. We are witnessing the obsolescence of a literary form.

Beyond literary almanacs, which have a particularly rigid relationship to environmental time and are therefore more prone to obsolescence, other forms of phenological writing are shifting. As Alastair Fowler notes, although "obsolescence is the most noticeable change a genre may suffer.... it is only one—and not necessarily the last—of a series of changes that generic forms continually pass through."[101] Seasonal rhythms embedded in works like *Walden* now register as historical baselines, rhythms that continue to exert an anticipatory force, even as seasonality grows increasingly volatile. Rhythms, Paul Fussell argues, establish a "metrical contract" with those who experience them: they are fundamentally patterns of anticipation.[102] Once this metrical contract has been established through sufficient repetition, a rhythmic pattern will proceed as a silent, underlying temporal force, even as a text's rhythms begin to deviate. A brief discrepancy between the metrical contract and the text's rhythm will produce "prosodic tension," interesting and even pleasant variation, but sustained or severe discrepancies will produce a feeling of arrhythmia.[103] For instance, when Walden Pond's ice cover lasted only ten days in the winter of 2012, it surpassed the point of prosodic tension, registering as a disruption of seasonal form. Reading a work like *Walden* can reinforce a metrical contract based in bygone phenological rhythms, exacerbating contemporary experiences of phenological uncertainty.

In this sense, warming is producing climate arrhythmias, and these arrhythmias register in literary writing and reading, as well as scientific studies. As Richard Primack imagines Thoreau returning to Walden Pond in the year 2064, these arrhythmias predominate his vision:

> Thoreau would notice many changes. The winter weather is no longer as cold as it used to be; the daytime temperatures are mostly in the pleasant 50s, and the nighttime temperatures are above freezing. Walden Pond no longer freezes over, and wood ducks remain on the pond all year long.... In the spring, there are hardly any wildflowers in the forests; the climate is now suited to more southern species, but they have still not migrated to the area. The trees are leafing out in March rather than in early May, and many seem sickly because of attack by newly arrived invasive insects. And there are not as many migratory birds as he remembered. Walden Pond has become too warm for trout. The swamps and bogs where the naturalist

used to enjoy spring choruses of peepers and other frogs have now dried up and are silent.[104]

Walden crafts a correspondence between spring and rejuvenation, the season's arrival at the close of the narrative serving as reassurance of environmental continuity. If the arrival of spring now highlights climate change's arrhythmias, is Thoreau's joy in the thawing sand and clay based on a historic form of seasonal significance? Is it possible to rejoice in Thoreau's textual spring if the contemporary rendition of the season produces an anxious affect? There is a recursive argument to be made about the interplay between literature and seasonality in the age of climate change: part of the unease generated by disrupted phenology and weather is attributable to the disruption of seasonality's literary resonances, and unstable seasonality and unpredictable weather shift established literary tropes in turn. Put more simply, climate's literary significance impacts the way that climate change is perceived while climate change's effects on seasonality and weather impact the way that literature is interpreted.

To comprehend the continuing force of the composite year and the literature that embodies it, an analogy to Primack's phenological fieldwork may prove useful. Resuming phenological observations in Concord in the twenty-first century, Primack and members of his lab searched in vain for some of the plants mentioned in Thoreau's *Journal*, concluding after years of fruitless searching that they were "botanical phantoms, plants that have vanished from the landscape." In the surrounds of Concord, these species are "locally extinct."[105] If, in botanical terms, warming produces "ghost plants," then in literary terms, warming may produce ghost forms. The composite year, as a literary device, now haunts seasonal writing, often present as reminiscence or elegy.

ANTHROPOGENIC PERIPETEIA

In 2005, as literary discussions of climate change were gathering steam, the writer Robert Macfarlane theorized that "forms which are chronic—which unfold within time" will prove indispensable.[106] Speculating about the future of environmental literature, Macfarlane pointed to a need for chronic forms "capable of registering change, and weighing its consequences."[107] Phenological records are among the most chronic of forms—in comparison to other accretive works like serial fiction, phenological records have the capacity to unfold over the course of centuries, layering each new year's leafings, migrations, witherings, and frost upon the last. In their sparseness—skeletal lists of dates for a given landscape—their maintenance passes easily from recorder to recorder, from generation to generation.

As climate change intensifies, these records are indeed waking from dormancy, revived through fresh contributions by a new generation of phenologists and galvanized by anthropogenic climate change. If colonial activity rendered 1852 a banner year for phenological activity, the feverish early decades of the twenty-first century mark another peak in phenological interest, a reminder that colonialism and climate change are inseparable processes. After a lapse of twenty-nine years, Nina Leopold Bradley, Aldo Leopold's daughter, resumed phenological observations near the shack. Her observations, extending from 1976 until her death in 2011, prolong the record that Jones and Leopold initiated in southeastern Wisconsin. Likewise, observations by Richard Primack and members of his lab are revitalizing the phenological log initiated by Thoreau, new entries accumulating as Primack "repeat[s] the same observations made a century and a half ago."[108] These repetitions are eerie echoes, a reminder that settler scientists now struggle to discern fluctuating pulses of environmental time, catching them only as they ebb and thud.

A similar impulse to renew observations is occurring within seasonal prose: *Returning North with the Spring*, a seasonal travelogue by John Harris, retraces the 1947 cross-country road trip of Edwin Way Teale and his spouse Nellie. Teale's account of chasing "the long northward flow of the season" formed the first volume of his seasonal quartet, *North with the Spring*, and Harris's repetition of this journey in the early twenty-first century documents how climate change and other pressures have altered the landscape during the intervening years.[109] Similarly, in *Early Spring*, published in 2009, the ecologist Amy Seidl invokes Rachel Carson's *Silent Spring*, reflecting on Carson's magnum opus as she recounts seasonal anachronisms cropping up in her own backyard. She describes a rainy January in her New England garden:

> I find two onion plants, holdovers from last summer that we missed during the harvest.... they are shooting up, responding to the ice-free earth and "expecting" continued warmth from here on. Nearby, the rhubarb plants remain thankfully underground, but the climbing yellow roses that were in bloom when December arrived retain the last of their tired pendulous blossoms; they have been flowering since July.[110]

Seidl's onion plants, sprouting prematurely, produce local evidence of disjointed times. The ceaseless roses prevent a sense of seasonal closure, lingering well into winter—also unexpected. Across phenological records and seasonal prose, we are witnessing a wave of revivals, an impulse to collate historical and contemporary seasons.

As charts and logs, as columns recording annual ice-out dates and migratory arrivals, phenological records maintained prior to anthropogenic climate change lacked narrative force, generating little interest among literary critics. They were, borrowing Hayden White's classification, akin to annals, consisting "only of a list of events ordered in a chronological sequence."[111] But while annals imply a linear temporality, each entry in these phenological records implied repetition, or in Wai Chee Dimock's expression, "the sense that there will be more, that whatever is happening now will happen again, a dilation of time that makes the future an endless iteration of the present."[112] Before the onset of climate change, the meaning of the records initiated by Thoreau, Jones, and Leopold coalesced with each new entry: each notation was a further accretion of seasonal form, a further crystallization of the composite year. In this sense, as Laura Dassow Walls notes, the science of phenology resists literary conventions because its phenomena emphasize "continuance, rather than narrative closure."[113] These phenological records were understood as documenting stable seasonal patterns, texts that elucidated the contours of the composite year in Massachusetts and Wisconsin.

However, as phenological work enters the twenty-first century, the purpose of these records alters. The force of a narrative, according to White, is generated through peripeteia: a sense of change over time, a shift in meaning. And with the onset of anthropogenic climate change, the significance of phenology has shifted: unlike Thoreau and Jones and Leopold, who practiced phenology as a means of intuiting the environment's temporal order, current phenologists track environmental events to intuit change. They take the pulse of a shifting environment, attending to seasonal rhythms just as environmental temporalities begin to respond to an overheated world. Contemporary phenologists record the annual ice-out on Walden Pond and the blossoming of phlox in southern Wisconsin in order to detect environmental arrhythmias, not to confirm established rhythmic forms. As current phenologists and writers juxtapose contemporary arrhythmias with the rhythmic forms that phenologists like Thoreau and Jones and Leopold observed during the nineteenth and early twentieth centuries, the peripeteia necessary for narrative emerges. Phenological pulses no longer signify the climate's continuity and vitality, but rather serve as indicators of climatic disorder. The climate crisis looms over these resumed records, an inevitable context for interpreting alterations in bud-burst or hatching dates. This shift in meaning constitutes the "passage from one moral order to another" that characterizes a "fully realized story."[114] Phenology has become "the means to track such shifts of meaning, that is, narrativity."[115] The records that Thoreau and Jones and Leopold meticulously compiled now generate their ethical and affective force from the emerging story of anthropogenic impact on environmental time. Each year is now understood as seasonally singular, as unrepeating and unexpected. In an age of arrhythmia, the future loses its form. It is no longer easily anticipated.

2

REPEAT PHOTOGRAPHY DURING THE GREAT ACCELERATION

A pair of photographs: In the first, an arctic fox, strikingly white against a rusty brown tundra. The landscape's dark soil and winter sedges contrast so sharply with the fox's milky fur that the photo feels tense. The polarity is sharp, volatile: the colors push against each other like repellent magnets. In the second photograph, the photographer's mittened hand holds out the first photo, positioning it within a snow-covered arctic scene that renders the fox's white coat a perfect camouflage.[1] The second photo eases the seasonal tension produced by the first: it reconciles the palette, restoring the visual consonance between pelt and icy drifts. The arctic fox—*vulpes lagopus*—is once again in concert with the snow.

This pair of photos, "Difluo Animalis," taken between 2010 and 2011 by the American photographer Christina Seely as part of her series "Markers of Time," captures a phenological mismatch in the arctic. Phenological mismatches—time-based relationships thrown out of joint—multiply as capitalism and military action in the Global North char the world. In Canada, a severe 2012 heatwave forced female ground squirrels to cut their hibernation short, leading to a mismatch in mating season with the less heat-sensitive males.[2] In Greenland, caribou winter on lichen along the coast and then

FIGURE 2.1 Christina Seely, *Defluo Animalis: Vulpes Lagopus Diptych*, 2011. Courtesy of Christina Seely.

migrate toward their interior calving grounds, but the tundra grasses that sustain newborn caribou now emerge too early to fully nourish the herd.[3] And as the exhibition label next to Seely's photographs notes, the arctic fox "is a coat-changing species now out of synch with new climate patterns."[4] Like the snowshoe hare and the stoat, the arctic fox's coat continues to molt in accordance with the photoperiod—the length of daylight—even as winter snow cover shortens in a warming arctic.[5] This new dissonance between seasonal light and temperature leaves the arctic fox exposed, "bright white and vulnerable on the brown tundra for weeks at a time on each end of the winter coat-changing season."[6]

Light, color, exposure, time. These elements lie at the heart of the arctic fox's seasonal mismatch, but they also underwrite the art of photography. This chapter explores the crosscurrents between phenological research and photographic art, tracing longstanding efforts to visualize phenological change in glacial regions through a camera lens. Three forms—repeat photography, time-lapse film, and long-exposure photography—augment the camera's capacity to capture change over time. As they tinker with photographic rhythms, adjusting repetitions, intervals, and durations, scientists and artists strive to condense or accelerate time. In the post-1945 proliferation of environmental crises often referred to as the Great Acceleration, these photographic projects become eerily resonant; photographic form and environmental context mirror each other.

In what follows, I construct an argument about temporal optics, advocating for the necessity of thinking about—and viewing—anthropogenic climate change within seasonal time frames rather than defaulting to the vast rhythms of deep time. The regions and places that the geographer and Indigenous studies scholar Jen Rose Smith terms "ice-geographies" have become associated with geological time, their icescapes framed in relation to eons rather than more tangible seasons of melt, emergence, movement, deposit, and freeze.[7] Much of this deep-time framing can be attributed to the essays, films, and photographs that keep the climate culture industry churning.[8] Literary scholars speak often of master narratives or master metaphors—dominant cultural scripts or topoi—but deep time now functions as a master temporality, a chronological scale controlling climate discourse. I argue that the optics of deep time fail to capture human and nonhuman life in the Arctic and other ice-geographies. Deep time obscures the relationships and everyday interactions that play out on more visceral timescales, including the historical and the seasonal. It blurs over the caribou, searching for the tender grasses that once prevented hunger.

In the process of constructing this argument about temporality, I also bring the work of contemporary women photographers into focus. With a few crucial exceptions, the history of phenological art and photography is a history interested in men behind cameras. Key figures in this chapter—Seely and the scientists Isla Myers-Smith, Alison Beamish, and Mary Caswell Stoddard—train their camera lenses on seasonal time, capturing phenological mismatches and multispecies arrhythmias. Likewise, the ecomedia theorists and temporal interlocutors in these pages—Allison Carruth, Bathsheba Demuth, Isabelle Gapp, Elaine Gan, Heather Houser, Dani Inkpen, Melody Jue, Stephanie Krzywonos, Naomi Klein, Jen Rose Smith, Kathryn Yusoff, and others—collectively signal the robust contributions of women and nonbinary thinkers to conversations about visual narrations of glacial rhythms. Impelled by Lisa Bloom's caution that the "welcome reemergence of interest in polar narratives and art" during anthropogenic climate change "often comes wrapped in a colonial nostalgia for white male heroism," the overwhelming majority of contemporary voices in this chapter stem from alternative outlooks.[9]

When I ask Seely about her diptych, she offers a story. The first photograph of the arctic fox, she tells me, was taken in October of 2010 in Svalbard, Norway; the lack of snow cover at that point in the year felt disconcerting. As she hiked back from an abandoned American coal mine once operated by the Arctic Coal Company, the fox appeared, starkly visible against the dark terrain. This narrative context feels vital: American imperialism in the Arctic is visible just beyond the photographic field, the emissions from the coal it unearthed contributing to the photograph's color contrast. Seely knew that the image resulting from this encounter was not a work of nature photography—not a portrait of an arctic fox as much as a portrait of a season out of joint—but without a companion shot, it could easily be mistaken by viewers. She took the second photograph a year later, clarifying the stakes. As I study the second photo in Seely's diptych, the photographer's hand remains enigmatic. It covers nearly a third of the image, looming over the snow.[10] Perhaps it signals a gesture of restoration, a phenological realignment generated through photographic art. But perhaps it just materializes the way that anthropogenic activity in the Global North now separates the arctic fox from the icy rhythms of its surroundings, the photographer's hand nothing more than a visual synecdoche. I do not ask

Seely to explain, allowing the photograph to balance between these two possibilities.

THE MASTER TEMPORALITY OF DEEP TIME

In the first decades of the twenty-first century, a flurry of trade books and public writing addressing anthropogenic climate change correlated glaciers with immense timescales. "To drill through ice is to descend backwards in time," the science writer Elizabeth Kolbert argued in her 2006 *Field Notes from a Catastrophe*. "In the Greenland ice there is volcanic ash from Krakatau, lead pollution from ancient Roman smelters, and dust blown in from Mongolia on ice-age winds."[11] The poet and printmaker Nancy Campbell, in a 2018 book titled *The Library of Ice*, waxes lyrical about Antarctic glaciers, describing polar ice as "the first archive, a compressed narrative of all time."[12] The scholar and photographer Anne McClintock suggests that "ice is the custodian of deep time, sealing the past in its frozen crypts. The Arctic's white domes are the keepers of the earth's memory."[13] And the geologist Marcia Bjornerud, in a 2018 book titled *Timefulness*, explains that "the gas bubbles trapped in polar ice.... tell us that over the last 700,000 years, global temperatures have been correlated at the very highest level of statistical significance with the concentrations of the greenhouse gases carbon dioxide and methane." She posits: "Fathoming deep time is arguably geology's single greatest contribution to humanity."[14] Throughout recent climate writing—by scholars, reporters, and scientists—glacial regions have become synonymous with colossal chronologies, with climate rhythms that play out over the course of millennia.

The rise of deep time as a master temporality within the climate culture industry coincides with the popularization of the Anthropocene as a geologic epoch. Although this proposed unit of geological time is omnipresent in scholarly and public environmental writing, I avoid it in this chapter—and in this book—for three reasons. First, as scores of critics have noted, the "anthropos" of the term is dangerously sweeping, attributing responsibility for extreme environmental damage to the human species as a collective whole, rather than distinguishing between those who wreak environmental havoc and those who are subjected to it. Second, the Anthropocene is too often employed as sloppy shorthand for climate change; they are not synonymous concepts. Many of the geologic markers associated with the Anthropocene—plastics embedded in the fossil record, the presence of radioactive fallout in sediment deposited after the mid-twentieth century—lie beyond the scope of this book, and I refrain from using the term partially in hopes of increasing precision. Third, and most crucially for my purposes here, the Anthropocene immediately invokes geologic timescales, cementing deep time as a master temporality within environmental discourse. It produces what the geographer Kathryn Yusoff describes as "selective perspectivism," one that overlooks the violence inflicted on Black and Indigenous peoples in the process of geologic extraction, but also—and not unrelatedly—enforces a temporal optics that obscures seasonal, lived time.[15]

What would it mean to focus, instead, on the seasonal rhythms of glacial places? To render these environments in palpable tempos rather than immense eons and eras? Small glimmers of seasonal time are present in recent writing from glacial regions. Rather than portraying these icy habitats as inert geological tomes, the historian Bathsheba Demuth describes the Bering Strait as seasonally dynamic: "When the sun returns, water pools overflow, jewel blue and green, on the ice. Then the streams roar. By midsummer, rivers erode their banks, opening walls of permafrost to the sun. The annual pulse of freezing and thawing, raining and running downriver, reshapes the land."[16] Jen Rose Smith attends to the lives that pulse within this northern hydrology, describing glacial "soil that grows cabbages the size of planets, thousands of pounds, weighed every year at the fair." She recalls summers in Alaska, when kids would "pack into a friend's truck and hotrod out the road" to the glacier's edge, building a fire to roast hotdogs "with our flannels pulled high around our necks to shield from the glacier air that sighed in our direction."[17] Stephanie Krzywonos, reflecting on her years in Antarctica and the astronomical calendars of her Mexican ancestors, describes the shifting seasonal light: "Dozens of us gathered, performing the Antarctic ritual of watching the last sunset. . . . But the deeper I went into winter, the more I entrusted myself to its dark womb, I found light. The flow of green auroras fed my eyes, my heart, my belly. The freckled Milky Way, too."[18] These depictions of vibrant, lively glacial places—their seasonal lilts and shifting hues—blur to nothing on the scale of deep time. But these passages are the ones I cling to as this argument proceeds—they flicker in the background, waiting for someone to adjust the narrative lens and bring them into focus.

REPEAT PHOTOGRAPHY

"Evidence," the historian Dani Inkpen writes as she reflects on repeat photography of glaciers, "has a history."[19] And as a form, repeat photography is associated with the science of glaciology, emerging through scientific rather than strictly artistic innovations. In 1888, the German mathematician and glaciologist Sebastian Finsterwalder conducted a photographic survey of glaciers in the Austrian Alps. Returning a year later to the precise locations of his original shots, Finsterwalder captured new images from the same vantage points, photographically assessing topographical change over the course of the year. As the story goes, he thereby "pioneered the technique of repeat photography involving deliberate and careful matching of older photographs with newer photographs from the same camera station."[20] While there are notable precedents to Finsterwalder's photographic repetitions, this glacial origin story grounds repeat photography in questions about glacial change over time.[21]

The promise of repeat photography lies in its accumulative potential and its temporal reach. Advocates of repeat photography as a scientific methodology encourage practitioners to maintain "a continuous image record of a consistent field of vision for as long as possible," thereby generating deep visual records of an icescape.[22] Indeed, scientists tracking glacial recession and changes in snowpack find that repeat photography's "main benefit is its ability to offer longer temporal scales of analysis."[23] A repeat photographic study can produce a record spanning decades or centuries, particularly if photographers return to the location of historical photographs and replicate the viewpoints of these images. As the art historian Melissa Miles explains, the archives resulting from these projects provide "a means of visually comparing a subject in order to highlight change.... together the photographs attest to absences or differences over time."[24] Repetition's capacity to detect—and substantiate—change over protracted timescales constitutes its formal power.

While juxtaposed photographs portraying glacial retreat have become a hackneyed visual in the climate culture industry, embellishing news articles, lecture slides, and glossy fundraising materials, repeat photography has quietly flourished as a phenological practice. Poring over a series of photographs, taken weekly between 1978 and 2007 at the Abisko Scientific Research Station in Sweden's northern subarctic, a team of phenologists assessed trends in the duration of lake ice, melt date of snow cover, and time of peak foliage in local mountain birch. Although clouds and dim light rendered some of the snapshots unusable, they found that the visual archive documented "a decrease in the length of the winter season and a subsequent increase in the length of the growing season."[25] Over the course of the photographic series, high-elevation snow cover shortened by 3.1 weeks, while the birch trees attained full leaf cover 1.6 weeks earlier in the final years of photographs. Phenological records can be visual as well as written, the rhythms of environmental time gauged through a photo album.

But in these efforts to stretch the camera's temporal purview and employ it as a phenological tool, repeat photography enforces a particular visual optic. Riffing on one-point perspective, a geometric technique used during the early European Renaissance in which all lines converged on a single horizon point, Elaine Gan theorizes "one-point temporality," a phenological tactic that isolates a particular life or material from its surroundings and follows it along a linear time line toward a predetermined point of ripeness or maturation. Within the optics of one-point temporality, Gan argues, "assemblages of animals, plants, microbes, and others have to be ignored or eradicated. The logic of one-point temporality makes attending to co-constitutions or contradictions between and within these assemblages irrelevant."[26] Temporal optics control currents of attention, dictating the focus and priorities of observations.

A similar myopia is at work in repeat photography, often referred to as fixed-point observation.[27] Thinking alongside Gan, a fixed-point temporality enforces its own limited vision, insofar as it inherits a point of view. An ecologist rephotographing a scene to compare a historical image with the present conditions on the ground is bound to the vantage point that they inherit. In scientific studies employing repeat photography, point of view is often classified according to spatial angle: ground, aerial, or aerial oblique. But points of view—in photography as in literature—are ideological as well as spatial, and might also be classified as proprietary, sublime, surveilling, or colonial. As the art historian Isabelle Gapp documents, glaciologists interested in accelerating melt will turn to nineteenth-century paintings and sketches "to articulate historical glacial fluctuations," viewing the current state of ice in relation to these often sublime views.[28] Other comparative studies are aesthetically related to colonial surveillance: a team of glacial scientists led by Allison Curley relied on sketches made of Ellesmere Island's glaciers during the 1875–1876 British Arctic Expedition to "extend the record of change," incorporating these imperial viewpoints into current climate research.[29] As paintings, sketches, and photographs are repeated, views of wilderness, beauty, adventure, and conquest fix the point. Yet again, art and ideology inflect scientific data, and the crucial question for repeat photography is, always, who fixes the point from which change will be assessed.

Critiques of repeat photography—particularly the ubiquitous pairings of present and historical glaciers that circulate in the climate culture industry—often center on their aloofness toward disparity. As Rodney Garrard and Mark Carey note, "most repeat photography analyses of glaciers leave society invisible, thereby concealing all the factors that create differential vulnerability to climate change and natural hazards, such as wealth, education, class, race, gender, infrastructure, building codes and protection policies (or lack thereof), access to government aid, and many other variables that affect risk to glacier loss."[30] To chip away at the invisibility of the structures that generate these differential vulnerabilities—including colonialism and the fossil fuel industry—I turn now to two Arctic case studies, tracing the way in which power and hegemony are often engrained in the practice of repeat photography.

In some repeat photographic studies, the physical infrastructure of colonialism anchors the present to the past. A team led by the ecologist Dr. Isla Myers-Smith investigated the spread and height increase of willows on Herschel Island in the Canadian Yukon, relying on a set of fifty-five historical photographs that captured tundra vegetation—hare's-tail cotton grass, Arctic lupine, mosses, open sky—throughout the twentieth century.[31] Eleven of these photographs date from 1898 to 1920, taken while whalers, likely employed by the Pacific Steam Whaling Company, slaughtered bowheads in the Beaufort Sea and occupied the Inuvialuit's island. Ice houses and graves from the whaling settlement are visible within the camera's frame. Twenty-two photographs date from 1953 to 1956, taken by members of the Royal Canadian Mounted Police posted to Herschel Island, part of an extended police occupation marked by the rape and assault of Inuvialuit women and the first execution of Inuit men under Canadian law. And the final twenty-two photographs date from 1978 to 1987, gleaned from surveys preparing for the Qikiqtaruk Territorial Park, established during the Inuvialuit Final Agreement, a land claim signed in 1984. I think of Melody Jue's writing on milieu-specific analysis, "a mode of media studies and literary criticism that involves close attention to the conditions of perception in a given environment, and to the techniques of mediation possible within that environment," and ponder how a milieu weighted with such violence alters repeat photography itself.[32] What happens to a camera and photographer bound to these fixed points? As Myers-Smith and her team updated these photographs in the twenty-first century, they used the weathered fence posts and gravestones of this violent history as visual landmarks, indicators that allowed them to locate the exact sites and photographic angles of the historical snapshots. The structures of colonialism and police violence allow photographers to align the past and the present, facilitating this study of willow expansion in a warming Arctic. Studying these contemporary images—the gravestones of whalers and police now tilting in the glacial deposits and unstable permafrost—I wonder if we should view these updated photographs as an acknowledgment or an unawareness of climate science's colonial inheritance. Those fence posts—linking views of the tundra over the years—begin to feel eerily symbolic, the fraught stakes of repeat photography and inherited viewpoints.

Even when using photographic archives devoid of visible infrastructure, military imperialism and the drive for fossil fuel can saturate the practice of repeat photography, linking climate science to the institutions driving climate change itself. Examining shrub expansion in Alaska between 1945 and 2002, a team of American scientists relied on a repeat photographic study to determine that alder, dwarf birch, and willows multiplied along hill slopes and valleys, spreading rapidly in a warming Arctic. Their baseline set of historical photographs, which documented an area between the Brooks Range and the Colville River, were "taken out of the side door of an airplane that sometimes flew just 50 m off the ground," producing images "of exceptional quality and resolution."[33] But what the scientists deemed a "remarkable set of oblique black and white photos" was compiled by the United States Navy, prospecting for oil as the Great Acceleration commenced.[34] It is a photographic collection that enabled the drilling of exploratory oil and gas wells in an area now known as the National Petroleum Reserve-Alaska, west of the Arctic National Wildlife Refuge. There is something grimly ironic about repeating this photographic survey in the name of climate science, assessing the expansion of willows in the Arctic just years before President Biden's administration approved the Willow Project, giving ConocoPhillips the green light to construct more than two hundred oil wells in the National Petroleum Reserve-Alaska. The entanglement of repeat photography and the American military—the Department of Defense uses more petroleum and produces more greenhouse gases than any other institution in the world—may continue: as the geographer Dawna Cerney notes, declassified military reconnaissance images are a photographic archive thus far "largely unexplored."[35]

As digital cameras become less expensive, and as imaging technologies improve, phenologists increasingly employ "phenocams"—digital cameras designed for repeat photography or time-lapse films that will be analyzed in phenological research. Automated cameras reduce the time-intensive manual labor of returning again and again to a photographic site, particularly when the site in question is remote or difficult to access. In some studies, solar panel-powered digital cameras, installed at a fixed location, methodically generate an archive. For example, a Canon camera, protected by a fiberglass shield, was installed 3,356 meters above sea level in Uttarakhand, India, programmed to photograph alpine rhododendrons at 10 a.m., 1 p.m., and 4 p.m. each day from 2017 to 2020. The camera, the phenologists reported, worked especially well in the glacial Himalayas, capturing "strange incidences that might go unnoticed, especially in areas with no permanent habitation," including a skipped flowering in 2020 after unusually warm soil temperatures at the timberline eliminated the chilling period necessary for bud formation.[36] As phenocam use increases, reducing the labor of image collection and enabling scientists to amass colossal photographic archives, repeat photography gives way to time-lapse film. In this sense, time-lapse films are an example of what Heather Houser calls a technomedia, a visual perspective made available "through developments in technology and media that are inextricable from each other."[37] We turn to them now.

TIME-LAPSE AND ACCELERATION

In the wildly popular book *Rising: Dispatches from the New American Shore*, Elizabeth Rush describes watching a film clip of the Jakobshavn Glacier calving, the most monumental glacial calving ever captured on video. She contextualizes this clip within a longer acceleration of melt: "from 1900 to 2000 the glacier on the screen retreated inward eight miles. From 2001 to 2010 it pulled back nine more; over a single decade the Jakobshavn Glacier lost more ice than it had during the previous century. And then there is this film clip, recorded over seventy minutes, in which the glacier retreats a full mile across a calving face three miles wide."[38] Watching massive blocks of ice break off into the churning bay, torrents of meltwater coursing down, Rush resorts to the language of climate arrhythmia: "In medicine, a pulse is something regular—a predictable throb of blood through veins, produced by a beating heart. It is so reliable, so steady, so definite that lack of a pulse is sometimes considered synonymous with death. A healthy adult will have a resting heart rate of sixty to one hundred beats per minute, every day, until they don't. But a meltwater pulse is the opposite. It is an anomaly."[39] The crafted pulse of Rush's writing—"so reliable, so steady, so definite"—splits apart as she reaches the surge of meltwater. The glacial arrhythmia reverberates, transmitting from environment to film, from film to prose.

In all likelihood, the film clip that Rush references was filmed by members of the Extreme Ice Survey, in Greenland to collect photographic footage for time-lapse videos of retreating glaciers. Ubiquitous in the climate culture industry since the film *Chasing Ice* debuted in 2012, time-lapse films are a classic example of what Allison Carruth and Robert Marzec call "environmental visualizations," optical forms that shape "ways of seeing and also perceiving twenty-first-century ecological realities."[40] If glaciers have attained "celebrity status" in the climate culture industry, it is worth noting that repeat photographs and time-lapse films are the forms of ecomedia that enable their prevalence.[41] Part of their popularity is due to these forms and their ability to manipulate environmental time.

The story of this particular environmental visualization begins in 1888, when the German physicist Ernst Mach envisioned the possibility of time-lapse photography, suggesting that "the principle of *temporal diminution*," if applied to a rapidly exhibited photographic sequence, might render prolonged phenomena—such as plant growth, embryo development, and evolution itself—visible within the span of a single film."[42] In addition to being scientifically valuable, Mach believed that accelerating environmental processes "would have to elicit an aesthetically and ethically grandiose effect."[43] Mach's theory was first put into practice by the German plant physiologist Wilhelm Pfeffer, an early pioneer in the field of chronobiology. Pfeffer dedicated his career to determining whether the rhythmic movements of plant leaves were autonomic, internal rhythms or whether they were aitionomic, driven by external rhythms like daily fluctuations in light or temperature.[44] Between 1898 and 1900, Pfeffer transformed repeat photographs depicting a range of botanical phenomena into short time-lapse films that he displayed during his lectures at the University of Leipzig: the twenty-eight-day life of tulips; the movements of *Desmodium gyrans* and *Mimosa spegazzinii* over the course of three days; the development of a gravitropic curve in impatiens plants; and the development of fava bean roots over the course of eleven days.[45] From its inception, therefore, time-lapse photography lay at the intersection of art and science: it produced proof while captivating an audience—it was simultaneously fact and spectacle.

Time-lapse moved from the didactic—from photography as a mode of demonstration—into narrative in Yosemite National Park in 1912. Concerned that his still-life photographs of wildflowers "lacked life and movement," Arthur Pillsbury, Yosemite's official photographer, had begun keeping notes on certain species in Yosemite Valley, observing "when they started to open and how long it took."[46] Retrofitting an old camera with a motor gear, Pillsbury crafted thirty-second videos of unfurling petals: "a film thirty seconds, or thirty feet, long contains 480 individual pictures," he noted, "so if it took a flower four days to open it was only necessary to divide the 5,760 minutes in four days by the 480 desired pictures, which gave twelve minute intervals between each picture."[47] He played the resulting time-lapse films at evening entertainments attended by tourists visiting his photography studio in the park, gradually adding species to his repertoire. As tourists viewed Pillsbury's films, he gauged their reactions, noting that "seeing a reel of flowers growing and opening was to instill a love for them, a realization of their life struggles so similar to ours, and a wish to do something to stop the ruthless destruction of them which was fast causing them to become extinct."[48] During this period, park service officers routinely mowed the meadow to obtain hay for their horses, a practice which endangered some of the species that Pillsbury filmed. At a conference of park superintendents in Yosemite, Pillsbury screened his films, "talked conservation," and contrasted "pictures of the meadows taken in early days in '95 showing them covered with flowers waist high and the same meadows as they were at this time."[49] As Pillsbury's photographic evidence of change over time acquired ethical weight, transforming into a declensionist story of anthropogenic impact on the environment, time-lapse photography produced a conservationist narrative. From these early screenings on the open porch of the Studio of the Three Arrows, it became clear that time-lapse's particular capacities—its ability to bring the gradual into focus and its natural emphasis on setting—made it particularly adept at narrating environmental damage.

The most well-known environmental time-lapse films began with an assignment for the climate culture industry. In 2004, the *New Yorker* needed an arresting photograph of glacial runoff to illustrate "The Climate of Man," the series by Elizabeth Kolbert that would eventually form the basis of her book *Field Notes from a Catastrophe: Man, Nature, and Climate Change*. The photographer James Balog, with a graduate degree in geomorphology and substantial experience photographing large-scale natural forms, was an obvious choice for this assignment. Working in Iceland, near the warm Gulf Stream current, he began to suspect that glaciers enabled climate change to manifest aesthetically: "you could feel the end of the glacier happening right in front of you through the shapes and through the sculptures," he reports.[50] Upon his return from Iceland, he contacted *National Geographic*, pitching a 2006 follow-up feature on the glacier to depict its retreat. He returned to the Sólheimajökull Glacier in October of 2006, placing stakes into the ground to mark the precise positions of his camera, and then returned six months later, in April, to retrace the route of his initial expedition and rephotograph the glaciers from his fixed vantage points. Balog was so startled by the extent of glacial retreat that he initiated a long-term repeat photography project of twenty-four glaciers, installing Nikon D200 digital, single-lens reflex cameras to record ice geographies across Antarctica, Greenland, Alaska, Canada, Austria, and the Rocky Mountains.

Turning his footage of Iceland's Sólheimajökull Glacier into a time-lapse film that runs for one minute and eight seconds, Balog dramatizes glacial retreat: as the clip opens in 2007, meltwater flows off the ice, leaving the base of the glacier riddled with small grey lakes that spread until their shorelines merge into a stream. Over the next eight years, as the glacier's lower layers of ice disintegrate, disappearing into the growing river below, the top layers begin to resemble fragile shelves that eventually crumble into the frigid water, the larger blocks floating for a second or two on the screen before vanishing into the current. To watch the Sólheimajökull Glacier retreat over the course of this film is to witness the aesthetic manipulation of time: on the screen, environmental temporalities accelerate, tempos of melt, wind, and currents progressing nearly four million times faster than in ordinary experience. Within the world of time-lapse photography, environmental change acquires a new pace: it escalates, intensifies. At the beginning of the clip, on April 1, 2007, the glacier occupies almost 2/3 of the screen, and by the close on July 23, 2015, it inhabits perhaps 1/6 of the screen's top left corner.[51] In just over a minute, a massive ice form has morphed into piles of dirty snow. This film is an extreme form of time-lapse, specifically designed to make change over years—and if the images keep compiling, over decades—visible within a single, easily circulated clip. Its declensionist narrative is visually calculable on the screen of an iPhone or a laptop's web browser.

Integral to time-lapse film, rate is also a pivotal concept in climate science. As historians J.R. McNeill and Peter Engelke argue, climate change boils down to the fact that corporations and societies in the Global North "have removed carbon from the Earth and placed it in the atmosphere at rates much faster than occurs naturally."[52] Moreover, the rate of fossil fuel emissions dramatically accelerated in the second half of the twentieth century: by 1970, the Global North burned over 4 billion metric tons of carbon annually; by 1990, over 6 billion tons; and by 2015, 9.5 billion tons. The pace of glacial melt followed suit. Detailing these statistics, McNeill and Engelke write again of rate: "Glaciers in the European Alps, for instance, melted at the rate of 1 percent per year between 1975 and 2000, and at a rate of 2 to 3 percent after 2000. This was a global trend. Scientists tracking of thirty 'reference' glaciers scattered around the globe revealed that melting after 1996 was four times as great as between 1976 and 1985."[53] This escalation is paradigmatic of the post-1945 period commonly referred to as the Great Acceleration. As its moniker implies, the Great Acceleration is a period of breakneck rates: runaway consumption manifests as runoff.

The impacts of the Great Acceleration are particularly acute in the Arctic. Commonly referred to as polar or Arctic amplification, strong feedback loops triggered by the loss of sea ice and snow cover magnify melting and heat, rendering the poles extremely sensitive to climatic change. In this sense, glacial regions are accelerated geographies, their rapid melt an indication of global disruption registering through a place-specific temporality. Between 1979 and 2021, the Arctic warmed almost four times faster than the globe, and climate scientists note that regions of the Arctic Ocean near Europe and Asia have warmed up to seven times as fast.[54] Late autumn—November—is the most accelerated season in the Arctic, while in the warmth of July, the rate of warming is less accelerated compared to the remainder of the globe.[55] Even the rate of Arctic warming shifts with seasonal time.

In technical terms, a time-lapse film is produced by a purposeful discrepancy between the frame rate of a camera and the frame rate of a projected film. Frame rate—measured in frames per second (fps)—has been standardized at 24fps since cinemas incorporated audio in the late 1920s.[56] 24fps became the conventional rate of projection because it approximates the pace of human vision, the rate of the images flashing on the screen producing a seamless view for the audience.[57] Most film cameras also capture frames at 24fps, and since this matches the projection speed, films appear to move naturally. However, if a camera records at the standard rate of 24fps and this same footage is then projected at the accelerated rate of 48fps, time in the film will appear to pass twice as quickly. Viewers will be forced to consume the recorded footage in half the time that it took to film. In other words, if each frame collected by a camera is understood as a beat, then time-lapse films are created through the reduction of the intervals between a camera's snapshots. As the intervals between the metered clicks of a camera diminish, time is severely compressed.

Similarly, the climate during the Great Acceleration is often articulated as a climate of altered intervals, a climate in which events that ought to be spaced out over time now occur without their established interlude. This elimination, or reduction, of the interval is another mode of environmental condensation or compression, another way in which climate change is experienced as an environmental time-lapse. The rhythms of environmental time are shifting, events occurring with dramatically reduced intervals, as though environmental time is an accordion being compressed. In November of 2016, *The Guardian* reported that "2016 will very likely be the hottest year on record and a new high for the third year in a row ... [which] means 16 of the 17 hottest years on record will have been in this century.... the impacts of climate change on people are coming sooner and with more ferocity than expected."[58] Similarly, when Hurricane Irene hit the Caribbean in 2012, analysts suggested that it was a hundred-year event, the kind of storm that occurs once a century. But climate change will produce these types of storms more frequently, perhaps establishing a recurrence interval of every three to twenty years. According to projected models, even five hundred-year floods could, in the new climate, occur once every 25 to 240 years. The "storm of the century," climate scientists postulate, may become the new "storm of the decade."[59] The rhythms of environmental time are compressing, events occurring with dramatically reduced intervals, as though environmental time is accelerating.

As climatic rhythms shift, they produce a sense that we are witnessing phenomena beyond the established range of human temporality, living through a series of records and storms that previously would have occurred only in deep time. This extension of human time is the promise of the time-lapse—as Charles Tung notes, the cinematic form holds out the possibility of "grandiose access to inhuman deep time."[60] Allan Cameron and Richard Misek emphasize this point, noting that time-lapse converts nonanthropocentric rates to anthropocentric tempos: "time-lapse underlines the limits of anthropocentric temporal perspectives by bringing long-duration time scales to the forefront," they write.[61] Time-lapse films are therefore resonant because they serve as a metaphor for the experience of living in the Great Acceleration, a form that exemplifies the intensification or condensation of environmental time. But, as a form associated with deep time and its narratives, they also blur out images of humans moving within a landscape, visually exonerating the cultures and corporations causing the very change that they depict. Climate-themed time-lapse films offer a world of deteriorating landscapes without human characters, which may explain their viral popularity among audiences in the Global North.

These accelerated rates are associated with cinematic crisis. Prior to the adoption of sound, both cameras and film projectors were hand cranked, and the frame rate within a single scene often ranged wildly, accelerating or decelerating according to the camera operator's hand and the aesthetic preferences of the projector operator. In fact, as the film preservationist James Card notes, "it was taken for granted that early films would not be shown at a constant speed at all."[62] To accelerate the frame rate was often to indicate a state of emergency: the collection of instruction manuals that the Triangle Motion Picture Company sent projectionists along with their film reels repeatedly associate crisis and accelerated frame rate. "The two big battle scenes," Triangle notes in its instructions for a 1916 film, "should be speeded up considerably. Following the subtitle 'The Alarm,' shoot through it fast."[63] To accelerate frame rate was to craft a sense of crisis, the pace of cinematic temporality a crucial ingredient in a film's emotional impact. But as cinemas integrated sound, these variations in tempo became problematic because a film reel had to keep pace with the recorded soundtrack. Frame rates, therefore, had to be standardized, and once the pace of cinematic time was regulated, accelerations or decelerations became rare aesthetic effects. But this legacy of early cinema lingers: an accelerated frame rate still evokes intensity, apprehension, or unease. To respond to a glacial time-lapse film is to respond to the absence of intervals, to a drastic rhythmic condensation—to a disrupted temporal order evident not only through the disappearing ice on the screen but also through the very speed of the footage.

COLORS AND SPECULATIVE FUTURES

A study carried out by Alison Beamish and her colleagues in the Alexandra Fiord of Ellesmere Island in Nunavut—the same location that Allison Curley and her team relied on nineteenth-century sketches to assess glacial change—documents how seasonal change can manifest as a shift in color palette, an alteration in tints and tones. Tracking phenophases—including melting, leafing, and withering—through color changes in ongoing photographic surveys, Beamish and her team analyzed the RBG pixel values of digital repeat photographs. In each photograph, they calculated the relative intensity of red, green, and blue lights on a screen to reveal seasonal progression. Tracking the rate of green-up in a variety of sites across the island, some comprised primarily of willows, some of arctic avens flowers, and some of sedges and mosses that grow in wetlands, they documented the close correlation of color and time in the Arctic through their RBG data:

> The first images taken on day 165 were dominated by red/brown litter with little to no green with the exception of bryophytes. Images taken on day 179 showed a greening and new vegetation growth penetrating through the standing litter. By day 188, the majority of the canopy was green in all sites and the major species were flowering. In the remaining 3 days (191, 196, and 213), the changes in greenness were subtle and difficult to detect by eye. There was a gradual senescence of all flowers and the evidence of the commencement of leaf senescence in some images by day 213.[64]

Notably, the digital images allowed the phenologists to identify color shifts not visible to the human eye. Their digital Nikon D40 SLR cameras—and the Adobe software used to analyze the RBG composition of the photographs—enhanced their understanding of the rhythms of Arctic colors in 2012.

Beamish's study was also speculative, capturing photographs of plots on Ellesmere Island that have been artificially warmed since 1992. These plots, each one-meter square, had transparent fiberglass panels tilted over them, producing a 1–3°C warming in relation to current temperatures, replicating future climates. These warmed plots have been the focus of manual phenological observations for over a decade, the subject of a speculative phenological practice, but these photographs were the first images of futuristic color. Photographs of these experimental plots contained far more green than the control sites, an effect particularly visible early in the field season, suggesting an accelerating rate of green-up, with "significantly earlier mature leaves in warmed plots."[65] Speculative Arctic futures are both greener overall and greener earlier. With time, printed photographs fade—through exposure to sunlight, humidity, and smoke—the climate gradually dulling their colors. But with time, the actual Arctic grows luridly bright when exposed to the elements. Photographs taken decades from now will be colored with a new palette.

Speculating futuristic color is even more complex beyond the realm of human vision. In the Arctic, reindeers' inner eyes change color with the season, moving from a summer gold-turquoise to a winter deep blue.[66] This shift is synced to the astronomical seasons, the tapetum lucidum of a reindeer's eye reaching peak gold during the long daylight hours near the summer solstice and then deepening to blue as long nights set in near the winter solstice. The seasonal vision shift allows the reindeer to locate both eatable lichen and lurking predators as low winter light floods the snow-covered landscape in blue wavelengths. This carefully calibrated seasonal vision is already shifting in response to light pollution—reindeer exposed to artificial light can develop green winter tapeta—but it is not yet clear how diminishing snow cover will impact reindeers' vision of winter, especially if the rhythms of light and snowpack separate.[67]

To approach related questions, and to think about time-lapse work on the scale of the seasonal rather than the scale of the geologic, we head to the Rocky Mountain Biological Laboratory—set in alpine meadows nearly 10,000 feet above sea level. Located in the abandoned silver-mining boomtown of Gothic, Colorado, the climate research conducted at this laboratory unfolds in a place haunted by geologic extraction, by efforts to delve into deep time and generate capital. For most of the year, these meadows are buried under feet of snow, but as June approaches, only the glaciers on the nearby peaks remain. In the fields, lupines bloom and it smells like fresh grass. Broad-tailed hummingbirds—metallic green, some with a magenta throat—arrive, migrating north from their winter grounds in Mexico. The ecologist and evolutionary biologist Mary Caswell Stoddard also arrives with the members of her lab, here to discern how hummingbirds see color. "Birds have four color cone types in their eyes," she explains. "We humans just have three color cone types in our eyes . . . Birds are probably experiencing an even more colorful world than we imagine."[68] Stoddard installs hummingbird feeders next to lights enabled to display the full range of colors that the birds can see, gauging their ability to identify changes in color saturation and pigment. These labors recall Jue's avowal that the perceptual capacities of nonhuman organisms, often gauged "through scientific instrumentation and sensing devices," ought to "humble us into considering how our own sensory attunements are a very narrow band through which parts of the world might be perceived."[69]

Increasingly, Stoddard's work on avian vision is intersecting with phenology. Since hummingbirds use color to locate flower nectar, anything that alters the flower population during their weeks in the Rocky Mountains—including wildfires and altered blooming times—can impact their ability to source nourishment. Part of the problem is a classic phenological mismatch, a matter of presence and absence: "If climate change accelerates flower bloom times, then... hummingbirds—remember, they're migrating from Mexico—may no longer be able to coincide the time of their breeding behavior with the peak bloom of wildflowers," Stoddard explains.[70] But color also plays a vital part. Based on longstanding phenological research at the Rocky Mountain Biological Laboratory, it is possible to determine the relative proportion of meadow flowers in a given week in the historical phenological record. As Stoddard and her team note, the hues of the "visual landscape" are shifting: "We can actually go back in time and look at a particular week in 1988 and we can see that in this week the hummingbirds were mostly seeing yellow erythronium flowers. But during the exact same week in 2012, the hummingbirds mostly saw blue delphinium flowers."[71] For the broad-tailed hummingbirds, climate change registers as a shift in color, an unexpectedly blue world.

Moving fifteen time-lapse cameras across the meadows, Stoddard and her team now capture close-up footage of a variety of flower species, hoping to document hummingbird feedings. After four years of filming, their collective archive contains 40,000 hours of film—over four and a half years of video. Stored online, these years of video footage recall an infrequently discussed indicator of the Great Acceleration: the accelerating accumulation of digital data. "In 1993," Allison Carruth remarks, "the total amount of information on the Internet could be measured in gigabytes. Today an affluent household in the United States is likely to have upward of one terabyte of data stored on the cloud."[72] As Carruth indicates, storing this ballooning online data is highly energy intensive, and yet, Stoddard's archives contain knowledge inaccessible without technological intervention. The footage is beyond the capacity of human attention—either behind the camera in the field or in the lab on a screen—and accelerating the frame rate in a typical time-lapse would blur the brief seconds in which a hummingbird alights on a flower. The seasonal, the fleeting, these moments of lived time in a meadow, disappear within accelerated time. Instead, the ecologists employ a machine-learning algorithm to extract the frames of film containing hummingbirds, locating the 2,040 feedings that occurred as the cameras rolled. This technique is a powerful confirmation of Heather Houser's prediction that representing "the odd pulses of the climate crisis will increasingly ... be aided by advanced supercomputers and graphic technologies."[73] In the extracted clips of hummingbird figures, the ecologists discovered that in 2018—a scorching season "with conditions that we will expect as the climate warms"—erythronium flowers, a key source of nectar, had wilted by the time the migrating flocks arrived.[74] And in the erraticism of the anthropogenic climate, migrating flocks arriving in 2019, a season with excruciatingly late melt, struggled to locate plants that offered any nectar. Population surveys suggest that broad-tailed hummingbirds are decreasing in number. If they disappear, a particular vision of the world—one that exists beyond the bounds of human sight—will vanish with them.

CODA: LONG-EXPOSURE

Another series of photographs in Seely's collection is titled "Metra Simulti," Latin for "simultaneous rhythms." At first glance, two of the photos resemble abstract paintings, dominated by strokes of color, set off against black backgrounds. But upon closer inspection, they come into focus as long-exposure photographs, their lines and streaks generated by lights moving across the subarctic darkness. Seely adjusted the rate of her camera's shutter to make these images, leaving it open longer than conventional photography, allowing her to capture an extended period of time from a fixed point. In one of the prints titled *Metra Simulti: Rhythmis: Tidal/Industrial*, cargo flights heading to and from the Anchorage airport generate lines against the night sky while below, ice floes buoyed by a tide create a gauzy horizontal streak. In the other, *Metra Simulti: Rhythmis: Celestial/Industrial*, the neon green blur of the northern lights floats above thin lines

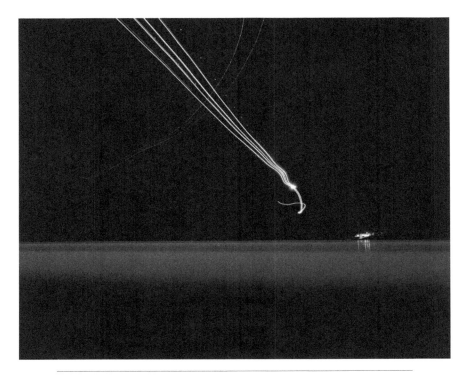

FIGURE 2.2 Christina Seely, *Metra Simulti: Rhythmis: Tidal/Industrial*. Courtesy of Christina Seely.

FIGURE 2.3 Christina Seely, *Metra Simulti: Rhythmis: Celestial/Industrial*. Courtesy of Christina Seely.

generated by the headlights of a freight truck. The traces of these industrial rhythms—their sharp lines—contrast with the rhythms of ice and the aurora borealis, which shade across the darkness.

Examining these photographs, I think of Naomi Klein's reminder that phenologists are studying seasonal mismatch "among dozens of species, from Arctic terns to pied flycatchers. But there is one important species they are missing: us. *Homo sapiens*. We, too, are suffering from a terrible case of climate-related mistiming.... the mismatch between climate change and market domination has created barriers within our very selves, making it harder for us to look at this most pressing of humanitarian crises with anything more than furtive, terrified glances."[75] Seely's photographs—which force the camera to maintain its gaze, unable to look away—invite their viewers to contemplate the disjunctures of the Great Acceleration. Long-exposure is both a photographic form and a stance within the climate crisis. Her camera stays trained on the industrial activity of the Global North, its frenetic rates registering as lines that bifurcate the photographic field and cut through other rhythms at play.

In these photographs, light and time feel simultaneously aesthetic and profoundly material. Their sharp lines are drawn by electricity and speed, generated by fuel or coal. I wonder what these planes and trucks are hauling north. Perhaps photography supplies: glass or toner cartridges, bottles of hydroquinone or phenidone. Perhaps paper, stacked in their trailers and holds like white drifts. They might be full of books, heading from a publisher's warehouse or an Amazon fulfillment center. A paperback book—including fiber acquisition, pulp production, printing, and transport—made in North America but distributed internationally, produces roughly the equivalent of 5.97 pounds of carbon dioxide.[76] These emissions hold on too, present in the atmosphere for the next three hundred to one thousand years. But before slipping into the abyss of deep time, where it becomes all too easy to detach carbon dioxide from the corporations and cultures that produced it, I return to the photographs and the industrial rhythms cutting through the gradations of the ice floes. A Boeing plane in the winter sky. A Freightliner semi-truck on a road bordered by gravel encased in ice. A photographer wearing a thick sweater and bulky coat as she stands outside beneath the iridescence of the northern lights, her breath visible in the air. Seely's shots make it almost impossible to look away.

UNSEASONABLE
NOVELS

3

URBAN PHENOLOGY AND MONSOON REALISM

In the coastal enclave of Urur Kuppam—situated in south Chennai, along the Bay of Bengal—urban phenological practices are alive and flourishing. The hook-and-line fisher S. Palayam and the environmental writer Nityanand Jayaraman walk along Besant Nagar beach in the pre-dawn light, examining plastic flotsam deposited near the tide lines.[1] Scanning the litter—"from bottles, used injection syringes to small packaging and empty, sea-worn convenience sachets of pickles, coconut oil and spice powders"—they analyze its distribution along the shore to determine the season.[2] In March of 2022, they noted that the debris was not dispersed evenly along the sand but clumped together in patches. The appearance of these plastic patches on the shore is a seasonal indicator, a sign that currents are shifting, the northern vanni beginning to give way to the southern thendi. Palayam explains to Jayaraman that "at this time of year—at the cusp of a new season" a clump of beach plastic "signals that a change is in the offing with the northern forces tiring, and the southern breeze and current asserting themselves."[3] Even plastic litter is governed by seasonal time, its appearance and configurations conditioned by the winds. I think about one of my favorite verses of classical Tamil poetry, attributed to an anonymous woman writer and translated by A. K. Ramanujan: "the rains, already old, / have brought new leaf upon the fields."[4] Now, along Besant Nagar beach, the winds have brought perforated tires and plastic bags upon the sand.

As Jayaraman notes, Palayam—who watches for bioluminescence in the Bay of Bengal, sinks his feet into the mud of the beach's intertidal zone to forecast storms, and confers on his cell phone with other fishers along Chennai's coast—is "a walking almanac."[5] Here on the coast, the winds and currents form seasons: Kachan naal, when they arrive from the south, is followed by Vaadai naal, when the monsoon comes from the northeast.[6] Since 2018, Palayam and Jayaraman have collaborated on a daily record of currents and winds in the Bay of Bengal. "Today's sea data is like this," Palayam observes. "The near shore current is thendi, flowing from south to the north. Whenever you have olini—the current flowing from the deep sea to land—we have thendi on the shore. In the Tamil month of Puratasi, usually, you have northerly winds and currents (Vaadai naal), but now it's different—we have southerly currents. Though at 3 a.m. today there was a light drizzle, the current has not changed from the southerly thendi—so the typical rains and northerly currents of Puratasi month are just not happening."[7] Palayam jots down his observations in Tamil, using paper charts that he stores in overflowing file folders—"I haven't taken a day's leave, despite heavy rain, wind or storms," he explains—and Jayaraman translates his entries into English, transferring them into an Excel spreadsheet.[8] As Palayam's "mental database" and the phenological "baselines committed to the collective memory of his community" are transcribed into Microsoft software, they generate a log that Jayaraman draws on as he drafts essays in English about Chennai's coastal phenology, publishing in *The Wire*.[9] Here, as elsewhere, phenology and writing go hand in hand.

For Jayaraman, this project of documentation and narration has a political valence. In Chennai, institutional meteorological observations date back to 1792, when the English East India Company acquired a meteorological observatory in the Egmore neighborhood. When I ask Sekhar Raghavan, the director of Chennai's Rain Centre, about precipitation records, he laughs and explains that "thanks to the British who ruled us," the Indian Meteorology Department contains extensive records of rainfall. He then quickly adds that he would not thank the British "for any other reason."[10] In contrast to these institutionalized climate sciences, which Jayaraman asserts "produce predominately elite and upper-caste experts," the project in Urur Kuppam is invested in Palayam's "subaltern" expertise.[11] Palayam's knowledge of seasonality and climate is produced through "a hand-me-down science refined over years of intimate observation of natural phenomena and the behaviour of native life-forms."[12] It is also produced through a particular trade, by four generations of labor within a coastal habitat. As I listen to Jayaraman and Palayam converse, small white egrets pick their way along the contaminated waters of the Adyar River where it meets the Bay of Bengal. I think about the credence granted through Excel spreadsheets and bylines, how phenological records gain authority via print. I hope Jayaraman's essays now stand as a testament to the stores of climate knowledge circulating through communities like Urur Kuppam.

Like other almanacs, both Palayam's internal records and Jayaraman's literary accountings are beginning to strain under climate change. In 2022, as the northeast monsoon arrived in Chennai almost a month late, Palayam noted, "It never used to be like this in my father's days . . . Seasons arrived as they ought to."[13] For the fishers along Chennai's coast, these phenological changes carry visceral consequences: without a storm lashing the Bay of Bengal and churning the fish, nets remain empty, months of income evaporating. The move from institutional observations to phenology conducted through labor brings climate injustices into focus: a delayed monsoon leads to financial precarity for people dependent on seasonal rhythms. When Jayaraman asks Palayam what has caused the shift in oceanic seasonality, Palayam alludes to inequitable consumption: in his fishing community, he observes, "we are repeatedly taught by our elders to control our greed. Just because you have the ability to take much, you should not. It is dangerous; it is immoral. Perhaps the state of our seas has to do with the replacement of these morals by a culture that does not know the meaning of the word 'enough.'"[14] I think of U.S. universities and the talks that I attend on carbon removal technologies, corporate net-zero targets, and electric vehicle sales. So much depends upon whether one thinks climate change is caused by chemical alterations to the atmosphere—increased proportions of carbon dioxide, methane, and other greenhouse gases—or by a culture of greed. These are not mutually exclusive views, but the distance between them feels vast, like ocean currents headed in different directions.

In this chapter, I strive to expand standard conceptions of phenology and the kind of writing associated with it. Rather than focusing solely on nonhuman arrhythmias and nature writing from the Indian subcontinent, I turn to prose detailing the political ecologies of water in the city of Chennai, tracking monsoonal arrhythmias as they manifest in empty pipes, altered livelihoods, dry wells, and lines of plastic buckets near neighborhood pumps. Reconceptualizing phenological observation to encompass its practice in megacities of the Global South, where the pulses of seasonal water percolate through infrastructure inherited from colonial regimes, it becomes possible to trace phenology's imprint within city fiction.

Chennai, often referred to as a motor city—Michelin and Bridgestone plants manufacture tires, while Nissan, Hyundai, BMW, and Caterpillar plants produce vehicles—is also a software hub, its IT Corridor lined with corporations like PayPal, Adobe Systems, Cisco, and IBM. Its geography functions as a mode of analysis here, this chapter moving from the coastal fishing enclave of Urur Kuppam to the neighborhood of West Mambalam to the Anglophone bookstore Higginbothams Private Limited. Recently, Chennai—like Cape Town and Phoenix—has become a metonym for water crises. In 2019, after an exceptionally deficient northeastern monsoon, its eleven million residents faced "Day Zero," the moment when tap water ceased running. Urban sprawl, which prevents rain from saturating the city's reservoirs, combined with proliferating bore wells that lower the water table, renders Chennai particularly vulnerable to water shortages. In a city like Chennai, the seasonal rhythms of water are inseparable from industry and a pipe system inherited from British colonialism. During 2019, those who could afford the expense purchased water from private tankers carted in from the countryside, those who could not scavenged for water, sometimes collecting it from leaking air conditioners.[15]

To examine how the monsoon inflects seasonal activity in fiction, I turn now to the novella தண்ணீர், *Thanneer*, or in its English translation, *Water*. Written by Jagadisa Thyagarajan, a modernist Indian writer more commonly known by his nom de plume Ashokamitran, it portrays the 1969 drought in Madras—the city was renamed Chennai in 1998, freed from its colonial moniker—and the struggles of the inhabitants to obtain sufficient water. First serialized in the Tamil literary magazine *Kanaiyazhi* between July and November of 1971, Ashokamitran's story was compiled into a book in 1973 and then translated into English in 1993.[16] In present-day Chennai, where residents speak Telugu, Urdu, Malayalam, Hindi, and English in addition to Tamil, some readers encounter Ashokamitran's fiction in the original Tamil, and others—like me— through its English translation. Rather than close reading turns of phrase or the accents of particular sentences, both of which are difficult to retain as a story seeps across languages, I examine the novella's patterning of scenes and narrative structure. Taking inspiration from the historian Sunil Amrith's reminder that "human lives and voices" are difficult to enfold into "meteorological data... readings of pressure and wind and moisture," I argue that *Water* provides an alternative accounting of urban drought.[17] Indeed, the formal patternings present in Ashokamitran's work suggest that literary realism is uniquely suited to capturing the everyday disparities of water scarcity. Attending to the climate rhythms that shape realist narrative can train readers to identify climate change not solely through spectacular occurrences, but also within ordinary routines.

URBAN PHENOLOGY IN THE GLOBAL SOUTH

Ashokamitran positions Jamuna, the main character in *Water*, as an urban phenologist. She surveys predawn Madras, observing her neighbors "speeding here and there with their pitchers and their water pots and their buckets, either on foot or with their vessels tied to their cycles."[18] She listens for the rhythmic "sound of those vessels being carried back, full of water," checks the ground for "those long streaks of water, left by the overflow of the vessels into the street."[19] Indeed, the novel opens by stressing Jamuna's attention to the pulses of her neighborhood's water infrastructure:

> As soon as she detected a slight difference in the sound of the water pump, Jamuna who had been lying in bed for the past half hour listening to the owners of that house working their pump, instantly shook herself awake. Switching on the light to the room, she lifted up the two brass water pots that were standing ready and ran downstairs.
>
> Water pumps were working away in all the houses of the neighborhood. In all those streets, in the one and the next, and the one next to that, in each one of the houses there, you could

hear very clearly at that early morning hour, the noises that were unique to its own water pump, separately and in unison.[20]

Jamuna's environmental observations are daily and precise, intensely local, and undertaken with the kind of dedicated attention that marks skilled phenological practice. And yet—because she resides in a densely populated megacity, rather than a rural locale; because she is a tenant threatened with eviction, rather than someone in possession of property; because she conducts environmental observation as provisioning, rather than pastime or sanctioned science; and because she measures drought via plastic buckets and used kerosene containers, rather than a rain gauge—her observations do not match prevailing representations of phenological study. The climate rhythms that interest her—the rise and fall of groundwater and the arrival of the rains—percolate through municipal infrastructure and the social stratifications of the city. They are entangled with socioeconomic divisions and therefore all too easily discounted.

Building on Ramachandra Guha and Joan Martínez Alier's influential dichotomy between the "full-stomach environmentalism" of the Global North, focused on conservation and wilderness, and the "empty-belly environmentalism" of the Global South, focused on access to natural resources, I contend that *Water* depicts not the full-stomach phenology of the Global North, but rather a variety of empty-belly phenology undertaken in the Global South.[21] I think of the observations depicted in *Water* as a form of social phenology in which attention is motivated by need as well as appreciation. Jamuna tracks environmental occurrences in her urban habitat—when rings are lowered into neighborhood wells to raise the water level and when a tank is installed on the street—not out of sheer curiosity, but out of the need for water to cook and bathe. She is a fluent interpreter of what the anthropologist Karen Coelho calls "waterlines," urban signifiers that occasionally register as "graphically readable, like the rows of plastic pots that appear behind water tankers near informal settlements, early indicators of a coming city-wide shortage."[22] Jamuna's internal phenological record captures the arrhythmias of the 1969 drought as they reverberate and echo across Madras:

> It was now months since the water had stopped coming out of their taps in that house. For the past month, there was only water enough in their well to fill perhaps four buckets in a day. It was over fifteen days since the water stopped coming to the one house right at the end of the street. Once in two or three days, the lorry came to fill up the water tank in their street. But because of the increase in numbers of the families who came to collect water there, they each got two plastic buckets' worth instead of the original three.[23]

Her log demonstrates how subtle shifts in the climate are detected "when we know a place deeply, not just as scenery but also as sustenance."[24]

Ashokamitran's novella quietly—but adamantly—grants Jamuna credence. It forces an acknowledgment of her environmental proficiency: she knows precisely where to obtain water, running to the house at the end of the street whenever the pump at her own apartment building runs dry, and she tracks relative water quality, noting that water drawn from the nearest tube well "seemed good enough. But within half an hour it would become discoloured. You could not use it for cooking, nor for washing clothes. You could keep it for washing your hands and feet."[25] Even more, the novella's repetitive descriptions of water collection enact her labor in discourse time, the accumulating pages a testament to her perpetual surveillance of pumps and wells.[26] One of the most revelatory moments in *Water* occurs as the rains finally commence in Madras: Jamuna appears at the very close of a vignette focalized on another character, a neighbor who ventures out with her umbrella and tins to collect rainwater in the middle of the night. As this neighbor arrives at the water spout attached to her building, she encounters "another form" there in the darkness, covertly filling a water pot.[27] The novella's readers and the unnamed neighbor are both unsure who has intruded on this scene, but as the neighbor calls out—"Who is it?"—Jamuna greets her.[28] Jamuna admits that she scaled the nearby wall, trespassing in her neighbor's yard—and, formally, in her neighbor's vignette—to collect water.[29] Throughout *Water*, Jamuna's furtive presence on the edges of vignettes focused on other characters' experiences gives the impression that she is continually monitoring water in the background, even as Ashokamitran's prose attends to other neighborhood residents.

SEASONAL INFRASTRUCTURE

The timing of the initial publication of *Water* in 1971 is worth noting: the novella is set during the prolonged drought that struck Madras in 1969, and the water shortages driving its narrative would have been fresh in the minds of the work's audience in Tamil Nadu. The 1969 drought was caused by irregularities in the monsoon: as *The Times of India* reported in March of 1969, "the rains failed this year. The shortfall was 25 per cent in the case of the south-west monsoon and 40 per cent in the case of the northeast monsoon."[30] As the monsoons failed, groundwater tables fell. By April, *The Times* reported that "wells and irrigation tanks by the thousands have run dry and even the Madurantakam tank in Chingleput District, one of the biggest in the State, is now a vast dust-blown bowl. . . . in at least one place, water ration cards have been issued by the panchayat to the people."[31] This detail adds historical texture to *Water*: Jamuna explains that her ration card allows her to obtain two pots of water from the tank installed in the street, filled by a lorry every two days. As pipes ran dry and pumps ceased to draw water, the subdued monsoon season altered the everyday rhythms of water in Madras. Climate percolated into hydrosocial routines, schedules, and habits.[32]

Water unfolds within the radius of a lower-middle-class neighborhood in Madras—when I speak with Ramakrishnan Thyagarajan, one of Ashokamitran's sons, over chai in his home in Velachery, he suggests that the novella is likely set in West Mambalam, a section of the megacity hit particularly hard by the 1969 drought.[33] Ashokamitran was a flâneur on a bicycle, he explains, and his repeated rides through West Mambalam presumably provided material for the various street scenes in *Water*. The specificity of this setting is crucial because access to municipal water varied by neighborhood during the drought. In a vignette depicting four laborers digging a trench to expose the street's cast-iron water main, a neighborhood resident stops to ask the laborers' supervisor—a city bureaucrat, employed by the Corporation of Madras—why other neighborhoods are faring better. "Sir," he ventures, "they say that places like Mandaveli and Mylapore are not suffering that much. It seems there is water in their taps at midnight. They are able to collect all that they need at that time."[34] The insinuation of this statement is partially about caste—Mandaveli and Mylapore are neighborhoods with large Brahmin populations—and partially about the inequities inherent in a water infrastructure inherited from a colonial regime. "As in other postcolonial cities," Coelho notes, "Chennai's pipe network is structured by historical geographies of power, embodying the exclusions and classifications of colonial rule."[35] Designed during British rule to funnel water toward areas of the city inhabited by colonists, the city's initial pipe network left lower-caste neighborhoods dependent on well water. As Madras expanded and new pipes were installed, neighborhoods like West Mambalam, that were located at the end of a pipeline—farthest from the city's stored water and distribution centers—were the first to experience a shortage. Therefore, the Corporation bureaucrat's response to the neighborhood resident—"The entire pipe system on this street was only recently laid"—is less a testament to its efficiency than to its distance from the city's water. Coelho argues that "the tail-end is both a location within a hierarchical piped water system and a trope encompassing all the challenges of politics, pollution and disorder that compromise the grid."[36] I would add that the pipe's tail-end, which serves as the setting of Ashokamitran's narrative, its cast-iron starkly visible because of the trench dug in the street, is also a timepiece.[37] It is a segment of infrastructure rendered especially sensitive to the monsoonal rhythms of rain and groundwater, an example of what Pamila Gupta calls "seasonal infrastructure."[38] For Jamuna and her neighbors, the tail-end functions as an urban phenological instrument, a gauge of both climatic conditions and the infrastructural legacy of colonialism.

Even within the tail-end milieu of West Mambalam, those who rent experience the water shortage more acutely than those who own property. To my knowledge, *Water* has not been read as a commentary on tenant rights during periods of environmental stress, but the mounting tension between landlords and tenants over scarce water pervades its pages, housing infrastructure contributing to the monsoonal rhythm structuring the arc of its narrative. Jamuna and her sister Chaya have no claim to the property held by their extended family—their uncle promises to deliver deeds allotting them a portion, but by the conclusion of the novella those documents have yet to materialize. In the meantime, as the owners of Jamuna's building fill their second brass pot from the pump, all the tenants gather, standing nearby with empty water vessels and asking for access:

> The landlady's son replied curtly, "There are ten of us in the family, all needing baths and drinking water. Just stand aside, please."

Another tenant put in, "All of us have to have baths too, where are we to go if you pump all the water from the tap for yourselves?"

The landlady declared, "But you people use up the water from the well and empty it completely without even waiting for dawn to break. Is it possible for us to compete with you there?"

One tenant said, "I've been trying to tell you for the past week. If you remove the pulley and rope as soon as it gets dark, then you yourselves could ration the water from the well, say two buckets of water each in the morning. You just refuse to do that. Then of course we have to push and shove at each other every day."[39]

Navigating the city without property means navigating it without water rights, and by the close of this scene, none of the renters have managed to obtain water. Jamuna's phenological record—measured in brass pots and plastic buckets—documents a more extreme drought than that experienced by the landlords on her street. Her notations register what the geographers Jamie Linton and Jessica Budds call the "hydrosocial cycle" of the monsoon, accentuating that how "water flows over space and time is also shaped by human institutions, practices and discourses."[40] Jamuna's phenological record documents how housing policies and class norms inflect seasonal timings across Madras. Her observations are particularly fine-grained, detailing seasonal tensions at the tail-end and occurrences within a distinct economic class.

CLIMATE CHANGE AND THE FIVE LANDSCAPES OF TAMIL LITERATURE

To appreciate the formal intricacies of seasonality in Ashokamitran's novella, we detour now through classical Tamil poetics. Musing on the uncertain future of South Asian monsoons, the historian Sunil Amrith turns to a Tamil poem dating from the first three centuries CE, translated into English by A.K. Ramanujan:

These fat *ko_nrai* trees
are gullible:

> the season of rains
> that he spoke of
> when he went through the stones
> of the desert
> is not yet here
> though these trees
> mistaking the untimely rains
> have put out
> their long arrangements of flowers
> on the twigs
>
> as if for a proper monsoon.[41]

Now, as the "season of rains" grows haphazard, swayed by greenhouse gas emissions and aerosols, these verses call out for a presentist reading. "Who knows what a 'proper monsoon' looks like any more?" Amrith asks as he parses the poem's premature blooms. "Over the past few decades, South Asian monsoons have swung between greater extremes of wet and dry.... Accelerating climate change brings even more uncertainty."[42]

These uncertainties about the monsoon reverberate forcefully in current readings of the *Ku_runtokai*, the anthology of classical Tamil poetry containing this poem. Within its pages, the seasons—the rains, the cold season, early frost, late frost, early summer, and late summer—are not backdrop, but components of an expressive syntax.[43] As Ramanujan explains, reflecting on his translation, "the poet's language is not only Tamil. . . . the world is the vocabulary of the poet."[44] The blossoming *konrai* trees and rains are conventional features in poetic depictions of the wait for a loved one's return; their presence evokes the yearning for reunion. "The rains, already old, / have brought new leaf upon the fields," my favorite anonymous woman poet writes. She continues: "In jasmine country, it is evening / for the hovering bees, / but look, he hasn't come back."[45] And yet another early Tamil poet compresses the rains and the longings conventionally associated with them: "As from rainstorms pouring / on a distant green land / my heart runs muddy."[46] I think about that translated line—*my heart runs muddy*—again and again during my time in Chennai, struck by its intermingling of seasonality and the interior currents that run through us. In classical Tamil poetry, the monsoon and the phenological occurrences bound to it comprise a "language within language," functioning not as independent images but as signifying motifs. Particular storylines and images are bound to particular temporal settings. In this way, newly distorted rainfall patterns garble the grammar of a literary convention.[47]

More materially, Amrith's impulse to read this poem from the *Kuruntokai* in light of climate change is almost uncanny: the anthropogenic climate has forced the *konrai*—the *Cassia fistula* or kanikonna trees—out of season in southern India. SeasonWatch, an Indian phenology collective with a dedicated cohort of observers in Kerala, reports that peak bloom no longer coincides with the festival of Vishu, held on April 14 or 15 each year.[48] Instead, to the chagrin of everyone accustomed to gathering vibrant yellow blossoms for the Vishu celebrations for the customary decoration of their homes, the trees now blossom erratically throughout the year. Aggregating data from their network of observers, SeasonWatch now charts "the pulse of the trees," attempting to track arrhythmias in recent blossoming. As Geetha Ramaswami explains, most *konrai* trees in Kerala reached peak bloom in 2017 before Vishu, and in 2018—despite yet another early blossoming—the trees came back into bloom after the celebrations had passed.[49] The botanist Jacob Verghese clarifies that these recurrent arrhythmias are due to altered groundwater: "The plant senses the fall in the water, becomes stressed and resorts to the survival strategy—blooming and reproduction. However, these days, the groundwater level falls numerous times throughout the year and whenever that happens, you can see the plant blooming. There is no particular season attached to it anymore."[50] He notes that air pollution also stresses the konrai, the ethylene released in vehicle emissions exacerbating these untimely profusions of buds.

But arrhythmias are never simply botanical. Mistimed konrai buds unsettle livelihoods based on seasonal markets, exacerbating financial precarity for those depending on a timely flower harvest. Flower vendors interviewed by *The New Indian Express* in 2022 attributed the season's shortages to climate change, citing both a premature blooming period and intense rains that felled the blossoms. Increasingly, plastic konrai flowers, imported from Delhi or abroad and sold for seventy to one hundred rupees in market stalls, are replacing fresh flowers in Vishu celebrations. Kalesh, a vendor interviewed by the *Times of India* in 2017, remarks that plastic enables people to buy flowers at any phenological phase: he sells bunches "with and without leaves, with buds and flowers, and those with flowers only."[51] These plastic konrai buds will never open, their petals will never wither. They are a seasonless adaptation, indifferent to the moisture of the monsoon and its percolations underground.

For his part, Ashokamitran concurs with Ramanujan's assessment that climate is its own language within Tamil literature. "It is almost a part of grammar that the setting should be specifically related to the human mood depicted in the poem," he writes in his analysis of Sangam poetry, the classical Tamil works including the *Kuruntokai*.[52]

He toys with this poetic grammar in *Water*, a novella set primarily in *pālai*, a parched place where dry wells and stagnant water predominate. As the literary critics M. Vinothkumar and V. Peruvalluthi note, the depiction of drought in the novella "knowingly or unknowingly" extends the *pālai* tradition into the twentieth century.[53] *Pālai* works are associated with the summer and often feature bandits—in twentieth-century Madras, Ashokamitran transforms these ancient robbers into those taking advantage of residents in West Mambalam: a character complains that "some dishonest fellows came to our street one evening claiming that they would make us a bore-well. They had to make connection with the electricity at my house and left a hundred-watt bulb burning through the night. You can get neither wind nor water from the pump that they put in."[54] But most crucially, *pālai* literature details the hardships of separation from a lover. In classical poetry, these relationships were between a woman and a man, and although contemporary critics comment on Jamuna's "tawdry affair with a film director," a man who abandons her once she learns she is pregnant, I do not read this relationship as central to the novella.[55] Instead, in a notably progressive twist, the separation that causes Jamuna genuine pain—and the separation that occupies the majority of the narrative—is from her beloved sister, Chaya. After a fight during the early days of the drought, Chaya moves out of their shared room, departing for a hostel, and Ashokamitran intertwines their separation with the water crisis in a manner reminiscent of *pālai* poems. The characteristic stagnant water of *pālai* literature appears as Jamuna laments the water that Chaya is drinking during their separation: "These drums which were being carried along now had been cleaned perhaps eons ago and had been filled in the dead darkness from any decaying well. The water could contain roots, droppings, rubbish, leeches, snails, cockroaches, even frogs. Chaya had gone away to that hostel. Was this the water that she was drinking? Was she drinking tea that had been made with this water? Chaya. Chaya."[56] As the novella shifts from a *pālai* setting to a *mullai* setting, entering the rainy season in its final pages, Chaya returns, and the two sisters patiently confront their domestic tribulations together: "There is no end to this, Chaya. We could hold on to each other and sob our hearts out all day. But must we do that? You stand in front of me; I stand in front of you. Isn't that enough?"[57] In this way, Ashokamitran mobilizes the climatic grammar of Sangam literature to tell a tale of contemporary drought and the bonds of sisterhood. Rereading this scene of *mullai* reunification, I am struck by the echoes it creates with Palayam's explanation of disrupted seasons along the Bay of Bengal, a change caused "by a culture that does not know the meaning of the word 'enough.'" *Isn't that enough?* In *Water*, recognizing what is enough marks the resumption of the rains.

In fact, in its portrayal of Jamuna's friendship with Teacher-Amma, a woman about ten years her senior, *Water* details the solidarities that can form in response to climatic stress. During Chaya's absence, Jamuna and Teacher-Amma join forces to obtain water. "It was only because Teacher-Amma and Jamuna plied the pump together that they were able to get some water," Ashokamitran narrates as the women gain access to a pump within a gated residence. "By the time their two water pots were full their hearts were thumping and they were sweating freely."[58] These efforts strengthen their bond, Jamuna comforting Teacher-Amma in the midst of her demeaning domestic labors and Teacher-Amma consoling Jamuna when it becomes apparent that she is expecting. Anjana Shekhar, a writer based in Chennai, points to these moments of alliance between women as she reflects on reading *Water* now:

> I'm no stranger to this setting. A distinct memory from the early 2000s came back to me as I read *Thanneer* for the first time a few years ago. On weekday late afternoon[s], I would telephone my

mother at work, announce the arrival of the water tanker to our street and quickly join the procession of (mostly) women carrying pots. I knew the drill. My mother would arrive a few minutes later, on permission, and carry back the pots filled with water from one end of the street to our house. The exercise would be repeated a couple of days later. We survived the water scarcity of 2002 only to find ourselves back in one, less than two decades later.[59]

In these repeating seasonal solidarities, the possibility of organizing comes into view. Ashokamitran is not lauded as a progressive writer, particularly in relation to issues of caste—in fact, as A. R. Venkatachalapathy documents, the Tamil Nadu Progressive Writers and Artists Association condemned the Sahitya Akademi, India's National Academy of Letters, for honoring him with the Sahitya Akademi Award in 1996.[60] But his attention to women's solidarities during drought remains remarkable. As the environmental activist Chittaroopa Palit, one of the key leaders of Narmada Bachao Andolan, the Indian movement against megadams, notes, "the rhythm of activism is also dictated by the pattern of the seasons."[61] During a delayed monsoon, people gather. Waterlines form, tension builds, connections grow.

MONSOONAL RHYTHMS

"Monsoon is not another word for rain," the Indian writer Khushwant Singh insists.[62] Seeping into English through the Portuguese word *monção*, monsoon derives from the Arabic word *mawsim*, which translates as "season."[63] In its winds, currents, and precipitation, the monsoon orchestrates seasonality across India: "What the four seasons of the year mean to the European, the one season of the monsoon means to the Indian," Singh explains to his Anglophone readership.[64] Similarly, the anthropologist Pamila Gupta conceptualizes monsoons as "a sort of seasonal habitus for people on the South Asian continent."[65] Rather than sheer meteorology, Singh describes the monsoon as a recurrent shift in color, scent, and activity:

> With the monsoon the tempo of life and death increases. Almost overnight grass begins to grow and leafless trees turn green. Snakes, centipedes, and scorpions are born out of nothing. At night, myriads of moths flutter around the lamps. They fall in everybody's food and water. Geckos dart about filling themselves with insects until they get heavy and fall off ceilings. Inside rooms, the hum of mosquitoes is maddening. People spray clouds of insecticide and the floor becomes a layer of wriggling bodies and wings.... The monsoon has its own music. Apart from thunder, the rumble of storm clouds and the pitter-patter of rain drops, there is the constant accompaniment of frogs croaking.[66]

Here, the monsoon's arrival registers as an increase in tempo, a quickening, an amplification. It has the makings of a rhythm.

In Chennai, the monsoon's rhythm is a matter of time and intensity, and both are changing as the globe heats. The northeast monsoon, responsible for the majority of annual rain, typically arrives in mid-October and lingers until mid-December, a cool, dry spell follows, the southwest monsoon blusters through, and then the heat sets in until the northeast monsoon arrives again. These intervals are a matter of wind and rain, ocean currents, and the rise and fall of groundwater, all forming a complex seasonal habitus that clocks the year along the coast of the Bay of Bengal. Deepti Singh, a climate scientist specializing in the South Asian monsoon, notes that precipitation has diminished since 1950, a reduction driven by greenhouse gases and land use. She forecasts "a continued weakening of rainfall into the twenty-first century," but notes that the "internal variability of the monsoon could be a major confounding factor."[67] Suhaas Raje, a groundwater expert, emphasizes increasing erraticism at the intraseasonal scale: "We have the same amount of rainfall, but instead of falling in 90 days it's falling in 30 days."[68] In such intense rains, the water does not percolate into the ground before it runs into the rivers and the Bay of Bengal, causing a deficit in groundwater. These shifts in duration also jumble the monsoon's composite year: "There is no more typical monsoon," residents of Chennai told Beth Cullen, an anthropologist, when she asked about monsoon rhythms. "All those days are gone. Now it is a time of extreme precipitation. There will be one day of 15 cm of rain and that's all, you will not have any more. Or you will have continuous rain, like we had in 2015."[69]

But as Cullen observes in her fieldwork in Chennai, rhythms are not solely a matter of intervals. They also require a patterned intensity: "the successive build-up and resolution of tension is ... a critical component of rhythm and in monsoonal terms tension comes with the build-up of heat and humidity before the release of the monsoon rains."[70] Attending to rhythmic tensions, as well as rhythmic time, is therefore especially crucial when reading monsoon fiction and searching for the climate's imprint on literary forms. "It is not enough to read about the monsoon in books, or see it on the cinema screen, or hear someone talk about it to understand what it means to India," Singh warns. But despite this caution, we return now to *Water*, tracking its seasonal tensions as they register via urban infrastructure and in the novella's form.[71]

MONSOON REALISM

If you search for Amitav Ghosh's *The Great Derangement: Climate Change and the Unthinkable* at Higginbothams Private Limited—an Anglophone bookstore founded in the colonial era and now owned by the Amalgamations Group, which also manufactures pistons, batteries, and paint for Chennai's auto factories—you will not find Ghosh's treatise nestled beside his novels, but displayed prominently in the science section. This placement feels almost apt: the book that sparked the spirited and ongoing debate over fiction's capacity to represent climate change is concerned with the ratios and probabilities of realist literature's form. In realist fiction, Ghosh argues, a narrow "calculus of probability" prevails: quotidian "everyday details" must far outweigh anything improbable that occurs during the course of the narrative in order for a work to register as realist.[72] The hitch, according to Ghosh, is that "we are now in an era that will be defined precisely by events that appear, by our current standards of normalcy, highly improbable: flash floods, hundred-year storms, persistent droughts, spells of unprecedented heat, sudden landslides, raging torrents pouring down from breached glacial lakes, and . . . freakish tornadoes."[73] An anthropogenically altered climate, Ghosh contends, is "not easily accommodated in the deliberately prosaic world of prose fiction" because it alters the ratio between the customary and the dramatic, tilting a work toward fantasy or legend.

Scholars who concur with this correlation between realism and quotidian life articulate realism not so much as a style or a mode, but instead as a form, as a particular patterning recognized as realist fiction. Roland Barthes distinguishes between "hinges" and "fillers" in realist fiction: some scenes "constitute actual hinges of the narrative . . . others do no more than 'fill in' the narrative space."[74]

For Barthes, the ratio between moments that "are functional in terms of action" and moments that are functional only "in terms of being" distinguishes fantasy and folklore from realist writing.[75] Frederic Jameson theorizes along similar lines, arguing that realism is "the triumph of everyday life . . . over the rarer and more exceptional moments of heroic deeds and extreme situations."[76] Crucially, critics following this logic argue that this patterning of realist texts occurs, not via style or mode, but via form: through fillers, the everyday "pervades *the very rhythm and form of the novel*."[77] Realist fiction is predicated on a rhythm that inculcates readers into a narrow zone of variability—perhaps even a narrower zone of variability than actually exists in the nonliterary world.

While Ghosh's hypothesis that realist form may not easily acclimate to the changed climate is provocative, I suspect *The Great Derangement* overlooks the myriad of ways in which climate change infiltrates the everyday, the ways in which it registers not just in extreme weather events but in the smaller, everyday rhythms that constitute the bread and butter of realist form. If climate change is understood not solely through the lens of sudden cataclysm, but instead as an environmental shift that registers in ordinary moments, suffusing the "fillers" in which the realist novel trades, then climate change will not necessarily render realist form obsolete but instead begin to manifest through the small-scale rhythms of everyday life within it. The challenge, perhaps, is not wholly a challenge of inventing new forms for a new climate but instead a challenge of identifying how climate already suffuses realist narratives and then providing a methodology for elucidating how—in Ghosh's terms—climate change might cast a shadow on "the grid of literary forms and conventions."[78] Ghosh's central thesis, the stake of his argument, is that examining realist fiction's peculiar reluctance to engage the changing climate may help to explain "why contemporary culture finds it so hard to deal with climate change."[79] Perhaps the reverse is also true: identifying the climate rhythms already present within realist narratives may assist in acknowledging climate change's impact on everyday life.

In reviews and existing scholarship, *Water* is described as a work of "strict realism."[80] Ashokamitran likely would have approved of this designation—in an overview of the Tamil short story published in *Indian Literature* in 1994, he complained that magical realism "has almost become an obsession with everyone who has to comment on literature. . . . Magical realism per se is not a guarantee of good writing."[81] The novelist Aravind Adiga points out that "nothing much happens on the surface" in Ashokamitran's prose, a sentiment echoed by Venkatachalapathy, who notes that Ashokamitran "avoids the dramatic and spectacular" to cultivate an "aesthetic of the ordinary."[82] Lakshmi Holmström, who translated *Water* into English in 1993, characterizes Ashokamitran's style as "bare and understated."[83] This scholarly consensus is unsurprising given the form of the novella. *Water* is patterned by brief scenes—neighbors clustered around a pump, the installation of a water tank, five men lowering rings into a well to raise the water level, a taxi navigating a dug-up street—interspersed throughout the story of Jamuna's attempts to collect water and reunite with Chaya. Collectively, these scenes occupy a significant portion of the novella, generating only slightly less than half the narrative. *Water* is precisely the type of text—replete with workaday routines, devoid of any trace of the implausible—that Ghosh categorizes as "serious fiction." It is, by all conventional metrics, a work of realism. And yet, it holds the chronic stress of drought, the rhythm of its narrative synced to the climate's seasonal pulses.

To discern the narrative construction of *Water*, we head to Anna Salai Road, taking a brief foray into Kollywood, the hub of Tamil cinema and the former home of Madras's famed Gemini Studios. Ashokamitran spent fourteen years here—from 1952 to 1966—working in

Gemini's public relations department, perusing magazines and newspapers, carefully clipping and filing relevant content. Holmström asserts that *Water* is reminiscent of "sequences in a film," its prose "cinematic rather than novelistic."[84] She argues that the Tamil novel developed alongside the film script, "with its attention to single 'frames' and the juxtaposition of scenes."[85] Gemini Studios did indeed function as a literary incubator—Ashokamitran calls it a "favourite haunt of poets"—and a crossroads for Chennai's literati.[86] In *My Years With Boss*, his account of his time in the industry, Ashokamitran describes poring over film mock-ups: "I had access to the library at Gemini Studios which was also a kind of dumping ground for mountains of old files most of which were 'subjects,' or stories proposed to be made into films in the future. One was a rather fully worked-out treatment bearing the by-line of R. K. Narayan. . . . it seemed quite interesting."[87] As he read Narayan's sketch of *Moondru Pillaigal*, a Gemini film released in 1952, and perused the other stories filed in Gemini's library, Ashokamitran steeped himself in what the anthropologist Anand Pandian calls "the grammar of Indian cinema."[88] It is this manipulation of tension and ease over the course of a story—both the intensities and lulls of individual scenes and the overall rhythm generated by the scenes in concert with each other—that Ashokamitran absorbed from the Tamil film industry.

Ashokamitran applies this grammar of Indian cinema via the monsoon in *Water*, implementing the rhythms of the climate to generate tension and resolution within a narrative scene. An extended passage located near the close of the novella brings this technique to the forefront:

> Jamuna hurried to light her stove. She had not lit it since that morning. Out of the ten wicks, two or three refused to burn. After a while, as soon as the flames came through all the holes evenly, even the ones which would not light, Jamuna set the water to

heat in a vessel, and took down the tin in which she kept the tea-leaves. Teacher-Amma, rather than stand there doing nothing, began to pick up the saris and petticoats that lay scattered about, and to fold them and put them away. When Jamuna caught her eye, once again she smiled, very slightly. Jamuna wondered at the way things had seemed to resolve themselves, without her saying a word. Suddenly the room felt a shade cooler. There was a perceptible heaviness in the air. After a few seconds they heard a steady tap-tapping sound. Teacher-Amma was shaking out and folding a sheet. "What, is it drizzling?" She asked.

Jamuna went to the window and stretched out her hand. The window had a wide sun-shade above it, preventing her from reaching right out. She opened the door, went out and put her hand out once more. "Rain," she said. Meanwhile the water began to boil on the stove.[89]

This scene opens at the height of the water shortage in Madras—Jamuna's small copper pot of drinking water is chronically low—and the domestic stress of the crisis is palpable. The infrastructure of her rental's interior—like the tail-end pipe on her street—is malfunctioning, her stove failing to properly ignite. And within this domestic space, both Jamuna and Teacher-Amma are waiting for water, holding on until the heat builds in the vessel and it begins to boil. The tensions simmering in the realist narrative are connected to the tension of the delayed monsoon not through pathetic fallacy—the monsoon is not a literary adornment—but rather through the novel's multiscalar portrayal of water. By this point in the novella, readers understand the tea water on the stove, perhaps lugged back from a tube well near Pondi Bazaar, as a climate indicator, a measurement of drought. The resolution of the scene—the release of its tension—is simultaneously meteorological and psychological, the rain easing the atmosphere of the scene even before Jamuna spots it through the window. The rain's arrival is so entwined with everyday tensions in Ashokamitran's novella that climate shapes the rhythm of his realist depiction of afternoon tea.

However, the overarching structure of *Water*—its alternation between city scenes and Jamuna's story—is its true contribution to climate realism. The influence of Kollywood scripts on Ashokamitran's novella renders its form more overt than is typical in realist fiction, its narrative cut into distinct scenes. In this sense, the ratios and "calculus"—to use Ghosh's term—between its hinges and fillers are unusually calculable. Holmström insists that "the form of the novel is notable, made up on the one hand of many impressionistic street scenes, some shadowy, in the early morning or at dusk, almost like sequences in a film; and on the other, of a number of vignettes featuring unnamed characters, whose lives are all interconnected, nevertheless, through their common struggle" in drought.[90] These unusually delineated "filler" scenes, separate from the narrative focalized on Jamuna, are necessary to produce a traditional literary realism. They temporarily release the tensions of Jamuna's plight—her pregnancy, the threat of her eviction, her estrangement from her family—spacing out the calamity and pitching the novella away from melodrama. The larger rhythms of *Water*—the novella's tensions and lulls over the course of its pages—are dependent on these realist fillers. The fillers chronicle the passage of time in the drought and control narrative intensity. The novella's infrastructure—its grid of street scenes and vignettes and moments of Jamuna's interior life—is classically and unmistakably realist.

But like the infrastructure portrayed in *Water*—the pipes and buildings and wells—the novella's realist infrastructure registers climate stress. Its fillers keep the drought at the forefront of the text, an interminable presence. Indeed, they perform much of the novella's phenological accounting:

The lorry driver struck hard at his horn, twice. A householder who had been chosen to represent the street came running along with three rupees out of the sum of money that he had collected from all the people living there. He handed it over, the fee for having brought them the water. The lorry driver accepted the money and drove away.

After he had gone away, the queue re-formed itself in a manner of speaking, and waited for the street representative to ration out the water at the rate of nineteen litres per family.[91]

To value these fillers, these textual records of water's seasonal availability and the social events it elicits, is to value the novella's climate realism. In these scenes, the monsoon is present not only in hinges—in dramatic twists and turns of the weather—but also in the mundane waterlines of urban life. Like Jamuna, who can read the pulses of water in Madras through lorry arrivals, streaks of mud on the street, and sudden lines near a pump, Ashokamitran's fiction insists that climate registers in the everyday. Through its own rhythms, the novel works to inculcate its readers in the kind of social phenology that Jamuna practices.

CODA

On a blistering hot day late in September of 2022, M. Ravi and I head south from Chennai on the East Coast Road, the Bay of Bengal visible out the car's left window.[92] Many of the vehicles we pass are emblazoned with the logo of the Mahindra Group, the Indian automotive corporation that donated ten million dollars to the U.S. university where I teach environmental literature, earmarking it for the humanities.[93] The chairman of the Mahindra Group is an alumnus—he graduated with a bachelor's degree in film in 1977—and he now practices what Arundhati Roy dryly calls the "exquisite art" of corporate philanthropy.[94] A windfall, people say when they mention this donation. I think about the koṉṟai vendors whose livelihoods shudder when unseasonable winds fell blossoms: that too is a windfall. I remember presenting early drafts of this book at the rechristened Mahindra Humanities Center; I breathe in the carbon dioxide and ethylene emitted by heavy traffic on the East Coast Road. These are the global proximities of literary scholarship, and my heart runs muddy.

Passing the former French colony now known as Puducherry and driving by a series of salt fields, Ravi and I enter Tamil Nadu's Cuddalore District and turn off the main road. We are looking for the Pillayar Kovali Kullum, the reservoir of water beside the main temple in the village of Kumudimoolai. In Kumudimoolai, nearly two

FIGURE 3.1 The Pillayar Kovali Kullum. Courtesy of Sarah Dimick.

thousand residents grow rice by relying on water from the nearby Neyveli Lignite Corporation's coal mining operation.[95] Prior to 2021, the temple reservoir—the community's water source for cleaning and, during dry spells, even drinking and cooking—was in a state of disrepair, clogged inlets and broken retaining walls resulting in stagnant, cloudy water. Sanitation First India, a nongovernmental organization working in the area, mentioned Kumudimoolai's water troubles to Ravishankar Thyagarajan, Ashokamitran's eldest son, who decided to fund the restoration in honor of his late father and *Water*. "Reviving a water body," they decided, "would probably be the right tribute to him."[96]

Relying on directions given by a crew of men laying cement, we find the temple, its multicolored gopuram glinting in the afternoon sun. The reservoir beside it is placid, except for small ripples near the steps where a man is cupping handfuls of water to cool his face. A bright yellow plaque at the edge of the water is imprinted with a photograph of Ashokamitran—earlier today, someone draped garlands of fresh flowers across it. Standing here beside this sign commemorating a writer, I watch a woman in a pink sari approach the restored reservoir with an empty plastic bucket. I think of Corey Byrnes's writing on China's Three Gorges Dam and his profound reminder that infrastructure is built on "cultural and aesthetic grounds."[97] I think of the water crisis that hit Chennai in 2019, the depletion of tap water after two years of insufficient monsoons, and I remember Victoria Saramago's argument that the "trajectories of fictional works" in Latin America are entangled with "the fates of the environments they depict."[98] As Saramago attests, shifts in environments can alter the resonance of literary works. Here in the village of Kumudimoolai, on the southeastern coast of India, a work of fiction has precipitated a reliable supply of water, and Ashokamitran's novella feels increasingly pertinent.

It is late September, and the northeast monsoon is expected in a matter of weeks. Everything here is waiting for the rain. From the homes that ring the edges of the Pillayar Kovali Kullum, cooking smoke rises into the atmosphere, some particles heading out over the Bay of Bengal and drifting toward the northern coast of Australia. In 2019, as a delayed southwest monsoon lingered in India, Australia turned to tinder.[99] It is to Australia and its fire seasons that we now turn.

4

CLIMATE FICTION AND THE UNPRECEDENTED

On May 17, 2019—as bushfires scorched the Australian continent, as the sky burned orange, as plumes of black carbon extended into the stratosphere and ash settled across the land—the novelist Alexis Wright, a member of the Waanyi nation of the Gulf of Carpentaria, penned an op-ed in *The Guardian*. "There is not one among us in this country who is not feeling the heat of hotter and more extended summers," she declared. "We smell the smoke of major environmental catastrophes and ask how safe we really feel in hotter summers, and we will become more anxious, as each extreme weather event comes by."[1] This newspaper column was not Wright's first depiction of inflamed, bone-dry times. In the final pages of her acclaimed novel *The Swan Book*, published in Australia in 2013, the landscape burns: a "slow-moving drought left behind smoldering ashes and soil baked by the dryness . . . fires blew smoke across the lands on fast moving currents."[2] This resonance was not lost on readers of Wright's op-ed; an epigraph affixed to her column connected the bushfires raging in 2019 to her fictional depiction of climate change and charred times. Drawn from the final pages of *The Swan Book*, the epigraph dramatizes a singed habitat: "all the raspy-voice myna birds have come here, to this old swamp, where the ghost swans now dance the yellow dust song cycles of drought. Around and around the dry swamp they go with their webbed feet stomping up the earth in a cloud of dust, and all the bits and pieces of the past unravelled from parched soil."[3] As these lines are repurposed, copied from the conclusion of Wright's novel to the opening of her column, fiction transforms into a dispatch from a burning continent. It is as though Wright is positioning her editorial on climate change as a short sequel to her novel, deliberately gesturing toward their relation. Or, more radically, this epigraph positions *The Swan Book* as a precedent for the flames ahead.

The Swan Book has been read as bildungsroman, magical realism, and Indigenous science fiction.[4] It has been described as a "difficult text" that "draws on the tradition of literary modernism."[5] Here, I approach it as a work of unseasonable literature, paying particular attention to the novel's off-kilter phenological rhythms. *The Swan Book* is predicated on desperate hibernations and disrupted migrations. It is a novel alive to the disorientation of living within haywire seasonality: "Mother Nature? Hah! Who knows how many hearts she could rip out? She never got tired of it. Who knows where on earth you would find your heart again? People on the road called her the Mother Catastrophe of flood, fire, drought, and blizzard. These were the four seasons, which she threw around the world whenever she liked."[6] As the book's catastrophic seasons—distinctly colonial, in their four-part rendering—are strewn haphazardly across the globe, hearts are wrenched, pulses become difficult to locate. Arrhythmias abound.

In Wright's imagined future, seasonal disorientation is produced through toxic entanglements of settler colonialism and atmospheric warming, showcasing how the importation of British seasonal schemas aggravates the temporal contortions of the warming world. In Australia, a continent of variegated climates and intricate phenological patterns, the attempt to enforce seasons as "temporal blocks," rather than attending to seasonality as the "periodic dynamic[s] of social and ecological life," can produce dysphoria.[7] "Seasons," Wright tells me in a personal interview, "are things happening that trigger something else happening. If there's a certain tree flowering it means certain fish are coming. Seasons work like that, it's a feeling of knowing when those things are happening and how they trigger other things."[8] In arrhythmic times, this feeling of knowing—this informed expectation—goes up in smoke. In her scholarship, the ethnographer Deborah Bird Rose echoes Wright's assessment of seasonal knowledge among Aboriginal peoples: "the rhythms of things that happen simultaneously are crucial codes for knowing what is happening in the world." She notes that the local particularity of Aboriginal knowledges, "built from extremely long-term observations," means that when people "go beyond the bounds of their knowledge, they know that they are in the presence of a system they do not understand."[9]

Struggling to convey the intensity and duration of the 2019–2020 fire season, Australian residents, news commentators, and scientists landed on the term *unprecedented*. Alexis Wright uses the term herself: "this manmade global warming catastrophe," she declares in The Guardian, "is creating before our eyes unprecedented heatwaves [and] out-of-control fires."[10] Angela Burford, a spokesperson for the New South Wales Rural Fire Service, called 2019 to 2020 an "unprecedented" fire season. She elaborated: "To put it in perspective, in the past few years we have had a total area burned for the whole season of about 280,000 hectares. This year we're at 3.41 million and we are only halfway through the season."[11] A group of researchers at Western Sydney University calculated that "the 2019/20 forest fires have burned a globally unprecedented percentage of any continental forest biome" in a single fire season. They cautioned that "these unprecedented fires may indicate that the more flammable future projected to eventuate under climate change has arrived earlier than anticipated."[12] These fires were both historically cumulative—kindled by centuries of suppressed Aboriginal burning practices combined with centuries of emissions—and exceptionally severe. For those who fled their homes, those who weathered the smoke, those who waited on beaches for the flames to recede, *unprecedented* seemed to encapsulate the feeling of environmental disorientation that descended as flames leapt across the parameters of previous experience.

And yet, *unprecedented* is a charged word to apply to the changing climate. The Potawatomi philosopher Kyle Powys Whyte singles it out, pointing to *unprecedented* as a symptom of what he terms crisis epistemology: "The crises are *unprecedented*. That is, they are ones in which there are few usable lessons from the past about how to cope with the problems of today generated by crises. Sometimes today's crises are considered to have the novelty of being complex beyond anything previously encountered."[13] As Whyte argues, this usage erases the myriad ways in which climate change emerges from, recapitulates, and intensifies ongoing structures of colonization. "When people relate to climate change through *linear time*—that is, as a ticking clock," he writes, "they feel peril and seek ways to stop the worst impacts of climate change immediately. Yet swift action obscures their responsibilities to others who risk being harmed by the solutions."[14] Drawing on Indigenous studies research that builds on longstanding survival within colonialism, Whyte emphasizes epistemologies of kinship and knowledge of "how to organize a society to be coordinated in the face of realities of constant change."[15] In what follows, I take Whyte's caution seriously, working to position *The Swan Book* as a literary work emerging from historical—and ongoing—settler colonialism in Australia. At the same time, I am cognizant of reports from people in Australia, including Warren Foster, a member of the Yuin nation, who describes the 2019–2020 bushfires in distinctly presentist terms: "These are the worst bushfires in our history . . . It's never gone up like this. Our people never knew fires like this. The ancestors would be wild, I reckon, about what's happened to the country."[16] Contradictions sometimes need to linger, tensions need to hold, multiple truths need to be acknowledged: the fires were kindled by colonialism *and* they were unsettlingly extreme. Articulating extremity without disconnecting from history is the tightrope that this chapter balances upon.

In this chapter, I return to *The Swan Book* and read it in light of the 2019–2020 bushfires, attempting to elucidate the resonances between the text and the flames that ensued. There is not yet adequate language for moments when a book feels newly resonant, when a story begins to spark, when—as Lauren Berlant writes—"*circumstances* alter [a literary object] before our eyes."[17] Toward this end, I build to an argument about climate fiction itself. Rather than conceptualizing climate fiction as a genre marked by textual affinities—a constellation of books with similar plots or a recognizable narrative style—I theorize it as a genre marked by interpretive affinities. As climate change intensifies—flames crackling across Australia, Russia, Canada, Bolivia, Morocco, Brazil, France, Indonesia, and Lebanon—and fire seasons extend due to drought and heat, readers employ literary works as touchstones within a disorienting climate. I argue that this effort to understand or navigate the changing climate by the light of the fictional is the pattern that makes climate fiction coherent as a genre. Rather than being a dilution of the literary, a voiding of style, form, or literary history, I contend that defining genre in this way foregrounds the function and increasing necessity of fiction. As geophysical and historical precedents go up in flame, stories become the baseline by which expectations are set. Literature is the guidepost that remains.

ENVIRONMENTAL CAESURAS

A prolonged hibernation lies at the narrative core of *The Swan Book*. For ten years, an Aboriginal child named Oblivia Ethyl(ene) hibernates in a hollow at the base of an old eucalyptus tree until she is violently yanked out of the tree's root system by a European refugee named Bella Donna.[18] Bella Donna insists that while frogs and swamp turtles may hibernate underground during droughts, "it was impossible for a human being to shut down like a burrowing frog with cold blood.... [Oblivia] would not be able to sleep through the drought like a frog, or like a swamp turtle, by conserving energy from living on a single heartbeat for whatever time was necessary to survive through hibernation."[19] Bella Donna uses the vernacular term *hibernate* (from the Latin *hībernāre*, to winter), but frogs and swamp turtles in Australia *aestivate* (from *aestīvāre*, to summer), becoming dormant during hot, dry stretches in order to sustain themselves through otherwise unlivable times. The western swamp tortoise aestivates for eight months each year, while desert frogs remain burrowed underground for years on end, waiting for a downpour to rouse them from their torpor.[20] To caesura like this—to pause in accordance with seasonal time—is an acclimation to environmental extremity, a means of holding on through parched, uninhabitable periods. Drawing on Alexis Pauline Gumbs's words, "breathing in unbreathable circumstances" necessitates long intervals between beats, synchronizing life with arid times requires the ability to suspend a pulse.[21]

Oblivia's decade-long hibernation in the charred bowels of the eucalyptus might be read as an arrhythmia, a temporal indicator of climate disruption. She hibernates because when she was a young girl, no older than ten, she was gang-raped by a group of local boys "wracked out of their minds on fumes" after they sniffed "an endless supply of petrol" from empty Coca-Cola cans.[22] The rapists' derangement is the result of fossil fuel addiction, their minds wasted from the exhaust wafting out of a vessel emblematic of global capitalism. In a blunt allegorical reading, the boys' petroleum abuse and their rape of Oblivia might be cast as climate change incarnate.

Moreover, the interminable violence of this gang rape is mirrored in the interminable fumes of colonialism; the swamp where Oblivia resides is used for military target practice, and warplanes aim for empty wreckage floating on the water, shooting at the "foreign history sinking there" in Oblivia's country.[23] She recalls running through the smoke of a bushfire, perhaps sparked by one of these bombs, as she flees the rapists. Her hibernation is a response to this powerful synthesis of colonial exhaust and environmental destruction, the impact of centuries of fossil fuel abuse concentrating on Aboriginal life. Your hibernation, Bella Donna tells Oblivia, is accretive, the result of "having been gang-raped physically, emotionally, psychologically, statistically, randomly, historically, so fully in fact: *Your time stands still.*"[24] Petroleum fumes have—in a pun Wright is no doubt aware of—"petrified" Oblivia.[25] Fossil fuels route through language in *The Swan Book*, the morpheme *petro* transferring from the petroleum to Oblivia's body, forcing her outside human temporalities.[26] She is petrified both in the sense of inhabiting horror and in the sense of persisting through time.

And yet, this atypical hibernation is also a mode of survivance, a caesura that enables Oblivia's continuance.[27] Scholars have noted that Oblivia Ethyl(ene)'s parenthetical name associates her with the hydrocarbon that underwrites the plastic industry, but ethylene also alleviates pain, regulates temperature, and paces phenological change. In the early twentieth century, greenhouses reported that ethylene vapors delayed the blooming of carnations, and after speculation that the gas might also function as an anesthetic agent on human bodies, it was used to bypass unbearable pain during gynecological surgeries.[28] As ethylene glycol, it continues to be used as a coolant in air conditioners, allowing those enduring intense heat to survive. And as a phytohormone flowing through plants—including eucalyptus trees—ethylene hastens or pauses phenological rhythms, adjusting the timing of root growth, seed germination, and leaf fall.

In its various applications, ethylene is a chemical that facilitates preservation and continuance under extreme conditions. As it courses around Oblivia, who lies numbed in the old roots of the eucalyptus tree, an extended caesura allows her to aestivate, to survive the severe drought and colonial forces rumbling above ground.

Critics have read human hibernation in *The Swan Book* as magical realism, treating it as a sheerly literary phenomenon.[29] Wright's novel certainly toys with widely-circulating folktales and works of fantasy involving temporal suspension. Oblivia is referred to as an "Aboriginal Tinker Bell fairy": instead of sprinkling pixie dust on children to allow them to fly to Neverland, a place where the future is forever forestalled, she exits time in the swirling dust of the drought-stricken Australian outback, a place colloquially referred to as the Never Never.[30] She is also declared "just like that old Rip Van Winkle fella," a character the novel's Aboriginal community remembers as a man who "kept on sleeping for so many years that when he woke up and went home, his house was gone. . . . So bloody good job. Serves him right. You should always know where to find your home."[31] Their distaste for this magical tale is a useful reminder that magical realism is a highly vexed mode in Indigenous writing. "Unsurprisingly," Alison Ravenscroft notes, "the so-called magic falls on the side of the Indigenous colonised subjects and so-called reality remains on the side of the colonisers."[32]

But, if prolonged hibernations in *The Swan Book* are elements of magical realism, they belong to a mode that Jennifer Wenzel, writing about literature from the Niger Delta, refers to as "petro-magic-realism." Combining "magical transmogrifications and fantastic landscapes with the monstrous-but-mundane violence of oil exploration and extraction, the state violence that supports it, and the environmental degradation that it causes," petro-magic-realism punctures fantasies of fossil-fueled futures.[33] The fantasies at play are colonial dreams and corporate tricks, magic aligned with the ongoing colonialism of the fossil fuel industry. *The Swan Book* adds an additional twist to this mode, suggesting that the prosaic or routine becomes a dangerous fantasy during anthropogenic climate change. During the 2019–2020 fires, Australia's acting prime minister, Michael McCormack, denied that the blazes were anything out of the ordinary: "We've had these smoke hazes before. We've had bushfires before. We've had droughts before.... That is Australia. It is a land of droughts and flooding rains and that's just the way it is."[34] Weaponizing the inherent variability of Australia's seasonality to downplay climate change, McCormack and other politicians aligned with the fossil fuel industry denied the nearly otherwordly nature of the flames roaring around them. Within this context, Wright's work, which pushes toward the incredible, resists fantasies of the prosaic. During Oblivia's hibernation, massive sandstorms "cursed the place" and "freak weather" tormented the continent, generating an almost mythical scale of change.[35] Again and again, *The Swan Book* pirouettes with the magical to insist on the unprecedented. It pokes fun at the fantasies of government bureaucrats, noting that they do "not regularly use words like *once upon a time*" except "when it was hoped that the bad weather would change back to normal climatic patterns."[36] It is a book that taunts its readers, daring them to deny the veracity of its anthropogenic extremes: "You be the judge. Believe it or not."[37]

However, I find it most unnerving to read Oblivia's hibernation more or less literally, as a magnification of the way in which human rhythms are already transforming under the pressure of intensifying climate change. As bushfires raged in 2019 and 2020, people living in Canberra went into hibernation, closing their windows and air vents. "The smoke still gets inside," the writer Peter Papathanasiou reported. "With Air Quality Index (AQI) readings of 5,000, the air is 25 times what is considered hazardous.... The streets are deserted."[38] And on January 4, 2020, as the Gospers Mountain and

Three Mile fires blazed nearby, the Sydney suburb of Penrith registered as the hottest place on earth, local temperatures clocking in at more than 120°F. Residents with access to air conditioning sheltered indoors. These withdrawals portend others ahead: Mark Howden, a vice chair of the IPCC, envisions a regular "summer hibernation" for residents of Australia by 2050, unlivable heat forcing people inside.[39] Urban planners have begun to talk of constructing homes underground, reducing the effect of heat islands and allowing people to burrow—like western swamp tortoises or frogs—into the cool ground. But for now, in the city of Alice Springs, those without air conditioning take refuge in the public library. Security guards at the air-conditioned Yeperenye shopping center prevent Aboriginal people from entering during heatwaves—capitalism hangs Indigenous lives out to dry—so the library's stacks of books serve as shelter from the heat.[40] People cluster within cool rows of paperbacks. Consider Oblivia, nestled in the wood of the eucalyptus tree; consider the Aboriginal elders and children, waiting out the scorching hours of a changed climate among stories printed on wood pulp. *The Swan Book* is available in the adult fiction section of the Alice Springs Public Library, call number F WRIG.

MIGRATIONS AND BLACK SWANS

"When I started thinking about writing a book about swans, way back in 2003, I was living in Central Australia," Wright explained at the Melbourne Writers Festival in 2013. As the climate shifted, the black swans that are indigenous to Australia took wing, migrating toward the interior in search of water:

> People started telling me stories of swans that they had seen in the desert, sometimes on very shallow stretches of water. People

were surprised to see them in these places, so far away from coastal and wetter regions of Australia.... At the time I was doing research for the novel, people were also talking about seeing swans in the sewerage dam in Alice Springs, where they'd never seen them before, and further out in very isolated areas of land where there you would rarely see much water at all. And the same thing was happening up in the Gulf, where there are normally no swans.[41]

These unprecedented flights are replicated in *The Swan Book*, black swans appearing at the detention center where Oblivia and Bella Donna live out their days in the rusty hull of a war ship abandoned by the Australian Army. "When their own habitats had dried from perpetual drought," Wright narrates, the black swans "had become nomads, migratory like the white swans of the northern world, with their established seasonal routes taking them back and forth, but unlike them, the black swans were following the rainwaters of cyclones deeper and deeper into the continent."[42] Newly migratory, the black swans arrive at Oblivia's swamp—a site now renamed Swan Lake. A swan "deranged by drought" lands near the water's edge, "then another, and another."[43] The swans multiply faster than anyone can count, a phenological anomaly that accrues into symbol.

Black swans serve as the central figure in an intellectual history dating back to the Roman poet Juvenal's *Satire VI*, written at the turn of the first century. Juvenal likens the ideal woman partner to a "rara avis in terris, nigroque simillima cygno," which roughly translates as "a rare bird, a black swan or the like."[44] The misogyny of Juvenal's claim sharpens with historical context: prior to colonial expeditions in Australia, Europeans considered black swans an impossibility. All swans in their known world—and in their stories—were white. In the *Satires*, Juvenal employs the black swan as a figure of speech signaling extreme improbability, akin to "a snowball's chance in hell." But in 1697, as Willem Hesselsz de Vlamingh—sailing for the Dutch East India Company—navigated his ship up a channel he later christened the Swan River, he was astounded to glimpse flocks of *Cygnus atratus*, the swans with inky feathers and scarlet beaks that are indigenous to Australia. Bella Donna relates this history to Oblivia: "The facts, girl. Here are the facts. . . . the crew of Willem de Vlamingh's Dutch ship claimed to have seen superstition come to life, when they saw alive, two black swans—a beautiful pair, swimming off the coast of Western Australia. . . . a celebration for science, a fact stripped from myth."[45] For the Dutch East India Company sailors, these black swans were incredible, astonishing, unprecedented within a settler worldview.

Based on this story of a worldview thrown into upheaval, the financial risk analyst Nassim Taleb published *The Black Swan: The Impact of the Highly Improbable* in 2007, cementing the black swan as a symbol of the unexpected.[46] Taleb defines a black swan event as an occurrence that "lies outside the realm of regular expectations," produces a major impact, and begs to be interpreted retrospectively. Although Taleb does not invoke anthropogenic alterations to the atmosphere, he does suggest that "ever since we left the Pleistocene, some ten millennia ago, the effect of these black swans has been increasing. It started accelerating during the industrial revolution, as the world started getting more complicated."[47] I am not interested, as Taleb is, in the impact of black swan events on financial markets. Instead, I want to point first to the crucial humility of acknowledging the vastness of "what you don't know" in relation to the changing climate, of recognizing—in an echo of Deborah Bird Rose's words—that we are in the presence of a system we do not fully understand, an earth system altered and defamiliarized by the emissions of the Global North.[48] Despite the extensive advances made in climate science, the unpredictable will wield a serious force over the next decades. Secondly, I want to note the desire for narration in the wake of a black swan event—a desire that Taleb dismisses and I embrace. This connection between the unprecedented and the literary forms the knot at the heart of this chapter.

Taleb's *The Black Swan* is cited in the IPCC's Fifth Assessment Report, and the specter of black swan events continues to haunt climate scientists. In the Sixth Assessment Report, published between 2021 and 2023, in the wake of the Australian bushfires, black swans figure prominently: "the probability of low-likelihood outcomes associated with potentially very large impacts increases with higher global warming levels." The report further cautions: "low-likelihood, high-impact outcomes could occur at regional scales even for global warming within the *very likely* assessed range for a given GHG [greenhouse gases] emissions scenario."[49] Whether greenhouse gases reach expected levels or exceed them, black swans are coming, flying in a V formation through the overheated atmosphere. During the 2019–2020 bushfire season, the prevalence of pyrocumulonimbus clouds—which form over fires and hurl lightning and wind—exceeded all models of probability. David Bowman, a professor of environmental change biology at the University of Tasmania, stepped into Willem Hesselsz de Vlamingh's shoes as he described the buildup of these bushfire-generated thunderheads: "Something happened this last summer which is truly extraordinary, because what we would call statistically a black swan event, we saw a flock of black swans.... That just shouldn't have happened."[50] Bowman's words echoed conversations on the Dutch East India Company's ships in 1697, a reminder that climate change is an intensification of colonialism, but they also echoed *The Swan Book*, published just a few years before the bushfires. "Black swans kept arriving from nowhere," Wright narrates, "more and more of them, from the first one that had arrived unexpectedly and spoiled the swamp people's dinner."[51] The black swans in the novel acquire resonance as climate change accelerates, circumstances altering their signification.

The future portrayed in Wright's novel suggests that many of the black swan events now haunting climate scientists and other environmental observers—changes to the Atlantic Meridional Overturning Circulation, runaway melting of the Greenland Ice Sheet, the burning of the Amazon—have occurred, prompting both animal and human migrations. Set "when the world changed," the novel's characters "talked about surviving a continuous dust storm under the old rain shadow, or they talked about living out the best part of their lives with floods lapping around their bellies.... Elsewhere on the planet, people didn't talk much at all while crawling through blizzards."[52] Bella Donna describes climate catastrophe in Europe in terms of phenological disruption, relying on the language of frantic animal migrations: "the rich people were flying off in armadas of planes like packs of migratory birds. The poverty people like myself had to walk herdlike.... refugees marching onward just like deer would through winter steppes to nowhere. Hunger was constant."[53] This mass migration is echoed at the close of the novel as people flee from a southern city—likely Sydney—the affluent leaving in cars and paying to pass through highway checkpoints, while Oblivia and "those who had slept on the footpaths with cardboard blankets, or in empty buildings," head off-road through the swamp.[54] Bella Donna's similes—"like birds" or "like deer"—collapse, economically and racially marginalized Australians traveling "alongside" dogs, cows, and bantam roosters.[55] Oblivia tracks the flock of black swans flying overhead on her journey, but she also carries a half-grown cygnet, a fledgling, "inside her hoodie windcheater next to her knife," protecting this symbol of Indigenous Australia from the storms of climate change raging around the travelers.[56] She allows the cygnet to hibernate inside her jacket, regulating its rhythms, "its heart thumping with her heart."[57]

Migrations in *The Swan Book* reinforce the urgency of postcolonial criticism as anthropogenic climate change intensifies. Wright's narration of Bella Donna's arrival in Australia is designed to facilitate a postcolonial reading, inviting comparisons between climate migrations and the settlement of the continent. Stepping off her boat, Bella Donna "saw the Australian beach lined with pandanus, smelt bush fires, caught the dust in the breeze laden with the aroma of overripe mangoes . . . she would listen no more to the law of breaking waves slapping against the shores of a forbidden land," and so "this old woman invaded Australia" and proceeded "to plow the ground with her own eyes, and to be totally ignorant of the ins and outs of family histories," a process through which she "discovered" Oblivia hibernating in the eucalyptus tree.[58] Maria Kaaren Takolander, approaching this narrative from a perspective exemplary of postcolonial responses to the novel, explains that Bella Donna "not only heroically 'discovers' Oblivia, just as white Australians are said to have discovered their continent, but also sets about saving her from her people's ways in a manner that ironically resonates with the treatment of Aboriginal people throughout Australia's colonial history."[59] In the prevailing interpretation of this novel and its relationship to ongoing colonization on the continent, climate change forces history to repeat itself, the future figured as a neat replication of the past.

Significantly less has been said about the way that intensifying climate change renders Europeans refugees in *The Swan Book*, but the novel also encourages a reading of Bella Donna and other new arrivals as "the planet's nomadic boat people," folks "drifting among the other countless stateless millions of sea gypsies looking for somewhere to live."[60] While this projected future may be unrealistic—European wealth offers barriers against climatic devastation that the Global South confronts without adaptive mitigations—it is also true that the geopolitical order is likely to develop new fault lines as climate change becomes increasingly exacerbated. While history certainly positions Bella Donna of the Champions as a hegemonic figure, the environmental necessity of her migration also positions her as a destitute exile, a character eliciting sympathy within a changed climate despite the colonial overtones of her arrival. Climate change does not nullify colonial responsibility in *The Swan Book*—it does not allow European characters, as much as they might wish, "to be exonerated from history"—but it does trouble the clear distinction between invader and migrant.[61] In other words, while colonialism exerts an immense force in Wright's text—this novel is, after all, set in a continent where settler colonialism is an ongoing occupation, Aboriginal peoples detained in a swampy wasteland full of discarded military vessels—Wright's narrative does not assume that politics in a changed climate will neatly reiterate past politics of colonial expansion. While colonial pasts and presents shape geopolitics in *The Swan Book*, they do not offer prepackaged ethical stances or a ready-made script to guide encounters.

Instead, Wright's narrative depicts moments of proximity— forged through capitalist destruction and colonial histories— painful intimacies that hold out the possibility of new solidarities within environmental catastrophe. As Wright explains, the novel grapples with how "Aboriginal people are tied through globalization to the inequalities and suffering experienced by millions of others across the planet."[62] For instance, Bella Donna's arrival at Swan Lake echoes colonial conquest but also suggests the appearance of an asylum seeker:

Anyone there? She called.
  A bullfrog sitting in the *janja*, the mud, a lone tiny creature guarding the closed-gap entrance to the security fence of government transparency erected by the Army around the entire swamp answered *baji*—maybe. It was happy enough to grant her asylum when she asked for a look.

She turned up on an Indigenous doorstep, and the children called out: *A Viking! A Viking! An old, raggedy Viking!*

All covered with dirt, grass and sticks, she looked as though she had forgotten how to walk or comb her hair and had swum through scrub. Two laws, one in the head, the other worthless on paper in the swamp, said she was an invader. But! What could you do? Poor Bella Donna of the Champions! The sight of her made you cry. She was like a big angel, who called herself the patroness of World Rejection. This was the place for rejection: there was no hotter topic in the mind than rejection in this swamp, so to prove that they were not assimilated into the Australian way of life, the ancient laws of good manners about welcoming strangers were bestowed—Here! Stay! Have a go! We don't mind.[63]

The ethics of this moment are difficult to parse: Bella Donna is simultaneously an invader and a refugee, both a threat to the Aboriginal community of Swan Lake and an environmental exile in desperate need of asylum. She is "one of those people who had invented climate change" and a person who has lost her home.[64] Climate change inherits but does not precisely replicate the politics of colonial expansion, and human relationships must therefore be renegotiated.

SEASONAL HEGEMONY

Imposed seasonal expectations remain a signal feature of settler-colonial culture. As Philip Steer writes, "Australia is of particular interest" in this regard because colonization and profits from sheep farming were "predicated on the transplanting of British weather expectations. . . . The early publication of colonial almanacs testifies to settler expectations that Australia's weather ought to conform to regular and predictable patterns of annual sequential change along British lines."[65] But these expectations were continually frustrated: as the environmental historian Libby Robin argues, "even ideas like 'average rainfall' are a problem in a place where, for much of the country, rain might fall in winter or in summer, or not at all."[66] Phenology, as well as meteorology, was unpredictable for Australia's European settlers. Robin illustrates this point with a story: in the early twentieth century, scientific egg collectors in Australia could not discern the breeding season of Australia's banded stilts, a shorebird with a distinctive brown band around its torso. Moreover, the curator of the Western Australian Museum, Ludwig Glauert, threw up his hands, complaining that "information concerning the birds' 'winter migration' was of the vaguest possible character."[67] The stilts remained an enigma until the downpours of 1930, when a wheat farmer named Mrs. B. E. Cannon sent Glauert a package of twenty-three blown eggs and three photographs of birds, asking him to identify the species crowding the sandy lakeshore of her wheat farm. The stilt, as Robin notes, migrates in search of tiny shrimp that appear in the arid zone's ephemeral salt lakes: "its breeding season is simply 'after rain'—immediately after, when the brine shrimp population erupts.... The idea that nesting is not annual ... and not affected by day length defied all standard assumptions."[68]

Settlers were left debating the fraught status of Australia's seasons: some complained that the continent had no seasons—by which they meant, Robin notes, that "there are no long dark nights, and long evenings as Europe defines them"—while others oversimplified the intricate sequences of weather and life unfolding around them, demarcating simply a wet season and a dry season.[69] Tellingly, Steer documents the attempts of H.C. Russell, a nineteenth-century meteorologist in New South Wales who authored the 1896 *On Periodicity of Good and Bad Seasons*, to correlate rainfall in Greenwich, England to rainfall in the Australian colonies. Russell spent years searching for local climate data "that might prove its alignment with the British weather system."[70] He drew charts, mapping rainfall in Melbourne, Adelaide, and Brisbane against rainfall in Greenwich, hoping the rhythms of wetness and dryness might align or connect in some discernible way. Desperate to identify resemblances or affinities between English and Australian climates, settlers, meteorologists, and phenologists searched for congruities and returned empty handed. In Robin's words, Australia required "a different seasonal sensibility."[71]

Part of the climate disorientation coursing through Wright's novel is caused by a resultant seasonal hegemony, by settlers' enforcement of imperial rhythms in a continent following its own pulses of life. During Oblivia's captivity in an urban residence called "the Christmas house," she is caught in a place "where geography was lost," where Australian seasonalities are overwritten by the rigid shape of the British year.[72] The Christmas house is an environment generated through what Yuriko Furuhata calls "site-specific weather control," a contained work of geoengineering motivated by aesthetic desire.[73] The white settlers who own the Christmas house have designed it—inside and out—to imitate European winter: the roof is "lit up like the solar system" with twinkly lights, while the driveway is bordered by "a parade of adult-sized glowing snowmen."[74] The garden of "worse-for-wear Norwegian fairy-tale forest firs covered in glowing balls" is planted "to muffle the sound of the ocean, *because you get sick of it roaring day and night.*"[75] As a result of this seasonal colonialism, the Norwegian firs disorient local seagulls, who become unable to navigate back to the ocean and remain "lost somewhere in the needles."[76] Meanwhile, the interior of the Christmas house brims with "festoons of pine branches that were tied with red ribbons in big bows, and large silver bells tinkling automatically."[77] Like the lost seagulls, Oblivia wanders these wintry halls, her disorientation produced by the dissonance between her seasonal expectations and the imposed seasonal regime.

If colonialism generates the desire for seasonal hegemony, fossil fuels empower it. Brigid Rooney describes the Christmas house as "a node within an invisible grid of power—power derived from fossil fuels."[78] Indeed, seasonal hegemony is contingent on energy-intensive infrastructure: the strings of flickering lights and the robotic snowman singing carols in the backyard testify to rampant energy use. Like the snow machines used by Australian ski resorts during dry years, or the irrigation systems maintaining European-style lawns in arid times, seasonal hegemony contributes to global warming and environmental stress. To settle—in this case a continent—involves adjusting the setting of the local thermostat, enforcing the temperatures of the metropole. When the electricity short circuits at the Christmas house—the wet lights giving off a faint smell of smoke and the snowman breaking off mid-carol—the fantasy of imported seasons vanishes. In this sense, the seasonal hegemony is maintained through the consumption of fossil fuels, which become a less reliable resource as Wright's narrative progresses.

A new phase of seasonal colonialism is underway at the Christmas house by the time of Oblivia's arrival, the changes produced by imported seasonality compounded by the phenological shifts of global warming. The white nuclear family occupying the Christmas house complains about increasing energy restrictions in the city:

> They remembered a time when you could leave the lights burning all night, without anyone batting an eyelid. *Bring back the good old days when we could even cover the whole yard, trees and all, with the snowflake machine.* The only good thing apparently, was that it had been another bumper season for the growth of the Christmas trees. . . . Conifers loved the rain, and the perpetual mist, and

did not seem to mind if the sun never shone. . . . *All the trees must have grown approximately three meters, just since spring. Whatever happened to the good, old, hot Australian Christmas. . . . It will be snowing next thing.*[79]

Climate change generates further dissonance, altering the city's precipitation patterns so drastically that the phrase "good, old, hot Australian Christmas" carries the same seasonal nostalgia as the idea of European winter. As the house's imported forest of Norwegian spruce acclimates to the anthropogenic climate in a way it was never able to acclimate to the continent's earlier rhythms, phenological shifts amplify seasonal hegemony. In this sense, climate change accelerates the process of environmental change that began with the colonization of the Australian continent in 1788.

Doubly forced out of time—by seasonal hegemony and climate change, which reinforce and feed off each other—Oblivia is, like the seagull in the fir trees, "lost."[80] She wanders through the Christmas house, examining the small dioramas that replicate "in miniature scale nostalgic wintertime memories of foreign countries."[81] Each diorama creates an "elaborate world of dreams, where miniature winter people went about their business . . . among reindeer . . . [in] a countryside full of red robins singing in bare-branch trees, and miniaturized forests of pine trees laden with fake snow."[82] Wright describes these winter dioramas as "the theater of the remembered foreign lands," alluding to Tchaikovsky's ballet "Swan Lake," first performed at the Bolshoi Theatre in Moscow, and the military theaters of colonization. The emblems of European winter—the snow and the robins—are a theatrical set, a seasonal setting, forced on the Australian continent through settler colonialism. As Oblivia wanders the halls, inspecting these dioramas, the resident house cat delivers an anticolonial warning: *"Don't get sucked into other people's worlds."*[83]

Like Tchaikovsky's Odile and Odette, the black and white swan maidens of the ballet, Oblivia is held captive in this winter world, caught in the temporalities of settler Australia. She peers at the black swans—here, symbols of Indigenous Australia—in the dioramas, captive in the linear time of European history. Sailors from the Dutch East India Company chase black swans across the shallows, black swans in cages are carted to zoos and botanical gardens, "at Knowsley, in England, where they were bred in the Earl of Derby's menagerie, and also in France—in the Empress Josephine's ponds at Malmaison—and the waters of Paris."[84] Like these black swans, Oblivia "now belonged in the menagerie of exhibits," unable to reenter seasonal time, she fights nightmares of "being locked in this moment forever."[85] She yearns for her lost sense of phenology: "Where had time gone? How many seasons of swans' breeding had passed by and she had not noticed?"[86] As she and the swans escape, leaving the cage crawling with swan lice and coated with droppings, their joint migration is an effort to reclaim their own coordinates of environmental time.

To read *The Swan Book* as a story of how colonialism and climate change alter environmental time and space—swans dislocated by perpetual drought, children undertaking prolonged hibernations, populations displaced by uninhabitable conditions, and "*all of this mixed-up weather*"—is to read it as a deliberately unseasonable tale.[87] It is a novel of disorientation, a work focused on Oblivia's struggle to both navigate and narrate the weather—atmospheric and political—blowing through her. Oblivia must reintegrate herself in temporality: she must orient herself within changed times.

This project alters Oblivia's relationship with literature, turning her into an avid and susceptible absorber of stories. She latches on to literature about swans—stories she absorbs from Bella Donna, a poem by Ch'i-Chi about "the flight of swans in the night, like *a lone boat chasing the moon*," works by Baudelaire, Neruda, Heaney—she searches for a narrative to orient herself within changed times.[88] The highly allusive nature of the novel—its references to the nineteenth-century Finnish epic *The Kalevala*, ballads from the Baul singers of rural India, Yeats's "Leda and the Swan," and the folk rock of Leonard Cohen—is an indication of Oblivia's porousness as a reader, her search for a literary touchstone in the wake of the changing climate. Wright is cautious about embracing the circulation of world literature—"the swamp people were not interested in being conquered by other peoples' stories"—and Oblivia's tendency to soak up the books swirling through her dust-ridden land renders her vulnerable rather than knowledgeable.[89] In such disorienting times, the novel seems to suggest, selecting a story to travel with is a risky act. Stories are powerful enough to lead you astray, colonize your mind, suck you into other people's worlds. And yet, Oblivia continually finds herself navigating the topsy-turvy events of the novel via stories—she is Rip Van Winkle, Leda, a ballerina in Tchaikovsky's production. She approaches unprecedented times via the literary, which as I will argue, makes her an archetypal reader of climate fiction.

CLIMATE FICTION IN UNPRECEDENTED TIMES

One of the most interesting debates emerging in climate fiction scholarship centers on its fraught status as a genre. Some writers classify it as an emergent genre, some call it an offshoot of science fiction. Shelley Streeby describes climate fiction as a "sub-genre . . . best situated within the larger category of speculative fiction."[90] Other critics are wary of invoking genre. Alex Trexler refers to climate fiction as an "archive" of texts, a "literary movement," and a publishing "phenomenon," while Rebecca Evans calls it "a literary preoccupation with climate futures."[91] Adeline Johns-Putra and Alex

Goodbody reject the idea of genre explicitly, asserting that "cli-fi is not a genre in the scholarly sense: it lacks the plot formulas and stylistic conventions that characterize genres such as sci-fi and the western. However ... [cli-fi] provides a convenient term for an already significant body of narrative work broadly defined by its thematic focus on climate change."[92] In this vein of thought, climate fiction is not a genre but rather a collection of texts unified solely through topic, a shorthand for the books incorporating anthropogenic climate change into their plots or settings. To add to the mayhem of this debate, a few writers and critics have thrown up their hands, positing that all contemporary fiction is climate fiction.[93]

And yet, the energy surrounding—and the demand for— climate fiction feels indicative of genre. In print, on the airwaves, at libraries, and within book clubs, its recent propulsion cannot be explained by topic alone. Books coalesce into genre through collective cravings and inquiries. Or, as Ralph Cohen once argued, genres "arise, change, and decline for historical reasons.... The purposes they serve are social and aesthetic."[94] Partially shaped by the uncertainties and needs of their reading publics, genres are inevitably connected to nonliterary urgencies. Bruce Robbins suggests "there are social tasks that cause a genre to be seized on at a given historical moment and invested with special energy and representativeness."[95] In the early twenty-first century, as plumes of smoke from Australian bushfires dim the afternoon light in Santiago and stain the sunset in Buenos Aires, turning the sky red halfway around the world, climate fiction is being seized on, pored over. People are—quite literally—reading in light of climate change.

However, if climate fiction is a bona fide genre, it is not a genre that coheres through affinities between texts. Comparing titles often referred to as cli-fi yields more incongruities than resemblances. The tortured ruminations of the Egyptian-Canadian writer Omar El Akkad's *American War*, a future history set as the United States bans fossil fuels and the South secedes in protest, contrast sharply with the stream of consciousness that predominates the American author Jenny Offill's *Weather*, a realist novel centered on a present-day Brooklyn librarian: "put out kibble and water, peer open-heartedly into the fridge. The window is open. It's nice out. The pigeons aren't on the fire escape."[96] Likewise, the breakneck oceanic time-travel plot of Dominican writer Rita Indiana's *La mucama de Omicunlé* is worlds apart from the classic detective fiction of Finnish novelist Antti Tuomainen's *Parantaja*. For years, literary theorists have conceived of genre through textual kinship, identifying "family resemblances" in a collection of texts with discernibly connected plots, tones, or forms.[97] But climate fiction—which ranges from the historical to the futuristic, from speculative to realist, from dystopian to idealistic—resists assemblage at the level of textual similarity. Pondering this conundrum, I cannot help but hear echoes of Libby Robin's warning about Australia's climate: "even ideas like 'average rainfall' are a problem in a place where, for much of the country, rain might fall in winter or in summer, or not at all."[98] Climate fiction is a highly variable literature, one that requires a different genric sensibility.

Fortunately, other scholarship hints at more capacious definitions of genre. Attending to the impact of historical context, many critics are less interested in genre as a collection of innately connected texts and more interested in conceiving of genre as a set of texts curated through reading conventions. Rachael Scarborough King argues that genres emerge through "acts of association—made by writers, readers, critics, scholars, and/or computers—that generate usable configurations of texts."[99] Along similar lines, Caroline Levine insists that "any attempt to recognize a work's genre is a historically specific and interpretive act."[100] What possibilities emerge when genre is thought of, not as a set of texts itself, but rather as the move that assembles a group of texts? Or, what happens when Martin

Puchner's argument at the nexus of climate change and literature is taken seriously? "What matters is not only *what* we read," Puchner insists, "but also *how* we read."[101] I suspect that that *how* we read matters profoundly: it allows climate fiction to cohere.

My assertion is that climate fiction is defined by an effort to measure or understand the nonliterary climate by the light of the fictional. As this interpretive gesture—the reach for the fictional as a means of orienting oneself within changed times, a reliance on a story to navigate the anthropogenic climate—is repeated, it forms the pattern that allows markedly dissimilar books to coalesce into a genre. Building on Lauren Berlant's work, Stephanie LeMenager maintains that climate fiction represents a "struggle for genre," a "struggle to find new patterns of expectation and new means of living with an unprecedented set of limiting conditions."[102] In a time when expectations about the climate are unstable—when, as LeMenager observes, many people have a queasy sense of living within unprecedented times—fiction becomes a lifeline. Without histories or scientific studies to frame bushfires of this proportion, when carbon dioxide levels have not risen to these levels since the Pliocene epoch and black swans are gathering on the horizon—readers grasp for stories by which they might recalibrate their expectations. They search—in books and stories—for a feeling of knowing.

Teachers, scholars, and readers all recount grasping for a literary touchstone within the changing climate. I think of these accounts as a generic pattern playing out not between texts, but between interpretations. For me, it is this movement between text and anthropogenic experience—the way that a reader senses a heat wave or an anxiety brush up against a story—that marks a work as climate fiction. To illustrate the prevalence of this interpretive convention, I offer a series of brief examples derived from published scholarship and media. I divide the following examples into three types—prescience, resonance, and counsel—to elucidate variations within this generic pattern, but in practice, these types of reading bleed into each other, becoming all but impossible to disentangle.

First, readers often describe literary works as eerily prescient, providing a fictional backstory during climate disasters. As Taleb notes, there is a desire—in the wake of extreme disruption—to "concoct explanations" retroactively, rendering a disaster "explainable and predictable."[103] In May of 2020, as Cyclone Amphan hit the Sundarbans, the delta south of Kolkata and Dhaka, the Seattle-based professor Jesse Oak Taylor experienced the storm as an uncanny animation of a novel:

> At the time, we were reading Amitav Ghosh's *The Hungry Tide* (2004), a novel in which (spoiler alert) a major cyclone hits the Sundarbans. We followed Ghosh's *Twitter* feed, which was full of images and videos of the devastation, either because he was posting them himself or because people were tagging him in order to comment on the resonance between the scenes unfolding before their (and our) eyes and *The Hungry Tide*. It was as though we were part of a global conspiracy to bring the novel to life.[104]

In Taylor's account, Ghosh's novel functions as precedent for the cyclone gaining momentum in overheated waters. Fiction becomes the yardstick by which extreme experience in a changed climate is calibrated. This sense of prescience interests me, because if genre is understood thematically, if climate fiction encompasses texts that explicitly mention or engage with anthropogenic climate change, then categorizing *The Hungry Tide* as climate fiction requires interpretive acrobatics. As Subhankar Banerjee notes, cyclones hit the Sundarbans well before anthropogenic climate change took hold. While a cyclone takes center stage in Ghosh's novel, he argues, "climate change does not. The novel was published in 2004, prior to when we started to connect the dots between tropical cyclones in the Bay of Bengal and the escalating climate crisis. That conversation started after Cyclone Sidr of 2007 and Cyclone Aila of 2009, both of which had caused widespread destruction in the Sundarbans."[105] But as Taylor, the author of *The Sky of Our Manufacture*, which tracks the relationship between climatic shifts and Victorian literature, is well aware, *The Hungry Tide* is indeed a novel invested in portrayals of climatic vulnerability. As scholars of earlier literary periods have documented, literary history is rife with narratives that highlight human susceptibility to climatic shifts, and these narratives gain prescience in light of the events of the climatic present. If climate fiction is understood as a genre cohering through interpretation, then reading *The Hungry Tide* in conjunction with Amphan, a cyclone that demonstrated the forces of a warming Indian Ocean, enfolds it within climate fiction.

Other readers search for literature that resonates in new ways as climate change intensifies, seeking insight or modes of adaptation within chronic change. Isabel Hofmeyr, who taught the South African and Botswanan writer Bessie Head's oeuvre in Johannesburg in the 1980s, framing it as feminist writing, now thinks of these same novels as "stories that unfold on the edge of the Kalahari Desert, where too much or too little rain destroys lives."[106] For Hofmeyr, Head's work resonates anew as climate change exacerbates aridity in Botswana: "Reading her now returns us to the question of what it took then (and would take now) to create a drought-resistant literature."[107] Hofmeyr is interested in Head's work insofar as it is useful, applicable: her novels, she suggests, might be drought-resistant. Head's thought might be a resource, a tool for adapting to life within drought. Even more obliquely, Min Hyoung Song reads *Human Acts*, the novel by South Korean writer Han Kang, as a book that forces its readers to confront "death's expanding presence" during compounding climate change.[108] In Song's adept hands, Kang's novel—set in the aftermath of the 1980 Gwangju uprising and deaths of civilians—assists readers as they "prepare" for "the end of human life in numbers the human species has never before encountered."[109] Song anticipates widespread death through "extreme weather events, such as hurricanes, wildfires, and droughts, and the spread of pathogens borne along vectors of warmer weather, as well as draconian responses to the suffering and unrest that follow."[110] Rather than suggesting *Human Acts* foreshadows or depicts the mass deaths anticipated through anthropogenic climate change, Song reads it as resonant, as an aid in psychologically preparing for the unprecedented.

In the most fervent iteration of climate fiction as an interpretive genre, novels function as guides, providing counsel for action in changing times. In the podcast *Octavia's Parables*, the musician Toshi Reagon and the activist and writer adrienne maree brown discuss Octavia Butler's *Parable of the Sower* chapter by chapter, plumbing the text for direct guidance: "I kind of live by it," Reagon explains.[111] brown articulates their work with Butler's novel as "studying apocalypse," offering their podcast listeners and fellow readers of *Parable of the Sower* questions to ponder.[112] In September of 2020, on the heels of the Australian bushfires a hemisphere away, and in the midst of a severe wildfire season on the west coast of the United States, Reagon and brown mulled over a pivotal chapter in Butler's novel that features a decimating fire, the result of ongoing drought in Southern California. Reagon suggests that Butler's novel offers a blueprint for disaster planning. Building on the main character's efforts to pack a go-bag, Reagon asks listeners about their own preparations within a climatically altered world: "There've been floods and hurricanes and . . . the electricity goes out . . . do you have, like your bag that you can walk out of the house and exist for a couple of days?" brown continues these questions: "What resources will you actually be able to access in the condition of systemic failure?" she asks. "Do you have something buried? Do you have stuff under the mattress? Do you have gold bars? Do you have seeds?"[113] In this vein of reading, literature becomes a life manual or survival guide to weather a changed world. Butler's work is approached not as allusive or resonant, but as instructional. It is also seen as predictive of the unprecedented, as evidenced by the hashtag #OctaviaKnew that readers use as they post about current droughts and fires.

Amid these patterns of reading, it is worth noting that recent IPCC reports address two characteristics of a black swan event, improbability and high impact, but they remain silent on the third characteristic: the need—in the wake of an overturned world—to construct a story within the wreckage, to account for what is occurring. Consider the black swans alighting—one after the other—at Oblivia's drought-stricken detention camp, "coming to the swamp with no story for themselves."[114] As Wright explains, their arrival was disconcerting because "nobody knew what it meant."[115] The unprecedented annihilates worldviews, leaving those in its wake grasping for a story—or, in Lauren Berlant's words, "the violence of the world makes us flail about for things to read with."[116] The flocking of the black swans marks a turbulence, their presence a reminder of the danger and necessity of crafting stories as established precedents crumble and flames flicker across the horizon of expectation.

Climate fiction is the effort to clasp on to stories in a changed climate—to adapt, resist, navigate, mourn, or generally orient oneself to changed times via the literary. Wright recalls that when she first heard about the black swans migrating toward the interior of the country, her concern was about the challenge of crafting a story for the flock, of finding a narrative for their altered circumstances. Her quandary will be shared by writers and readers of climate fiction in the years ahead:

> Someone told me, I saw a swan out there and I didn't know if I should kill it or not. It's got no story up in our country. So what

do you do? What happens to a bird—or to anyone—who has no story for that country?

There was a change in the environment, in the weather patterns, so we were getting heaps of rain up in central Australia, with a lot of water lying around, and then down south for years there was a drought, and that perhaps explains the reason why the swans were moving.... They had to go somewhere. Where do they go and what stories do they have? How do you make stories for them in a new place?[117]

RHYTHM AND ENVIRONMENTAL PRACTICE

5

OCCASIONAL POETRY
IN STRESSED TIMES

On September 23, 2014, at the opening ceremony of the United Nations Climate Summit in New York City, the Marshallese spoken word poet Kathy Jetñil-Kijiner stood in front of an audience composed of more than one hundred world leaders and presidents—including the secretary-general of the United Nations, the chair of the Intergovernmental Panel on Climate Change, and the president of the World Bank Group. She looked out across the assembled representatives, seated behind platinum titles engrained with the names of countries and institutions, and performed a poem addressed to her infant daughter, Matafele Peinam:

Men say that one day
that lagoon will devour you

They say it will gnaw at the shoreline
chew at the roots of your breadfruit trees
gulp down rows of your seawalls
and crunch your island's shattered bones

They say you, your daughter
and your granddaughter, too

will wander
rootless
with only
a passport
to call home[1]

Jetñil-Kijiner's delivery intensifies as she describes the lagoon's rising waters, her voice gaining momentum and volume as the future gnaws and chews and gulps and crunches the Marshall Islands. This poem is ostensibly addressed to her daughter—it resembles a grim, anthropogenic fairy tale about children wandering through an insatiable, monstrous world—but it is also, circuitously, intended for the representatives gathered before her, the global organization that will decide to restrain or unleash the waters. Jetñil-Kijiner wrote "Dear Matafele Peinam" for this precise occasion, and her performance conveys environmental stress, conjuring the nightmares of small island nations into the UN chambers.

In parsing this poem, Jetñil-Kijiner's evocation of climate stress—the lore of rising seas and intergenerational displacement that she imparts—might be understood in relation to the rhetoric of climate injustice. Or, since much of the force of this poem is generated through live performance—through Jetñil-Kijiner's cadences, shifting facial expressions, and the volume of her delivery—it might be situated in relation to spoken word and the rise of slam poetry as a literary practice. But more compelling questions emerge when these two genealogies are parsed simultaneously, when anthropogenic climate change and slam poetry—which both gained traction in public consciousness during the late 1980s and became increasingly prevalent over the course of the next few decades—are understood in relation to each other. Read in tandem, these environmental and literary histories further theorize the concept of climate arrhythmias, foregrounding the role of stress.

FIGURE 5.1 Kathy Jetñil-Kijiner performing during the opening of the UN Climate Summit 2014. Courtesy of UN Photo / Mark Garten.

Arrhythmias are produced through temporal irregularities—prematurity or delay—but they also result from unexpected emphases. A pulse that arrives at the expected time but imparts a stronger or weaker intensity than anticipated will register as arrhythmic. Arrhythmias are a matter of stress, of heightened or diminished force relative to an established pattern. And although very little attention has been given to the prosody of spoken word performances, poetic performance conveys stress across multiple registers: the accented syllables of words, the shifting pitch of a poet's voice, the change in volume between words or phrases, the timbre or tone of an utterance, a hand gesture or facial expression that adds emphasis to what is spoken.[2] Spoken word performance is one of the most intricate and nuanced fields in which to consider literary stress, which makes it a particularly germane field for the study of urgency and its imprint on literary work.

Environmentally, arrhythmias also register through excessive stress. During the 2019 UN General Assembly in New York, Hilda Heine the president of the Marshall Islands, described how anthropogenic climate change is impacting her home: "Prolonged and unseasonal droughts are hitting us real hard, and salt water is creeping into our freshwater lands. We are on the very front line of climate change."[3] In addition to Heine's description of unseasonable droughts, environmental time feels strangely accentuated as tides reach further inland due to sea level rise. Tidal rhythms continue temporally, the water reaching its highest levels in February and March, as the earth nears perihelion and the moon nears perigee, the dual proximity of the sun and moon magnifying the gravitational tug upon the water. With sea level rise, however, high tides—referred to colloquially as king tides—stretch ever farther inland, a problematically emphasized pulse. In multiple ways—changes in the timing of droughts, overly emphasized tides, and unusually severe storms—watery time across the Pacific has entered the realm of the unseasonable.

In 2015, at the 21st annual United Nations Conference of the Parties, held in Paris and commonly referred to as COP21, four other spoken word poets from Southeast Asia, the Pacific Islands, and their diasporas joined Jetñil-Kijiner, forming a poetic lineup resembling a slam team. As world leaders negotiated what would come to be known as the Paris Agreement—a pledge to limit the rise in global average temperature "to well below 2° above pre-industrial levels"—these poets gathered through Spoken Word for the World, a global, multilingual poetry competition sponsored by the nongovernmental organization Global Call for Climate Action (GCCA).[4] The Spoken Word for the World competition was premised on literature's capacity to move an audience, to incite action in a way that sheer data may not: "We don't need another science lecture," the GCCA argued in its call for submissions, "we need poetry."[5]

From a pool of poets representing more than thirty countries, the panel of judges selected Eunice Andrada, a Filipina poet living in Sydney; Isabella Borgeson, a Filipina American slam poet based in Oakland; John "Meta" Sarmiento, a Filipino rapper and poet from Guam; and Terisa Siagatonu, a Samoan poet and community organizer from California's Bay Area.[6] As voices affiliated with areas of the world acutely affected by global warming, yet accorded little input in the arena of global climate negotiations, these poets' performances at forums, marches, and events during COP21 were inherently acts of representation. As Siagatonu explained in an interview with NBC during the summit: "It's hard to be at the biggest gathering on climate change in the world, and feel like no one from your community or homeland is around you or being represented."[7] At this occasion, poetry was performed as both art and advocacy.

In this chapter, I reflect on the poems performed at the UN climate summit in 2014 and the following year at COP21 to consider how climate justice activism is inhabiting slam performance. Cataloging the structures and stresses of these occasional performances reveals how writers and performance artists honed their lyrics to effect political and environmental change during the pivotal first decades of the twenty-first century. Moreover, as Jetñil-Kijiner and the poets performing at COP21 depicted intensifying storm seasons and other oceanic arrhythmias, they infused conference halls, auditoriums, and crowded streets with a sense of urgency. Their poems are now a case study in the literature of extremity—from the extreme winds of typhoons to the stresses of oral performance. Nearly out of time—in the sense of an unseasonable storm, but also in the sense of writing and performing within a quickly overheating atmosphere—these poets translated the stress of climatic precarity and displacement into poetic stress conveyed on a global stage.

SLAM POETRY AS REPRESENTATIVE PRACTICE

In the late 1980s—as decolonization continued its sweep through the Pacific, as the UN Trust Territory dissolved into sovereign nations, as headlines following James Hansen's testimony before a United States Senate committee raised concerns about anthropogenic warming—poetry slams emerged in Chicago and quickly migrated to the coasts. They settled in established performance venues like the Nuyorican Poets' Cafe, where Latinx and Black poets had gathered and performed for decades. In this sense, slam grafted onto performance practices developed through the Black Arts Movement and Nuyorican poetry, lineages that should not be obscured as slam becomes an increasingly global phenomenon.[8] Even in this initial era of slam performance, the form thrived within diasporic venues and communities.

During these early years, representation—speaking as a resident of a place or as a member of a community—became engrained in slam performance. For instance, at the first National Poetry Slam, held in San Francisco in 1990, poets representing Chicago, New York, and San Francisco took their turns on stage, competing on behalf of their localities.[9] Although some slam competitions—like the Individual World Poetry Slam—now permit individual poets to compete against each other, many national and international slams retain this original group structure, featuring teams of poets representing their local café, city, territory, or nation. This collective and affiliative structure—each poet contributing a performance toward a team outcome, each performance undertaken on behalf of a home literary community—would eventually translate into representative performances by poets from small island nations at UN gatherings. Slam performance, as a representative literary practice, has an affinity with the political.

Near the turn of the twenty-first century, poetry slams departed the continental United States, rapidly gaining popularity across, and beyond, the Pacific. As D. Keali'i MacKenzie observes, slam competitions initially surfaced in regions of the Pacific with a "forced orientation toward the United States": Youth Speaks Hawai'i was founded in 2005 and Guam's Sinangån-ta poetry slam was founded in 2007.[10] However, while the proliferation of poetry slams throughout the Pacific world followed routes engrained through American military imperialism, poets increasingly framed spoken word as a vehicle for what Rob Wilson and Hsinya Huang, both building on the work of Epeli Hau'ofa, call transpacific and transindigenous solidarity.[11] For instance, Youth Speaks Hawai'i—which became "a banner too small to represent the Pacific"—expanded into an organization called Pacific Tongues that includes partner spoken word groups in Guam, Palau, and New Zealand.[12] These solidarities only deepen as climate change intensifies: as Hi'ilei Julia Hobart notes, reflecting on Jetñil-Kijiner's collaborative work, "environmental change across the globe binds Indigenous islanders together into a kind of shared risk."[13] This sense of an oceanic literary community—islanders and diasporas joining voices—is crucial context for understanding the Spoken Word for the World performances in 2015. In representing frontline communities in the climate crisis, the cohort of poets assembled through Global Call for Climate Action built on this literary tradition of Pacific solidarity, performing as a collective within international climate negotiations.

By the time they arrived in Paris, Jetñil-Kijiner and the poets performing at COP21 were not debuting amateurs but rather award-winning artists who had honed their craft in the poetry slams and spoken word competitions emerging throughout the Pacific world. Jetñil-Kijiner began performing in high school with the Youth Speaks Hawai'i slam team and then taught and performed as an undergraduate student in California through Poetry for the People, an arts activism program founded by the Caribbean American writer June Jordan.[14] In 2012, Jetñil-Kijiner represented the Marshall Islands at the Poetry Parnassus Festival in London, quickly gaining international acclaim as a spoken word performer. Like Jetñil-Kijiner, Siagatonu and Borgeson also have roots in the Pacific coast slam scene: Siagatonu spent three years slamming in Los Angeles with the Da Poetry Lounge team, which took second place at the National Poetry Slam in 2013, while Borgeson also trained with Poetry for the People and competed as a member of the UC-Berkeley slam team.[15] Prior to his performance in Paris, Sarmiento was actively involved with the Sinangån-ta poetry slam in Mangilao and coached two of Guam's teams to the semifinal rounds of Brave New Voices, an international youth spoken word competition.[16] Further afield from the United States and its unincorporated territories, Andrada entered slam performance through The Rumble Youth Slam, the largest youth competition in Sydney.[17] These extensive pedigrees reveal not only the proliferation of spoken word competitions along the coasts and archipelagoes of the Pacific world, but also how slam and other varieties of spoken word serve as tributaries for literary climate activism. By the time they took to the stages and streets of Paris, the Spoken Word for the World poets were seasoned performers, accomplished in the multifaceted art of connecting with an audience.

Performing before world leaders and assembled crowds at the UN was a literary opportunity freighted with the task of representation. In 2014, when the UN Non-Governmental Liaison Service announced its open competition to address heads of state at the upcoming climate summit in New York, demographic representation was built into the call: applications were sought from women under the age of thirty in the Global South. Susan Alzner, the primary organizer of the competition, explained this decision: "Women disproportionately experience the impacts of climate change in particular because 70% of the lowest income people worldwide are women.... It is essential that we give women the space to speak on this critical topic that is an existential threat to humanity."[18] But if this representational task was structured in terms of gender, geography, and generational status, it was also entwined with cause-based advocacy. The UN hoped that Jetñil-Kijiner, selected from a pool of 544 applicants, would serve as an energizing emblem of—and spokesperson for—the climate crisis, much like Malala Yousafzai embodied and gave voice to educational gender inequities at the UN in 2013. Building on Jetñil-Kijiner's moving performance, the judges of the Spoken Word for the World contest—including members of the environmental nonprofit 350.org and the spoken word publisher Button Poetry—selected a team of young poets of color, primarily women.[19] This cohort, all from Southeast Asia, the Pacific Islands, and their diasporas, also represented the geographic frontlines of the climate crisis. Cause-based representation of this kind is inherently vexed: in the case of Jetñil-Kijiner and the Spoken Word for the World poets, the task of voicing climate change became nearly inextricable from functioning as its iconography on a world stage. It is possible to read these invitations to perform at the UN as an attempt at justice washing the climate negotiations, a simultaneous tokenization of frontline communities and poetry.

While slam poetry is now a globalized literary form, practiced everywhere from Los Angeles to Mangilao, it acquires local inflections and significance as it settles in a region—or, in Susanna Sacks's apt phrasing, slam "becom[es] local even as it maintains a global poetic ethos."[20] The founders of the Sinangån-ta Poetry Slam—which translates from Chamorro as "our spoken words"— view slam in relation to Chamorro literary practices: Fanai Castro observes that the audience participation of slam performance "evokes the system of call and response that is characteristic of Chamorro oral narration," while Melvin Won Pat-Borja notes that spoken word is "a way for our people to reconnect with the oral traditions that our ancestors practiced centuries ago. It may look a little different with stages and microphones, but it is still a vehicle that allows us to share our stories, songs, and histories."[21] Jetñil-Kijiner makes a related claim within a Marshallese context: "Spoken word was my introduction to the interaction between an audience and a poet—that collective, shared space, so reminiscent of storytelling," she explains, noting that involvement in spoken word performance "inspired me . . . to start to investigate our oral traditions, and the lineage of writing that came before me."[22] In this sense, Pacific slam performances exemplify what MacKenzie calls "a joining," an intermingling of "past, continuing, and adapting oral arts" within the Pacific.[23] Similarly, Samoan writer Albert Wendt suggests that Pacific literatures demonstrate "survival and dynamic adaptation, despite enormous suffering under colonialism in some of our countries. . . . We have indigenized much that was colonial or foreign to suit ourselves, creating new blends and forms."[24] Selina Tusitala Marsh observes that Pacific art practices "manifest continuous change," thereby resisting the "stultifying" or "essentialized" notion of a static practice frozen in time.[25] As slam poetry and spoken word spread throughout the Pacific, they fortify—and reciprocally, are fortified by—local oral literatures.

This joining of slam performance and local oral literatures allowed poets in 2014 and 2015 to represent their communities not only through the subject matter of a poem, but also through the evocation of Indigenous oral genres. In an overt instance of intermingling established and recent oral genres, Jetñil-Kijiner prefaced her 2014 poetic performance by sharing "one of our most beloved legends" with the leaders assembled at the United Nations. This prefatory legend about a sailing race is rarely mentioned in analyses of

Jetñil-Kijiner's performance, likely because it is not included in the printed version of "Dear Matafele Peinam." As Jetñil-Kijiner explains in her scholarship, "bwebwenato is meant to be live, not textual."[26] Just before she segued into her poetic performance, Jetñil-Kijiner interpreted this legend in light of the climatic future, interweaving a notable piece of Marshallese literature with current climate politics. She exhorted the audience before her: "I ask world leaders to take us all along on your ride. We won't slow you down. We'll help you win the most important race of all, the race to save humanity."[27] In this moment of interpretation, she adapted bwebwenato to the occasion, joining her country's literary traditions and Marshallese environmental advocacy.

Moreover, Jetñil-Kijiner's subsequent poetic epistle to her daughter might be interpreted in relation to her research on the Marshallese genres bwebwenato and roro, oral performances that can record lineages and preserve family history.[28] Understood apropos of bwebwenato or roro, Jetñil-Kijiner's poem acquires additional gravitas: in the Marshall Islands, daughters have traditionally been the inheritors of land, and by the time Matafele Peinem grows up, there might not be an island topography left for her to inherit. As Jetñil-Kijiner's voice shifts "upward in pitch and volume," her poem invokes a future family lineage rather than a historical one—"you, your daughter, / and your granddaughter, too" will have "only / a passport / to call home."[29] These lines forecast imminent citizens of a submerged landscape. In this sense, as she stood before delegates of the UN climate summit, Jetñil-Kijiner represented the Marshall Islands not only by reporting on the climatic prospects of her island home, but also through her evocation of these Marshallese genres. If performances by Pacific Islander poets are interpreted in relation to Indigenous literary practices, then spoken word itself has the capacity to represent a regional identity, even as it burgeons into a globalized literary form.

EXPERIENTIAL WITNESS

Partially due to their training in slam performance, the poets performing in Paris in 2015 articulated the climate crisis through what Angela Robinson terms "experiential and embodied knowledges."[30] Rhetorically, they positioned themselves not as scientific authorities but rather as community members engaged in more intimate acts of environmental witness. This authority rooted in "habitual evaluative practices," rather than scientific or bureaucratic data, is foregrounded in Siagatonu's "Layers."[31] Siagatonu explicitly rejects an ethos derived from scientific expertise, instead offering her audience a poem accentuating material evidence:

> I don't know much about how to talk about climate change
> but I do know a thing or two about water.
> I know that San Francisco, city of my birth, is running out of it—
> as in the state of California is losing its memory of what lakes look like
> because not enough rain has fallen to replenish them.
> I know that my island of Samoa is thriving off of the very thing that plans to kill it
> once the sea levels are too high to distinguish the difference between swimming and drowning.
> I know that the tsunami spared my grandpa and his home back in September of 2009
> but took two hundred others,
> how no one in my family ever dared to call this a blessing.[32]

Siagatonu's emphasis on tangible, palpable climatic change—her insistence that she is not conversant in climate change discourse and yet well-versed in water resources, storms, and sea levels—is exemplary of experiential knowledge. Throughout "Layers," she distances herself from professional environmentalism and its terminology, grounding her descriptions of the changing climate in the knowledge of a neighborhood forced below the poverty line:

> I don't know much about how to talk about the impact of fossil fuels or carbon footprints
> But I do know a lot about poverty and the paradoxes of being poor
> How saving the environment never means saving people who come from environments like mine[33]

As Robinson observes, "experiential knowledge, especially from Indigenous women and women of color, is rarely, if ever, taken seriously by those in power," and in this context, Siagatonu's work expanded the forms of knowledge and expertise available at COP21, her poetry serving as a surreptitious vehicle for her testimony.[34] Her performance insisted—in Robinson's phrasing—"on the inclusion of affective, felt experience as real knowledge" in climate summit discourse.[35] It was an invitation, as Rebecca Hogue and Anaïs Maurer suggest, for those assembled at the climate summit "to reconsider what counts as valid data and legitimate genres to be included at the highest levels of policy-making."[36]

While literary scholars have frequently commented on the experiential bent of poems performed at climate summits, particularly in conversations around Jetñil-Kijiner's work, it has yet to be noted that this stance—this emphasis on embodied experience—is a generic convention of slam performance. Rather than being unique to Jetñil-Kijiner's oeuvre, it is characteristic of a larger cohort of poets involved in the poetry slams of the Pacific world and its diasporas. For instance, Siagatonu's inclination to hold professional climate terminology at arm's length—"I don't know much about how to talk about the impact of fossil fuels or carbon footprints"—aligns with the nonelite ethos of slam performance, in which, to borrow

Maria Damon's words, "the criterion for slam success seems to be some kind of 'realness'" or direct experience rather than literary credentials.[37] In other words, as slam poetry's emphasis on what Ron Silliman calls "the poem as confession of lived experience" converges with the community science of climate change, poems of climatic witness are marked by these first-person accounts of the warming world.[38] Experiential witness is a fine needle to thread: de-emphasizing scientific expertise risks veering into anti-intellectualism, and yet—in the midst of a political backlash against climate science, as dark money is poured into debunking scientific authority and muddying climate politics—this rhetorical position, this grounding in experiential knowledge, may prove an indispensable rhetorical strategy.

In their emphasis on firsthand observation, the poems performed in New York and Paris are also tied to the genre of witness. Formative scholarship on the literature of witness stresses a writer's proximity to an event: Carolyn Forché, for instance, catalogs poets who "personally endured" severe conditions, producing poems that "bear the trace of extremity within them."[39] Similarly, poetry of climatic witness often underscores physical experience: performing "Island Haze" at COP21, John Meta Sarmiento vividly depicts smoke from forest fires in Indonesia and Papua New Guinea that drifted across Guam, "clinging too closely to shorelines and branches," but ultimately stakes his witness in his body, declaring, "I am choking on the smoke."[40] This embodied evidence was not the upshot of a persona poem or hyperbole: Sarmiento explained to CNN that "for me specifically, the forest fires in Indonesia and Papua New Guinea created a harmful haze . . . I was sick for weeks, coughing, and riddled with headaches."[41] This emphasis on embodied witness is especially resonant within slam performance, a poetic movement that, as Javon Johnson notes, rejects the idea "that what the body offers is somehow less relevant than what the mind offers."[42] In slam competitions, poets are required to perform their own work, their physical expressions and gestures contributing to their poems, which, as Susan Somers-Willet observes, pushes slam performance "beyond mere confessionalism" into "an outright proclamation of the authorial self."[43] As poets who have personally endured the extremities of the climate crisis take to the stage, this embrace of first-person testimony—what Jesse Lichtenstein, writing in *The Atlantic*, describes as a marked "resurgence of the first-person lyric" among a generation of poets "having come of age in the heyday of identity politics"—merges with climate discourse.[44] In this sense, slam poetry's commitment to progressive identity politics—to articulating and addressing injustices tied to identity—maps onto the climate crisis, making slam performance a particularly apt form for witnessing climate injustice. Poets affiliated with frontline communities bear witness to the severe climatic changes underway, their physical presence a reminder to their audience that the storms, heat, and smoke of the climate crisis have already touched skin and permeated lungs.

This proximity to acute climatic change allows poets from small island nations to act as situated informants within a global climate crisis, detailing climate extremity for those geographically or economically removed from discernible climatic change. For instance, in a poem titled "Tell Them," which Jetñil-Kijiner performed in Paris in 2015 as over 10,000 people linked arms in the streets to form a human chain in place of the planned climate march, in order to symbolize global unity, she addresses her friends in the United States and asks them to spread the word of rising sea levels in the Marshall Islands:

> tell them about the water—how we have seen it rising
> flooding across our cemeteries
> gushing over the sea walls
> and crashing against our homes

Tell them what it's like
to see the entire ocean_level_with the land

Tell them
we are afraid

Tell them we don't know
of the politics
or the science
but tell them we see
what is in our own backyard[45]

Building on Elizabeth DeLoughrey's influential assessment of the scalar disjuncture between "experience[s] of local weather" and "understandings of global climate" in "Tell Them," I note that Jetñil-Kijiner's rhetoric is characteristic of climate justice rhetoric.[46] Here, Jetñil-Kijiner offers a backyard form of climatic witness—we, the Marshallese, know that the world is warming and sea levels are increasing not because we examine the Keeling Curve or a graph of sea level rise, but because the water is level with the land. We have seen it rising, she insists. Proximity to acute climatic change—living on atolls positioned just above sea level—affords Jetñil-Kijiner a particular body of experiential knowledge within this era of planetary change. Her performance shares Siagatonu's rhetorical rejection of scientific authority—as DeLoughrey observes, the claim to not know "of the politics / or the science" is a literary trope rather than a statement of fact in Jetñil-Kijiner's case—instead gaining its rhetorical force from the speaker's position at sea level.[47] The visceral details of Jetñil-Kijiner's layman account—the inundated graveyards, the submerged seawalls at the edges of the Marshall Islands—function as bellwethers within a global crisis.

Proximity may initially seem at odds with a diasporic framework, and yet diasporic movements facilitate direct understanding of climate injustice. Situated experience in small island territories and nations, combined with familiarity with nations wielding power in climate negotiations—including the United States and Australia—allowed the poets at COP21 to juxtapose the frontlines of the climate crisis with political inaction by the most egregious emitters. Isabella Borgeson, performing "Yolanda Winds," first offers an eye-witness account, emphasizing her firsthand experience in the Philippines:

> When I arrive in Tanauan one month after the typhoon
> I do not recognize my mother's home
> Roof crumpled like a ball of paper
> The basketball court where I spent each childhood morning
> Is now an unmarked mass grave
> 13 holes for over 600 bodies[48]

Here, Borgeson demonstrates that situated witness does not require permanent residence but rather an intimate specificity: "five corpses stuffed into one body bag," she observes as she describes the typhoon's devastation, "names of entire families scribbled onto the premade crosses at the traffic circle turned mass grave."[49] Borgeson—who remained in the Philippines for two years after Typhoon Haiyan, assisting with relief efforts—confirms that situated witness is grounded in ongoing knowledge of a home and affiliation with the impacted community.[50] It is a testimony to continuous connection and commitment within diaspora.

But Borgeson's diasporic circulations also allow her to depict the United States, to serve as a witness not only of devastation but of apathy. In this sense, her work escapes the mode of tragedy or simplistic grief that so often accompanies climate poetry. Rather than turning the spotlight solely on the suffering in the devastation of Typhoon Haiyan, she turns the spotlight on another place she knows intimately, reminding her audience that embodied, lived experience occurs, not just in environmentally subjugated places, but also in the seats of power. She produces an account that is not about victimhood but also about the machinations of power:

> When I return to the U.S.
> Politicians label climate change a myth
> Deny our existence as if natural disasters only count when there are white bodies to bury[51]

Experiencing both frontline catastrophe and the environmental racism of the powerful, Borgeson brings climate injustice into sharp focus. Indeed, it is her mobility that enables this type of poetic work: introduced to slam poetry in the Bay Area, she relates the typhoon's impact on her neighborhood in Tanauan during an international gathering in Paris. These travels and returns bring a poetic skill, a situated experience in a small island community, and the platform to speak to a global audience into alignment.

DECOLONIAL OCCASIONAL PERFORMANCES AND ANTHROPOGENIC TIME

In addition to acts of witness, the poems performed at the 2014 and 2015 summits can be understood as occasional poems, a category of verse proliferating in recent climate activism. Although occasional poetry is a broad umbrella term, encompassing nearly all verse commemorating "events of a public character—a coronation, a military victory, a death, a political crisis"—I use the term here to refer to a particular subset of these poems: poems performed within the programming of a state function.⁵² More specifically, I am interested in poems crafted in relation to—and performed within or alongside—intergovernmental gatherings. For instance, in 2014, Jetñil-Kijiner's performance constituted part of the climate summit's opening ceremony, following speeches by Rajendra Pachauri, chair of the Intergovernmental Panel on Climate Change, and Al Gore, former vice president of the United States. Similarly, in 2015, the Spoken Word for the World poets performed in a variety of events affiliated with COP21, including forums, ceremonies, and demonstrations in the streets of Paris. They performed at parties and on the Paris Metro. At both intergovernmental gatherings, poets participated in occasions rather than retrospectively memorializing them, and in this way, these performances edged toward J. L. Austin's understanding of the performative: utterances that do not describe nor state but "*do* something."⁵³ Spoken word poetry brought portions of the 2014 and 2015 summits into being. Moreover, considering the way spoken word invigorated these international gatherings, infusing them with a sense of urgency, it is worth noting that *occasion* is both a noun and a verb: *an occasion* is a significant occurrence, an event of note, while *to occasion* is to "give rise to," albeit incidentally.⁵⁴ The verb form stops short of implying direct causality—it is difficult to claim that a poetic performance causes climate action—but it does suggest the creation of an opportune period. These performances at UN climate summits are occasional both because they generated portions of the summits' programming and because they intensified the opportunity for political movement on the climate crisis.

In a more granular sense of the occasional, these poems were crafted within—and through their performances, spotlighted—atmospheric occasions. These summits occurred at 395 ppm and 401 ppm respectively, at particular points in what Joshua Howe calls "anthropogenic time."⁵⁵ As carbon dioxide levels are forced into an exponential rise, occasions can be clocked atmospherically, parts per million serving as a chronological mode.⁵⁶ Marking time atmospherically foregrounds the momentousness of anthropogenic climate change in contemporary history, insisting that all occasions are saturated by the changing atmosphere. As a chronological mode, atmospheric time is inherently seasonal: embedded in the dramatic rise of carbon dioxide levels since the mid-twentieth century is a seasonal pulse, global concentrations of carbon dioxide dipping slightly each year as plants in temperate and boreal regions take up carbon dioxide in their leaves, then rising again as leaves fall and decompose. This seasonal pulse generates the subtle fluctuation visible on atmospheric charts like the Keeling Curve, and Howe evocatively refers to it as a signal of "the earth breathing," inhaling and exhaling carbon.⁵⁷ At the scale of the global, seasonality might be understood as the rhythm of planetary breath. And as the Spoken Word for the World poets performed in Paris at 401 ppm, each breath they drew in to utter their poems contained greater concentrations of carbon dioxide than the inhalations that supported Jetñil-Kijiner's performance at 395 ppm. On a molecular level, the occasional performances in Paris were weightier in carbon dioxide than the occasional performance in New York.

Beyond the sheer chemistry of breath, atmospheric time influences literary periodization. These spoken word performances occurred during a precipitous period for environmental writers and activists, a stretch of history when carbon dioxide levels still hovered around the 400 ppm boundary. During this period, the emerging climate crisis might yet have been curtailed, the extremities of anthropogenic warming partially averted. The 2014 summit in New York, intended to generate political will in advance of the Paris summit, drew international media coverage and ignited discussions of various climatic futures. In 2015, COP21 garnered a remarkable 196 signatories on a pledge to curtail the rise of global temperatures.

Moreover, while the Paris Agreement set 2° above preindustrial levels as a firm limit, the advocacy of small island nations is imprinted on the document through a collective promise "to pursue efforts to limit the temperature increase to 1.5 degrees C above pre-industrial levels."[58] In effect, the poems crafted for these summits were shaped by the galvanizing potential of these occasions, their articulations of the climate crisis reflective of their atmospheric moment and its promise. "There was a time," Andrada declares in her performance, "that could preserve us," a line indicative of both the urgency of the summit and—through Andrada's use of the past tense, with a hint of the conditional—a memorializing stance toward this pivotal period in anthropogenic history.[59] At 395 and 401 ppm, these poets performed during summits that could redirect the planet's carbon trajectory, their occasional poems crafted to stimulate intergovernmental response during these crucial yet fleeting days.

But understanding these performances as occasional—as rhetorically shaped for a particular state function—also links them to a political history of Pacific Islander testimony before the United Nations in response to environmental colonialism. Between 310 and 362 ppm, or between 1946 and 1996, the United States, the United Kingdom, and France conducted hundreds of nuclear tests across the Pacific, irradiating the landscape, triggering high rates of cancer and miscarriages, and producing a new class of "nuclear nomads" by forcing Pacific Islanders to relocate through either official edict or fear of ongoing exposure.[60] In the twenty-first century, the overlap between what Elizabeth DeLoughrey calls the "atomic cartography" of the Pacific and what might be thought of as an emerging climatic cartography is substantial: islands subjected to nuclear testing now face rising seas.[61] "It's the same story," Alson Kelen of Bikini Atoll explains to *The Guardian*. "Nuclear time, we were relocated. Climate change, we will be relocated. It's the same harshness affecting us."[62] And if climate change is the next iteration of environmental colonialism in the Pacific—yet another way in which the excesses of powerful nations erase or contaminate island landscapes, then the 2014 and 2015 performances at the United Nations can be read alongside past occasions of Pacific testimony. In 1954, Dwight Heine, an elementary school superintendent and a representative in the House of Assembly in the Marshall Islands Congress, was summoned to Washington, D.C. to testify before the UN Trusteeship Council, prior to his testimony on nuclear testing at the United Nations. He spoke at 313 ppm, on July 7, just a few months after the Castle Bravo nuclear test:

> Some of our people were hurt during the recent nuclear test and we have asked the aid of the United Nations, of which the United States is a member and to which it is answerable for its administration of the trust territory, to stop the experiments there. Or, if this is not possible, then to be a little more careful. I have noticed that it is illegal to set off fire-crackers in New York to celebrate the Fourth of July. I read in the paper that several people were arrested for violating this safety rule.[63]

The force of Heine's discourse—the searing charge of environmental injustice—is generated through his swift and subtle compression, his rescaling of a thermonuclear bomb into a firecracker. This shift allows Heine to denounce the United States for playing fast and loose with Marshallese lives, but it also allows him to convey this condemnation through juxtaposition, rather than direct accusation. His discretion is tactical, an approach to the fraught rhetorical task of witnessing before those who control the future of his environment.

Like Heine's testimony, the spoken word performances in 2014 and 2015 are perhaps best understood as decolonial occasional performances, a term I use here to designate performances by those representing occupied or formerly occupied lands and waters at occasions of state power. As Keith Leonard observes, the term *occasional poetry* tends to evoke an "old-school mode of patronized practice," a tradition of courtier verse and regal philanthropy.[64] It brings to mind scenes of wealthy elites congregating in imperial courts for commissioned entertainment, a literary history that echoes in unsettling ways when considering the performances of Southeast Asian and Pacific Islander poets for an audience of international leaders, particularly leaders capable of impacting the rate at which seas will claim island and coastal territories. To the degree that the United Nations intended Jetñil-Kijiner's 2014 performance as aesthetic ornamentation, as a touching moment within the business at hand, her appearance on the schedule is tinged by this history of literary patronage. However, as Stephen Wilson notes, occasional poetry is inherently representative: "the occasional poet does not write simply or primarily for herself or himself but speaks to, and on behalf of, a collectivity."[65] Jetñil-Kijiner and the performers at COP21 refused to be mere poetic embellishments for an international audience, taking to the stage to perform on behalf of their communities.

If occasional poetry, more overtly than other types of verse, is shaped by state power—Samuel Monk observes that it requires "tact as well as talent"—I would go further in the case of decolonial occasional performances, arguing that the discretion that often marks these performances is not a matter of etiquette as much as an acute awareness of the sanctioned limits of speech. The power inequities endemic to these performances require poets to tailor their demands in ways that remain palatable to the gathered audience of political authorities. As a result, these poems engage in what Giovanna DiChiro calls the "politics of articulation" marking the climate justice movement.[66] For instance, when addressing the audience gathered at COP 21, Andrada veiled her frustration with—and likely her condemnation of—political leaders' inaction on the climate crisis, opting for a plea rather than an indictment: "Tell me this fight for us doesn't end where your borders begin."[67] In a related maneuver, Jetñil-Kijiner employed the epistolary, addressing her performance to her infant daughter rather than the world leaders seated before her. In doing so, she referred to her audience obliquely, describing "blindfolded bureaucracies." She skirted what would have been an accusation if formatted in direct address: "there are those / hidden behind platinum titles / who like to pretend / that we don't exist."[68] These deflections highlight how the political conditions of decolonial occasional performances produce complex structures of address, conveying charges of climate injustice without antagonizing political authorities. While state power shapes all occasional poetry, it shapes the work of environmentally and politically subjugated poets most forcefully. When considering the poems of climatic witness performed at the United Nations, we might think less of Tennyson's readings as the British Poet Laureate than of Scheherazade's fabled performances in the Persian court: these were literary performances undertaken in halls of power in order to forestall or prevent a particular climatic future.

STRUCTURES OF ADDRESS AT THE UNITED NATIONS

When Jetñil-Kijiner was invited to attend the 2014 climate summit as the civil society representative, she was asked to perform a poem that spoke "not just for the Marshall Islands, not just the Pacific, but for the whole of civil society." "That's the entire world," she mused, perplexed by an invitation premised on the idea that her voice could represent humanity writ large, that it was possible to articulate a shared climatic future for an international audience.[69] The impossibility of world literature in this sense—one voice speaking for all of humanity—is compounded by the topic of climate change, a global, yet profoundly uneven, crisis. The representational choice Jetñil-Kijiner faced as she composed "Dear Matafele Peinam"—to articulate climate change as a crisis caused and experienced by the human species writ large, or to articulate climate change as a crisis caused by carbon consumption in the Global North, yet primarily inflicted upon communities in the Global South—often plays out at the level of writerly craft. As Rob Nixon notes: "A crucial challenge facing us is this: how do we tell two large stories that can often seem in tension with each other, a convergent story and a divergent one? First, a collective story about humanity's impacts that will be legible in the geophysical systems for millennia to come. Second, a much more fractured narrative. . . . that acknowledge[s] immense inequalities in planet-altering powers?"[70] These competing rhetorical agendas are particularly pronounced for Southeast Asian and Pacific Islander poets performing before a summit of world leaders: the occasion intensifies the stakes of this choice. In their work, these poets must retain an emphasis on climate justice without framing climate change as a solely regional issue. At the United Nations, emphasizing inequality risks alienating powerful members of the audience and forestalling collective action, but emphasizing universality risks a climatic form of strategic essentialism that blunts the political force of their witness.

Negotiating this rhetorical double bind, Jetñil-Kijiner contorts the universal, twisting the task of "speaking for the world" severely enough to expose its impossibility. She articulates a global future only as an inverse scenario, describing the rising waters that shall *not* come to pass. As she fends off nightmares of the climatic future, she reassures her infant daughter—and, by proxy, the international leaders in her audience—that collective and substantial reductions in emissions can prevent the direst climatic projections from physically manifesting:

no one's drowning, baby

no one's moving
no one's losing

their homeland
no one's gonna become
a climate change refugee[71]

And yet, far from providing reassurance, Jetñil-Kijiner's adamant refusal of this future, her litany of negated perils, only serves to underscore her alarm. A future of widespread refugeeism and rising tides is brought into stark relief, even as it is refused. In and of itself, this negated nightmare is a deft rhetorical move; it allows Jetñil-Kijiner to evoke the climate crisis in its full extremity without terrifying her audience to the point of immobilization, and it manages to strike chords of urgency and determination without dissolving into unadulterated optimism. But then, in a crucial rhetorical pivot, Jetñil-Kijiner acknowledges that the climatic future she just refused to envision has—in some areas of the world—already come to pass:

or should I say
no one else

to the Carteret Islanders of Papua New Guinea
and to the Taro Islanders of the Solomon Islands
I take this moment
to apologize to you
we are drawing the line
here[72]

As Jetñil-Kijiner's self-conscious pivot suggests, universal representations of the climate crisis—"no one's drowning"—fail to hold. This apology to the Carteret Islanders and Taro Islanders, the only moment in the poem that Jetñil-Kijiner directly addresses anyone other than her daughter, mimics the tone of an official acknowledgment of historical wrongdoing and allows Jetñil-Kijiner to go on record in the UN chambers as testifying that the threats of the warming world are universal, but not simultaneous nor equally distributed.

Structures of address—who is speaking to whom, and how—are endlessly complex in the 2014 and 2015 performances at the United Nations. For instance, who is the "we" who are "drawing the line / here" in Jetñil-Kijiner's poem? Who is she representing through that first-person plural? How do the politicians and leaders in her audience interpret this "we"? Do they identify themselves within its scope? Barbara Johnson's work on "interlocutionary strategy" provides a possible inroad through these matters.[73] Johnson insists that "questions of difference and identity"—here, questions of climate justice and the position of the Marshallese relative to the powers of the United Nations—"are always a function of a specific interlocutionary situation—and the answers, matters of strategy rather than truth."[74] The ambiguity surrounding the first-person plural that continues throughout Jetñil-Kijiner's performance may, in fact, comprise a poetic strategy. The mechanics of this ambiguity, and its function during this occasion, come to the forefront as Jetñil-Kijiner depicts the burgeoning climate justice movement:

> Because baby we are going to fight
> your mommy daddy
> bubu jimma your country and your president too
> we will all fight[75]

Jetñil-Kijiner's description of the climate justice movement expands, first, along genealogical lines—intimations of bwebwenato and roro are again present—from a child, to parents, to grandparents. But Jetñil-Kijiner continues, expanding to the scale of the national and political, culminating with "we . . . all" This final "we" might refer back to the actors just mentioned, declaring a Marshallese commitment to climate justice, but the momentum generated by Jetñil-Kijiner's rapid expansion from family to nation, and her intensifying delivery, opens the possibility that "we . . . all" represents a further expansion to the scale of the international, potentially encompassing the leaders assembled at the climate summit. The indeterminacy of Jetñil-Kijiner's structure of address allows her audience to decide whether she is making a promise on behalf of the Marshallese or on behalf of the world.

In Paris, continual shifts and reversals in structure of address were employed to simultaneously condemn high-emitting nations and induce consensus on climate policy. In Eunice Andrada's "Pacific Salt," the first person lyric characteristic of slam performance—"my hometown is still drying its feet"—spins out to encompass the collective "we" of an island community, broadens into the "we" of humanity, and then narrows back to a situated voice.[76] As Andrada seamlessly shifts between the specific "we" of small island communities and a vaster "we" enveloping the human collective, she interweaves accusations of climate injustice with calls for collective action. Initially, her performance distinguishes between high emitters and frontline communities: "Perhaps our hunger cannot look the same when yours demands that the ocean swallow itself to be filled and we are hungry for justice."[77] In this declaration, Andrada juxtaposes the Global North's greediness for fossil fuel with small island nations' desire to sustain themselves, separating the "you" who control the waters from the "we" who call for climate justice. Andrada delivers this line in a measured tone, but it is a clear indictment of the powerful politicians gathered at COP21, an accusation only possible to verbalize by dividing the initial "our," separating into "you" and "we." And yet, by the close of the poem, Andrada shifts back into a fully collective register, her "we" now encompassing the entire audience in an attempt to mobilize political action: "Let us not say there is nothing we could have done," she implores.[78]

In this moment, as she speaks for the entirety of the crowd in Paris, folding her audience inside the "us" who can impact climate policy, she performs an act of linguistic persuasion.

Throughout the climate summits, these shifting structures of address contained a subtle animating power. Barbara Johnson, writing on poetic address—specifically apostrophe in first-person lyrics like Shelley's oft-quoted "O wild West Wind, thou breath of Autumn's being"—argues that addressing an inanimate entity is "a form of ventriloquism through which the speaker throws voice . . . into the addressee, turning its silence into mute responsiveness."[79] Johnson theorizes this ventriloquism in relation to nonhuman and inanimate entities, but a parallel interlocutionary phenomenon is at work when poets envelop inanimate or resistant political leaders within the "we" of their poems. The line between persuasion and animation becomes more difficult to trace in these moments, particularly as poets speak on behalf of a sluggish bureaucracy. As Jetñil-Kijiner concludes her poetic address to her daughter—"we won't let you down / you'll see"—the collective "we" implies an inclusion of those assembled before her—we, here at the United Nations, gathered together for this pivotal occasion, won't let you down.[80] As Erin Suzuki notes, Jetñil-Kijiner often extends this collective "we" to her audiences, leaving open a question of "whether or not they will take up their end of the dialogue; whether or not they will . . . enter into the 'we' of mutual entanglement and mutual responsibility."[81] As she speaks on behalf of the mute and resistant political body before her, Jetñil-Kijiner performs a formal ventriloquism, what Johnson calls "the giving of voice, the throwing of voice, the giving of animation" to that which lacks the necessary words or will.[82] Without changing pronouns, she moves back and forth between the "we" of the climate justice movement—"we are / canoes blocking coal ships"—and this larger "we" of a full-throated UN commitment to reduce global temperature rise to no more than 1.5°C, working to enlist her audience within the climate justice movement.[83] Her shifting structures of address are designed to animate her audience, to galvanize the occasion, to breathe urgency into inert politicians.

THE RHYTHM OF EMERGENCIES

At the United Nations in 2014 and at COP21 in 2015, slam poetry rose to the occasion. Critics often dismiss slam as a heavy-handed form, an overly passionate art, but at these particular junctures in atmospheric history, urgency became a rhetorical necessity. At these summits, there was no time to spare: the earth was warming at an unsustainable rate, the names of those taken by the typhoon were being scribbled on premade crosses, the smoke was moving across the waters of the Pacific and entering people's lungs. In Eunice Andrada's estimation, poetic performance is particularly suited to these conditions: "Spoken word entails a sense of urgency different to the written text that you see on a paper, where you can dwell on it for however long you like," she explains. "When it's spoken, you know that I am *here*—what I'm saying is here."[84] As Andrada implies, poets trained in slam performance are capable of pitching their writing to impending crises, of crafting poetry tailored to deliver the urgency of frontline communities to stale bureaucratic occasions. The form of their poetic witness matters: it contributes to its political potency.

The idea of urgency percolates through discussions of activist writing, and yet its meaning is rarely clarified. In a material sense, urgency is a condition of pressure or stress, often related to atmospherics. The Oxford English Dictionary makes this atmospheric relation explicit: urgency is the "stress of wind, weather, etc."[85] Derived from the Latin *urgēre*, it compels or presses, as when a typhoon pushes waves far past the shoreline. In an overheated world, as storms and tides grow extreme, the urgencies of the material environment grow pronounced. In a second sense, urgency is a state of temporal pressure, a condition of imperativeness. Urgency is an intensification of time, a pressurized period. But what I find most striking is urgency's association with the rhetorical. A close relative of the verb "urge," it suggests "pressure by importunity or entreaty; urgent solicitation; insistence."[86] We are perhaps more adept at documenting environmental extremity than we are at discerning forces of rhetorical pressure. But there must be a way to think of these two conditions together, to link the water rushing through Majuro to the cadences of Jetñil-Kijiner's performance in New York, to connect the strength of the winds that compelled Typhoon Haiyan through the Philippines to the force of breath and language that brought Borgeson's poem into the streets of Paris. We have to find a way to think of these occasions not as separate occurrences but as a connected urgency. In this chapter, urgency is a stress conveyed from the climatic to the literary. It is an accent forceful enough to transect the environmental and the rhetorical.

To bring these mechanics of urgency into focus, and to consider their relationship to rhythm, I turn now to Andrada's videopoem "Pacific Salt," produced for the 2015 summit in Paris. Portions of Andrada's performance are deliberately tranquil, far removed from the urgent: she wades in the shallows, salt water lapping against her ankles. Watching Andrada's bare feet move through the translucent water, her poem spoken in voiceover, homonyms begins to surface: Andrada's feet, immersed in the rhythm of the saltwater, evoke the poetic foot, the unit of stressed and unstressed syllables that shapes accentual-syllabic verse. Rhythms—of the waves, of words, of Andrada's soles working their way across the sand—intermingle into a complex harmony in this videopoem. But to my mind, the most haunting line of Andrada's poem describes not the waves' lulling crests and troughs but a pounding sense of disaster: "Our pulses know the rhythm of emergencies," she intones, "just like our islands know the Pacific salt that cradles them."[87] Here, emergency is figured as a birthright, the throb of survival as pervasive as the ebb and flow of tides. Within the climate crisis, it is worth lingering on Andrada's phrase: what are the rhythms of emergency? Is it possible to understand this line not as an elegant turn of phrase, but rather an articulation of a vaster prosody?

A bare-bones, elementary sort of scansion may route us closer to an understanding of Andrada's phrase "the rhythm of emergencies." In a basic explanation of accentual-syllabic verse, poetic rhythm emerges from the relationship between stressed and unstressed syllables. Andrada's phrase is iambic, and more specifically, an alexandrine: our *pulses know the rhythm of emergencies.* Unstressed, stressed, unstressed, stressed, and so forth. Visually, the videopoems produced for the 2014 and 2015 climate summits are marked by this sort of pulse: they alternate between scenes of oceanic calm and environmental crisis. The video screens positioned on either side of Jetñil-Kijiner at the United Nations initially displayed a montage of halcyon scenes, including sunrise breaking over the lagoon and a clip of Jetñil-Kijiner walking barefoot through the shallows, holding Matafele Peinam in her arms. About thirty seconds into her performance, this montage shifted to images of environmental damage: a cemetery unearthed by the force of a storm, people carrying furniture to dry land in the wake of a flood, water gushing past the trunks of wind-battered banana trees. Just as the tension of the footage peaked, the video returned to panoramas of calm shorelines, its visual pulse ebbing back to relative tranquility. This rhythm is even more apparent in Andrada's "Pacific Salt": the visual footage steadily vacillates between scenes of Andrada strolling along the shoreline and scenes of environmental disaster and displacement. Human figures are more present in Andrada's video, emphasizing anthropogenic climate change as a humanitarian crisis: neighbors stand in waist-deep water and survey submerged buildings, a line of displaced residents slowly enter a rescue aircraft, canoes congregate in a flooded street to obtain bottled drinking water from an aid vehicle. In both Jetñil-Kijiner's and Andrada's videopoems, these fluctuations between shots of climate disaster and scenes of the tranquil shoreline might be read as documentary, as visual evidence of anthropogenic climate change and—simultaneously—island residents' long-standing and ongoing attachment to oceanic homes. But as the films flip repeatedly between these two elements, they do something more: they generate an emotional pulse that replicates the sense of precarity, the feeling of being on the brink of environmental distress. They envelop their audience in the pulses of a changing climate.

But in terms of language itself, a mechanical deployment of prosody—charting syllables and accents—is an odd approach to free verse works in which poets control the stresses and emphases throughout their performance. It is also a perplexing approach to works of Anglophone poetry whose influences stretch far beyond the tradition of English versification to which prosody remains tethered. For instance, in analyzing Jetñil-Kijiner's 2014 performance, the musicologist Jessica Schwartz detects a "crescendo upward in pitch and volume," an extended stress that she connects to "the animating force of roro."[88] As Jetñil-Kijiner employs anaphora, working to transmit the momentum of the climate justice movement to the audience assembled at the United Nations, the force of her poem builds: "and we are / canoes blocking coal ships / we are / the radiance of solar villages / we are / the rich clean soil of the farmer's past / we are / petitions blooming from teenage fingertips / we are / families biking, recycling, reusing."[89] This crescendo produces an extended accent within the poem, exceeding the bounds of the accentual-syllabic. In Anglophone poetry, accents are not textual—outside the pages of a dictionary, they are not visible orthographically—but rather oral. Accents emerge through speech, which makes spoken word poetry a particularly rich field for those interested in the power of the accentual and stressed. Slam and spoken word poets maintain a great degree of artistic control over the accents of their verse, conveying stresses not only through what is called "word-stress," the accents of a word's standard pronunciation, but also through the volume and pitch of the voice, the tempo of the performance, subtle changes in tone or inflection, and emphases produced by the poet's expression and gestures.

Urgency, or stressed times, bridge the environmental and the poetic. As Andrada's bare feet move along the shore, they evoke not only the poetic foot, but also the exposure to the elements produced by climate displacement. "Pacific Salt" is among the more lyrical poems performed through Spoken Word for the World—Andrada eschews repetitions, conveying her lines in an even timbre—but she permits herself one brief lapse into the statistical. "Two years ago," she informs her audience, "the number of people displaced by natural disasters tripled the number of war refugees."[90] This figure is a reference to a report by the Norwegian Refugee Council, which states that close to 22 million people fled their homes during floods, hurricanes, and other disasters in 2013.[91] Enfolded within this statistic are the 4.1 million Filipinos displaced by Typhoon Haiyan, the storm that Borgeson depicts in "Yolanda Winds." As the report notes, 19 million of the 22 million people displaced in 2013 lived in Asia, and as a Filipina poet, Andrada's inclusion of these numbers are a powerful moment of regional advocacy. Her quotation of this report is a moment worth marking—like Jetñil-Kijiner's direct address to the citizens of the Carteret Islands, it is a moment in which the poem approximates testimony. Andrada, like the other poets in Paris, testified to the ongoing humanitarian crises of the changing climate. These crises and displacements are also a marker of stressed times, of extreme moments.

The distress that Andrada references—the disasters and displacement of the overheated world—shaped the stresses of the poetic performances in 2014 and 2015. Turning to Borgeson's street performance of "Yolanda Winds" reveals the mechanics of stress and activism. As Borgeson exclaims with a look of anguish, people in the Philippines are "counting down the years before we are drowning in a rising Pacific."[92] This count is a rhythm of emergency, an urgency that Borgeson conveyed and drew upon in her performance. Indeed, accents within the live performances in Paris were impacted by the occasion itself—stresses can also be occasional, produced by the dynamics of a crowd or movement. Borgeson performed "Yolanda Winds" as hundreds of people linked arms along the route of the Paris climate march, cancelled due to recent bombings, and she modulated her performance to the ambient noise of the public demonstration and her dispersed audience. Contending with the wind, the crowd, and perhaps picking up on the energy of the gathering itself, she performs "Yolanda Winds" at a much higher intensity than in her staged video performance of the same poem. Her entire performance at COP21 is stressed, in the sense of emphasized or insistent. As a chant from a nearby group of climate activists begins, Borgeson amplifies her volume even more, the proximity of the climate justice movement creating a new charge within her line. As she looks out at the crowd flooding the streets of France's capital, she seemingly addresses the crowd directly: "Our islands are in your hands."[93] The timbre of her voice as she reaches the phrase "your hands" subtly changes, as though her poem, in this moment, can finally be addressed to those it was written for.

Here, rhythm, as it moves between the environment and the rhetorical, is not so much a matter of the unstressed and stressed, but rather a matter of distress and stress. Urgency forges a connection between environmental distress and stressed utterance. Although scansion—when employed judiciously—illuminates the visceral musicality and potency of a poem, there is something disconcerting about focusing too narrowly on alexandrines in the face of widespread displacement and flooded streets. Prosody is far from inconsequential, but there is a risk in retreating into iambs and trochees in the face of stark climatic injustices. In so doing, we miss the larger rhythmic forces shaping contemporary poetry, the rhythms connecting intense storm seasons in the Pacific to words performed on the streets of Paris. The climate extremities that the poets at these summits stressed—unseasonable typhoons, tides inundating local cemeteries, droughts that persist beyond their typical time frames—are moments of pronounced distress. But poetic stress is also a force. An accent foregrounds or calls attention to something, granting a syllable, a statement, or a moment weight and gravitas. In this sense, the form of the environment produces accents or stress within poetry as well, translating into urgent verse. The stresses of these performances intensified the atmosphere surrounding these negotiations, carrying the rhythm of emergency into the UN chambers and through the streets of Paris, working to animate those that had gathered. During this particular period of conjoined environmental and political history, as atmospheric carbon dioxide levels still hovered around 400 ppm, the stakes of these poets' performances were so high: they performed to witness the injustices of the rapidly warming world, and to incite intergovernmental response before climate change swallowed the places that they call home. On these occasions, the degree of these poets' conviction was commensurate with the dire environmental future that their communities faced.

6

KEEPING TIME

In Ontario and across the border in Michigan, the branches of sugar maples glisten as streetlights slant through the darkness. In alleys and along sidewalks, patches of snow linger beside trash cans—it will be weeks before the buds of these sugar maples burst open. But the cold, clear liquid moving through their sapwood contains 2 or even 3 percent sugar, compared to the silver maple's 1.5–1.75 percent, or the box elder's 1 percent.[1] Sugar maples are, in the words of the writer Callum Angus, "a conduit for sweetness in this world."[2] Boiled down, thirty or forty gallons of sugar maple sap will yield a gallon of syrup. During the few weeks each year when temperatures near the Great Lakes dip below freezing at night and thaw as the sun rises, maple sap flows. It seeps through metal spiles wedged into the trees' bark, slowly filling the buckets hung below. During these weeks, sugar maples season in multiple senses of the word, drawing forth their flavor on the cusp between coldness and warmth.

But in Toronto, trees planted on city property—and trees on private property that exceed thirty inches in circumference—are off limits for tapping. The city's municipal code dictates that "no person shall . . . mark, cut, break, peel or deface any part of a tree."[3] And across the border in Detroit, the Parks & Recreation Department's code suggests that trees along boulevards and alleys, in parks, golf courses, and squares, shall not be "cut" or "in any way defaced."[4] These regulations limit the seasonal practice of maple sugaring to landowners, or those willing to risk hefty fees and prosecution. Sap season is privatized. These prohibitions recall "Plight," a short story by the acclaimed Michi Saagiig Nishnaabeg writer Leanne Betasamosake Simpson. In "Plight," a character who is part of a Mississauga collective trying to tap maples in suburban Ontario protests: "It's the spring ... we just want to make syrup in my backyard without it being a goddamn ordeal."[5] In Simpson's prose, the land theft underwriting Canadian parks and boulevards intersects with the seasonal dispossession forced on renters, the unhoused, and anyone navigating the city without a property deed.

Compounding these barriers to tapping, the timing and character of sap season—like the other seasons tended to throughout this book—are changing. Unrelenting summer heat forces maples to increase respiration, depleting the sugars that would otherwise flavor their sap the coming spring. In the winter, without snow insulating the ground, the more delicate tree roots freeze, stunting growth and increasing mortality within a sugar bush. Extreme winds, heavy ice storms, and drought also stress the maples, leaving them prone to insect infestation. As these altered rhythms multiply, the interval of sap flow also changes: maple sugarers, working for decades near the border of the United States and Canada, report that sap runs earlier now, often flowing in mid-February instead of mid to late March, erratic warm spells making it difficult to know when to tap trees and harvest the liquid moving within them. Maple sap becomes bitter once the tips of a tree's buds turn green and burst, and premature bud burst on unexpectedly warm days can constrict or preempt tapping season.[6]

In this chapter, I gather scenes and ideas—from Simpson's writing; Amanda Strong's film *Biidaaban (The Dawn Comes)*; Callum Angus's

A Natural History of Transition and essay "The Climate of Gender"; and news reports of the Detroit police threatening a sugar bush in 2022—that point toward the future of seasonal practices in anthropogenic times. As a transnational collective, these stories and accounts intertwine Indigenous futurisms, trans literature, and the anti-capitalist stirrings of the early twenty-first century. Maple syrup makers are careful to space out their spiles, not tapping within six inches of a previous year's hole and not placing multiple spiles into young trees—sap extraction should not exhaust any given maple. Similarly, statements about the climatic future can risk overextraction, siphoning language, solutions, or theories from a single intellectual trunk. In this array of literary tappings, I try to work a wider forest. But boiled down, these stories and reflections all balance on the sharp edge between seasonal injustice and justice. They ebb from dispossession to moments of seasonal reclamation and back again. Thinking alongside these writers, organizers, and artists, I gauge how time is kept now—in terms of phenology and the changing rhythms of sap, but also in terms of artistic and literary forms. What does it mean to keep time amid the climate's arrhythmias?

UNSENTIMENTAL SEASONALITY

As she constructs her leaves, the Michif filmmaker Amanda Strong attends to their particular silhouette: the animated leaves that will drift from the top left corner of her screen have five smooth-edged lobes. She captures their variegated hues: each leaf is tinted ochre, dry brown, or rust. Strong is crafting sugar maples, making a film based on a constellation of Simpson's stories and poems. The resulting film adaptation, *Biidaaban (The Dawn Comes)*, released in 2017, depicts an urban sugar making project in the months leading up to *ziigwan*, "the first part of spring when the ice is breaking up and the snow is melting," the days when sap runs.[7] A thin crust of snow covers the ground as Strong's handcrafted puppets trudge through suburban Ontario, lugging a battery-operated drill, tobacco, tin buckets, and spiles to tap the boulevard's maples. Strong renders her puppets' breath visible in the film's darkness, indicating the frozen temperatures of the predawn. Her film, like Simpson's writing, captures this season of piercing dampness, these particular days of freeze-thaw.

Biidaaban, which incorporates elements of Simpson's short stories "Plight" and the "The Gift is in the Making," as well as her poem "Caribou Ghosts & Untold Stories," follows a genderfluid Anishinaabe young adult—the eponymous Biidaaban—as they tap sugar maples under the cover of night. This sugaring project takes place in a neighborhood that Strong describes as "not like downtown Toronto per se, but not quite suburban—something in between. Something with old growth."[8] In the film, as in "Plight," Biidaaban is mentored in the practice of syrup making by Sabe, a "beyond-ancient" Sasquatch shapeshifter.[9] As Biidaaban and Sabe make their way from tree to tree, avoiding home security systems and motion-activated lights, they encounter the spirits of wolves and caribou who once roamed this habitat. The film therefore unfolds in a temporality that Grace Dillon argues is characteristic of Native slipstream: "Native slipstream views time as pasts, presents, and futures that flow together like currents in a navigable stream. . . . It allows authors to recover the Native space of the past, to bring it to the attention of contemporary readers, and to build better futures."[10] The seasonal practice of syrup making that Biidaaban undertakes is a repetition of their ancestors' maple tapping and an anticipation of maple tapping by others in the years to come.

Prior to the onset of anthropogenic climate change, seasonal writing and art had a reputation—in Michael Kammen's words—for "sugary sentimentalism."[11] Prone to "nostalgia and romanticization," seasonal literature often veered into retrograde pastoralism.[12] It was—all puns intended—associated with a sappy or syrupy affect, designed to reassure or assuage. Like much of unseasonable literature and art, *Biidaaban* contrasts starkly with this tonality. It is a tense film, a piece that rumbles with the threat of a confrontation

FIGURE 6.1 Film still from *Biidaaban* (*The Dawn Comes*). Courtesy of Spotted Fawn Productions.

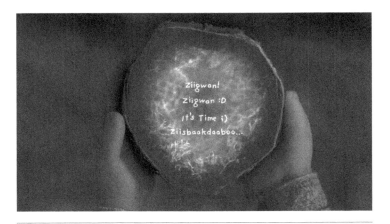

FIGURE 6.2 Film still from *Biidaaban* (*The Dawn Comes*). Courtesy of Spotted Fawn Productions.

with property owners or law enforcement. Twice during its nineteen-minute run, Biidaaban collapses, wrapping their arms around their knees as they heave with exhaustion, the camera zooming in on their breath. In and out, the puppet breathes the cold air of early spring, a heavy, taxed rhythm. These repeated moments speak to the physical exertion of the maple tapping project, the fatigue of working a graveyard shift to avoid skirmishes with property owners, and the strain of living as a young Indigenous artist within a colonized and gentrifying metro area.

Both Simpson and Strong steer away from seasonal nostalgia and the idea that Indigenous syrupers are naturally harmonized with the season. The characters in "Plight" are novices, spray-painting sugar maples in the fall when they are easier to identify: "Really we should be able to tell by looking at the bark and the way the branches hold themselves, but we're still too new at it."[13] Likewise, the figure of Sabe in Strong's film appears simultaneously ancient and futuristic. He wears a hooded garment that seems organic—as though constructed from moss, lichens, and vines—but also resembles a space suit. From the hood, small twigs—perhaps antennas?—point upwards. When Biidaaban refers to themself as his "client," Sabe "rolls his eyes," rejecting Biidaaban's corporate lingo for his mentorship in the art of maple tapping.[14] But they communicate with each other through electronic devices—reminiscent of smartphones or alarm clocks, yet shaped in a manner akin to a rock or clump of earth laced with roots or leaf veins—that provide them with glowing phenological indicators. *Ninaatigoog*, Sabe texts Biidaaban—the film's subtitles translate from Ojibwe: *maple trees*—reminding them to identify the trees in the fall while their leaves still cling to the branches. And then again, after the months have worn on and the snow has fallen, Biidaaban's device lights up with a message: *Ziigwan! Ziigwan:D It's Time;) Ziisbaakdaaboo*—the subtitles offer: *Spring! Spring:D It's Time;) Sap*... The sideways smiles and winks of Sabe's text gives a friendly refusal to any primitivist readings of this knowledge. This is not a nostalgic seasonality, not one that harkens backward, but a reclamation of maple season in the present, under the conditions of anthropogenic and settler time.

Rather than sentimentality or heartwarming assurances, unseasonable works are conditioned by a gritty heartbreak. Simpson's poem "Caribou Ghosts & Untold Stories," which is read in voiceover during Strong's film, attests to the flimsiness of sentiment during crisis: "we don't have time to feel these feelings / so we file that for / another day."[15] This hardened grit is explicated in "Plight" as Biidaaban ponders their love for Lucy, who is chain-smoking beneath a maple tree wearing a black leather motorcycle jacket: "For NDNs the tougher we act, the purer our hearts are, because this strangulation is not set up for the sensitive and we have to protect the fuck out of ourselves. I wish they'd soften for me. . . . I wish they could feel my warmth."[16] Survival within what Kristen Simmons terms "settler atmospherics" requires a well-armored heart, a strategic haptics of unsentimentality.[17] It requires weathering what Simpson describes as the "bad timing / & smashed hearts" of the unseasonable world.[18] Again and again in unseasonable literature, this sense of heartbreak emerges: in *The Swan Book*, the focus of this book's fourth chapter, the narrator cries, "Mother Nature? Hah! Who knows how many hearts she could rip out?"[19] In Cameron Awkward-Rich's poem "Meditations in Emergency," a throbbing rhythm surfaces: "I wake up and it breaks my heart," Awkward-Rich writes. His repetition builds toward a painful heartbeat: "I draw the blinds & the thrill of rain breaks my heart. . . . the city of tents beneath the underpass, the huddled mass, old women hawking roses, & children all of them break my heart. . . . Hand on my heart. Hand on my stupid heart."[20] Rather than sentimental, these writings are tender—as in bruised and aching.[21]

If Awkward-Rich's heartbreak unfolds beneath the underpass, a site in Canadian and U.S. cities associated with encampments of unhoused people living in tents or beneath tarps, the underpass is the site of anti-capitalist rebellion in Simpson's "Caribou Ghosts & Untold Stories." A revolutionary streak runs through this poem, and it concludes with a call to action:

> meet me at the underpass
> rebellion is
> on her way

Within this context, Biidaaban and Sabe's springtime labor comes into focus as a rebellion against economic inequality as well as settler colonialism: accessing a season prohibited to those who do not own land, gathering sap even as home mortgages spiral beyond what the working class can afford, this reclamation is an anti-capitalist stirring. It is a small hole drilled into what has been hoarded by settlers and the affluent.

ANTI-CAPITALIST PRACTICES

Keeping time is not always a generous act—to keep can mean to seize or to hoard.[22] As Callum Angus observes, an "exclusive cabal" called the Fédération des Producteurs Acéricoles du Québec controls a significant portion of the maple syrup market, maintaining a stockpile in three warehouses north of Montreal, facilities capable of storing a combined 216,000 barrels of syrup.[23] In these warehouses, syrup transforms into capital, an alchemy apparent in language. "When stocks decline," the Fédération writes, they may be replenished "by issuing additional quotas to maple producers. When inventories grow too large, incentives may be offered to buyers to stimulate markets and sales."[24] Like crude oil, syrup is concentrated carbon, a season of time condensed to its sticky essence. And like oil, it is kept in the hands of a few, hoarded through the years to buffer instabilities in the climate and market. These privately controlled barrels of syrup are referred to as the Strategic Reserve, a direct echo of the Strategic Petroleum Reserve maintained by the U.S. Department of Defense since the 1973 oil crisis. Angus describes the Fédération as eerily reminiscent of a "government-sanctioned, OPEC-like cartel," a reminder that capitalism and climate change are conjoined.[25] As Anne-Lise François argues, "the post-seasonal future of which climate scientists are warning is already here, to the degree that contemporary anthropogenic climate change originates in an economic system built on the homogenization of space and time, on the erasure of seasonal variation, and on the fiction of the permanent availability of labor, goods, and services."[26] Capitalism responds to climate arrhythmias by hoarding, by trying to contain what is otherwise transitory and ephemeral. Those 216,000 barrels are one way of keeping time, of seizing what is seasonal.

FIGURE 6.3 Film still from *Biidaaban (The Dawn Comes)*. Courtesy of Spotted Fawn Productions.

Against this backdrop, the DIY sap collection portrayed in "Plight" and *Biidaaban* can be read as anti-capitalist action, as a reclamation of sap season from corporations and federations. It is a different kind of time keeping, a reminder that obtaining one's keep is a pursuit of sustenance and livelihood, of generating "the requisites of life" while the sap runs.[27] As Biidaaban and Sabe stir their pot of sap over a backyard fire—cinder blocks and dry milkweed on the ground next to them, stars spread out above—they are contributing to a twenty-first-century revival of artisanship, craft, and repair efforts. Stephanie LeMenager refers to these efforts as "skilling up," noting that contemporary turns to foraging, refurbishing, provisioning, electrical repair, mending, and salvaging are a response to environmental, economic, and political breakdown. "My point," she writes, "is that as the U.S. state fails or willfully destroys itself, and as the global economy becomes increasingly volatile, a significant set of countercultural actors are skilling up the Anthropocene."[28] Skill, for LeMenager, is "where human craft meets worldly force," where knack and artistry allow practitioners to detour around the ecological dead ends of late-stage capitalism.[29] As Biidaaban and Sabe labor, boiling sap through the night, Simpson's poem read in voice-over accentuates the need to salvage and reforge in a smashed world: "a collection of old parts.... but / there's never / enough glue / we'll tie ourselves together / with bungee cords / and luck."[30] Anti-capitalist practices, like guerrilla-tapping urban maple trees, often require collective work and concentrated solidarities.

The film set Strong constructs for *Biidaaban* is crafted to subtly indicate Biidaaban's economic position. They rent a basement studio in a vinyl-sided building beside the railroad tracks, and a pair of shoes dangles from the telephone wires outside. "Train tracks / six pack/ riff raff," Simpson's poem intones, ventriloquizing the socioeconomic prejudices of wealthier Ontario residents. Biidaaban's furnishings are thrifted or homemade: a mattress lies on the floor, wire hangers stick out of a cardboard box, and a clay mug bears the imprint of a friend's early attempts at pottery. Their pants hang on a clothesline, perhaps an environmental practice, perhaps an effort to avoid laundromat charges. Unlike the maple sugarers in "Plight," who drive to reach their urban sugar bush, Biidaaban does not appear to have access to transportation: they navigate the predawn streets on foot rather than by car, dragging a wagon of supplies behind them. The puppet that Strong crafted to portray Biidaaban appears young, like a member of Gen Z saddled with student loan debt and skyrocketing rent. The recent rent strikes in Toronto—and the fact that in March of 2023 the average price for a one-bedroom in the city reached $2,501 a month—flutter around the edges of this film for viewers.[31] Watching Biidaaban keep the hood of their sweatshirt up as they navigate the cold sidewalks below the maples, one is reminded of how the frayed edges of capitalism leave people exposed in the chill of early spring. As a work of cinema, Strong's film has a subtle yet strong class consciousness.

Class struggle and the Land Back movement converge in "Plight," coming to a head during maple tapping season. The boulevards of large maples that Biidaaban and their friends hope to tap from March 21–23 are located in an affluent pocket of the city, a place where environmental aesthetics encode—and enforce—class-based enclosure: "They have perennials instead of grass. They get organic, local vegetables delivered to their doors twice weekly *in addition* to going to the farmers' market on Saturday. They're also trying to make our neighborhood into an Ontario heritage designation; I think that mostly means you can't do renovations that make your house look like it isn't from the 1800s or rent your extra floors to the lower class."[32] But if the environmental privilege of this neighborhood is safeguarded by economic class, it is underwritten by settler colonialism.[33] The irony of an Indigenous collective seeking permission to tap this neighborhood's trees is not lost on Biidaaban: "I think this in english because I don't know how to say any of it: This is our sugar bush. It looks different because there are three streets and 150 houses and one thousand people living in it, but it is still my sugar bush. It is our sugar bush."[34] To access a season requires access to land: for the characters in Simpson's story and Strong's film, the right to a season depends upon both economic justice and decolonization.

Tapping small holes in these maples is akin to boring small holes in capitalism, private property, and white supremacy, an act that provokes both systems of surveillance and threat. The characters in "Plight" are justifiably wary. They distribute a flyer in advance, alerting property owners to their tapping project—"No need to call the cops or the city; it's sustainable"—in hopes of avoiding the hypervigilance to city codes that Justin Mann identifies as advancing the agenda of empire in gentrifying neighborhoods across North America.[35] Biidaaban's friend Kwe dons a "Not Murdered, Not Missing" t-shirt as they head out to tap, which reads simultaneously as defiant and as an appeal to any law enforcement officers or settler vigilantes that they encounter while collecting sap. Biidaaban themself carries three pieces of maple sugar in their pocket to quiet their friend's infant, hoping the tapping can proceed quietly, without drawing neighborhood attention. Through this detail, the history of the residential school systems lurks on the edges of Simpson's short story: "If I get caught, hide my kids," Biidaaban thinks as they begin drilling into the bark.[36] In "Plight," the threats are anticipated, but the narrative concludes just as Biidaaban turns on their electric drill. Cutting off in media res, the story leaves readers guessing whether the syruping project will unfold without incident or whether Biidaaban and their friends—affectionately referred to as the Fourth World Collective—will face fines and violence.

In contrast, Strong's film climaxes in violence. Rather than setting out during the day, like the characters in "Plight," the cinematic renditions of Biidaaban and Sabe undertake tapping under the cover of darkness. As they tramp through the lingering crust of snow to collect their accumulated sap, the wealthier homes outfitted with security lights, garden hoses, and sprinkler systems menace them. The film's threatening infrastructure—the surveillance lights that track Biidaaban's movements and the animate orange plastic safety fencing wrapped around the maple trunks—are certainly cinematic representations of settler state violence. No human antagonists appear in the film, which increases the sense that the threats to Biidaaban's safety are systemic. As Biidaaban retrieves a pail of sap, loosening the orange plastic fencing on the trunk to reveal the spigot, the camera angle shifts, positioned for the first and only time in the film within an upper-story window of one of the houses on the street, as though surveilling Biidaaban's movements. Below, the plastic fencing ensnares Biidaaban, pressing them against the trunk and tightening to cover their mouth and nose in an act of strangulation. The houses lurch forward, closing in on Biidaaban as they struggle to free themselves and breathe.

This disruption of Biidaaban's syrup tapping is accompanied by an audible arrhythmia. Until this moment, the soundscape of the maple tapping is characterized by rhythm: a drill sound; a tapping sound as the spile is hammered into the bark; a metal clank as Biidaaban takes a bucket from their wheelbarrow and attaches it to the spile; a clunk as a lid is placed over the spile to prevent snow or dead leaves from drifting into the pail. This sound pattern repeats a few times, eventually condensing into just a repeated drilling. A steady drip of sap follows, then a rhythmic stirring of the collected sap over the backyard fire. But as Biidaaban is captured in the orange plastic fencing, the film's score increases in volume and quickens its beat, the string players furiously working their bows to signal alarm.[37] This audible arrhythmia corresponds with the interruption of a seasonal practice through the intertwined forces of settler colonialism and capital accumulation.

As capitalism tightens, constricting lives just as Biidaaban is squeezed by plastic fencing, it is worth pausing to reflect on the entangled flows of oil, currency, exhaust, and the literary arts. Petroleum, after all, quietly fuels literary preservation and publication as well as engines and heaters, and many of the works analyzed in this book are artifacts of petroculture. For instance, Frederick Koch was a significant donor to the Morgan Museum & Library where Thoreau's phenology manuscripts—discussed in chapter 1—are housed. And the oil fortune that contributed to the preservation of Thoreau's records was partially derived through theft of oil from Native American lands. Employing a technique some workers called "the Koch method," Koch employees falsified measurements and quality reports when they drew oil from wells on land owned by tribes or individual Native Americans. According to an investigation by the Senate Select Committee on Indian Affairs, carried out during the late 1980s, documents suggest that Koch Industries stole 803,874 barrels of oil in 1986; 671,144 barrels in 1987; and 474,281 barrels in 1988.[38] This contraband oil was valued at a total of $31.1 million dollars. As Christopher Leonard notes in his portrait of the Koch family and U.S. capitalism, the senate report on these hearings was definitive. "Koch Oil," the report stated, "the largest purchaser of Indian oil in the country, is the most dramatic example of an oil company stealing by deliberate mismeasurement and fraudulent reporting."[39] Evidence of this theft emerged through repeat photography: John Elroy, an FBI special agent, waited in Oklahoma cattle pastures with a 600mm camera, photographing Koch employees as they collected oil. "*Snap. Snap. Snap.* . . . The Koch Oil man approaching the oil tank. Opening it. Measuring the oil within. Writing a receipt. The images were crisp and clear. Inarguable evidence."[40]

I think of John Elroy, crouching in the dry pasture with his lens, and then of Amanda Strong clicking away in her studio to bring *Biidaaban* to life: two renditions of anti-capitalist photographic craft.

The issue of oil fortunes underwriting the literary arts becomes more pronounced in the coming pages as we turn to "The Climate of Gender," an essay on seasonality and transition by Callum Angus. In 2021, this piece appeared in *Catapult*, an online literary magazine and press funded by Elizabeth Koch, daughter of the multibillionaire Charles Koch. As the writer Hilary Plum notes, "we can only assume this press is made of Koch Industries money," its publications financed by the profits of a multinational conglomerate based in crude oil.[41] At the time of submission, Angus was—in all likelihood—unaware of the magazine's financing, so "The Climate of Gender" is a reminder of how easily even prose documenting and decrying the changing climate can be caught in the swirl of emissions and cash now heating the globe. To construct what Jennifer Wenzel calls a "commodity biography" of this essay—to trace its production and distribution through global networks—requires connecting the greenhouse gas emissions of Koch Industries to compounding financial profits to the anti-science lobbying efforts that permitted the fossil fuel industry and this fortune to grow unchecked.[42] It requires following the money that leaked into literary publishing—perhaps in an attempt to make over Elizabeth Koch's reputation—and eventually allowed an essay on the unseasonable to see print. In a sense, Angus's essay is an artifact of the same emissions that gave rise to its subject. When I read Callum Angus's piercing essay on climate change and the unseasonable, I cannot help but think about these barrels of dispossessed oil and the "exquisite art" of Elizabeth Koch's literary philanthropy.[43] Crude oil is refined into gasoline and other products, oil fortunes are refined into literature.

TRANS LIFE AND SEASONALITY

We return now to maples. Eli Clare writes while looking out a window at a pair of old maple trees, rooted in unceded Abenaki territory. "Currently leafed out, a luscious green, the trees worry me," he confesses. "A year ago, the power company not so carefully trimmed branches away from the electric lines, and this summer I'm noticing dead twigs among their greenery." Reshaped by the power company—by the wires and currents of petrocapitalist infrastructure—the trees now work to keep time. "Three months from now," Clare insists, slipping into a phenological account, "they will begin to shed leaves, becoming an orange-yellow luminescence on clear fall days, by November revealing the bare bones of their trunks and branches. Five months after that, leaves will emerge, pale-green fists unfurling themselves as the days lengthen and the nights rise above freezing."[44] Clare, who describes himself as "white, disabled, and genderqueer," is beautifully attentive to nonnormative futurities. With his pen, budburst as "pale-green fists" takes on an activist tone, a phenological defiance. And indeed, Clare notes how easily normativity can take on environmental overtones: "The standards called *normal*—sometimes in tandem with *natural*—are promoted as averages. They are posed as the most common and best states of being for body-minds. They are advertised as descriptions of who 'we' collectively are—a *we* who is predictably white, male, middle- and upper-class, nondisabled, Christian, heterosexual, gender-conforming, slender, cisgender."[45] Reading Clare's description of the normal, I think of climate, the average weather in a habitat over the course of years. I hear echoes of Zadie Smith's wry observation that "we can't even say the word 'abnormal' to each other out loud: it reminds us of what came before. Better to forget what once was normal, the way season followed season, with a temperate charm only the poets appreciated."[46] How can we acknowledge the grave impact of climate change without invoking harmful ideas of the normal and normative?

Within queer studies, discussions of temporality accelerated in the first decades of the twenty-first century. Building on Dana Luciano's concept of chronobiopolitics, Elizabeth Freeman argues that chrononormativity intends to make populations "feel coherently collective, through particular orchestrations of time."[47] Birth, graduations, jobs, marriages, reproduction, retirement, death. Not celebrating these milestones—through choice or otherwise—leads to "asynchrony, or time out of joint."[48] As Freeman notes, queer people, as well as people subjected to poverty and unemployment, are perceived as grating against chrononormativity. Jack Halberstam, in their groundbreaking *In a Queer Time and Place: Transgender Bodies, Subcultural Lives*, suggests that "once one leaves the temporal frames of bourgeois reproduction and family, longevity, risk/safety, and inheritance," once one lives on the margins of either heteronormativity or capitalism, one enters "queer time."[49] Responding to these theorizations, Kadji Amin observes that there is a "potential alliance between asynchronic temporalities and queer and sexual social practices."[50] Without treading carefully, it becomes easy to align the temporal damages of climate change with the asychronies of queer time, thereby failing to distinguish between temporal injury and temporal variation. Instead, I note that in a roundtable discussion on the subject of queer time, Annamarie Jagose cautions that "it's important to question . . . the credentialing of asynchrony, multi temporality, and nonlinearity as if they were automatically in the service of queer political projects and aspirations."[51] The arrythmias of the unseasonable, which often lead to disconnection and diminishment, are not the asynchronies of queer life, which open a plethora of habitable timings.

The writer working directly in relation to—and perhaps beyond—these theorizations is Callum Angus. Angus explains that he writes of gender "transition and climate change in the same breath because those are the two dominant forces of change in my life."[52] And indeed, in his essay "The Climate of Gender," Angus recalls his own transition as a period of intense phenological work, observing the melt and germinations of change: "I filled journals comparing myself to others, always collecting data for an experiment of one. I watched the seasons march across my body, the shelf of my breasts calving in the surgeon's office, the sprouting of male privilege and a five o'clock shadow after just a few weeks on testosterone. For me, this was the appeal of transitioning. The ability to track and measure and watch for hair growth and octave drops in voice and the redistribution of fat from hips to stomach, the way people started to ignore me in public, how men spoke to me differently."[53] This keeping of records is also an anticipation, an effort to keep time in the sense of watching for, or awaiting, what is to come.[54]

Likewise, in the short stories contained in the collection *A Natural History of Transition*, Angus leans on the language of seasonality as he writes of gender transition and gender fluidity. A mother observing her child begin weekly testosterone injections is "like a gardener monitoring the progress of a patch of summer squash."[55] Or, in "Winter of Men," a short work of historical fiction, the fluidity of gender flows according to seasonal change. Set during the mid-seventeenth century in Ville-Marie—the French colony that would grow into Montreal—the Catholic sisters in the congregation led by Marguerite Bourgeoys have the capacity "to slip through the cracks of man and woman as one season changed to another."[56] On November 1, as snowflakes begin to accumulate on the windowsill, Lydia, the main character, notices that her friend Jeanne's voice "cracked and croaked and dropped a raspy octave lower in a jarring split, like a log opening under the axe."[57] Jeanne's body continues changing as the days grow shorter: "rough stubble grew in along her jaw and at her temples . . . [her] hips had slenderized and her jaw hardened to the point where her silhouette, when seen in shadow or periphery, could pass for a young man's."[58] Her period ceases, not to resume until spring. Lydia calls Jeanne "a bear getting ready for winter with her thick coat of new hair."[59] Building on the shifts that many human bodies undertake during seasonal transitions in the temperate zone—slight hair loss as fall and spring commence, ebbs and flows in the immune system, and experiences of seasonal affective disorder—Angus imagines secondary sex characteristics also acquiring seasonal cadences. Throughout *A Natural History of Transition*, his short stories recall Nicole Seymour's concept of organic transgenderism, "a spontaneous, non-commodified, and self-directed process likened to the life-cycle changes of plants and animals."[60] In contrast to a medicalized, institutionalized process of transition, organic transgenderism occurs as phenological growth or cycle. Transition, in these stories, is profoundly seasonal.

In Angus's writing, climate change haunts the interconnections between seasonality and gender transition. In one story, a greenhouse employee—working double shifts in Massachusetts as the thermometer reaches eighty degrees in March—compares his deadname to a shell discarded during maturation: "Out front the rhododendrons bloom the third time this spring like nothing's wrong. The rain gauge is Seattle-full. Lawn moldy, worms drowned and decomposing. New England has lost its shit. On the kitchen table junk mail piles up: debt collections, library fines, student loans, all automailed in cellophane windows to my old name, husks of my former self collecting like the papery exoskeletons of dragonflies."[61] Here, the unseasonable world is composed not only of irregular blooms and soppy lawns, but also the trappings of capitalist captivity—fines and loans—and the repetition of a dead name. To the degree that organic transgenderism depends on seasonality and phenology, climate change destabilizes its foundations.

The analogy between climate change and gender transition at work in Angus's essay "The Climate of Gender" is not a simplistic one—anthropogenic climate change inflicts suffering while gender affirmation relieves it—but Angus's interweaving of gender and environmental transitions spotlights the insight of those who have intimate experience with shifted timings. His essay toys with connections between the failing rhythms of sap and the fading rhythms of menstruation but then relaxes into a looser—and more tenable—reflection on climate change as a kind of dysphoria: "This isn't about sap and flow and blood and menstruation as inherently feminine things to escape," he writes, "but the fact, instead, that we all have a territory to which we dream of returning, trees and people both."[62] Another way of saying this might be that maple trees and trans people share a yearning for habitable times, for livable rhythms. "The forces that may push us out"—and by us, Angus encompasses both maples and the trans community—"rising temperatures, warmth and hate caused by ten billion combustions every day in the hearts of greedy men (for they have mostly been men)—are already here."[63] In the northern United States, where Angus writes from, both arboreal and trans lives are regularly threatened.

For me, the gift of Angus's meditation on maple tapping is the reminder that life during climate arrhythmias requires a stance of radical openness. Whether they remain stationary or migrate, "trees and people live in transition now, perhaps permanently" and many of us will change from stranger to host and back again.[64] Commitments to restraining the profligate emissions of the Global North must be matched by commitments to value the lives unfolding within the arrhythmia that they created, to acknowledge—returning to Zadie Smith—that "there will be butterflies appearing in new areas, and birds visiting earlier and leaving later—perhaps that will be interesting, and new," and even beautiful in its own way.[65] As

Angus notes, transitions allow us to rewrite meaning, shift symbolics, reimagine relations. He writes:

> I am simply looking at the maple and wondering where it will grow next, how its meaning might change were its physiological rhythms no longer so uniquely adapted to the spring season.... I am simply looking at myself and how much change I've had to adapt to in order to still be here, how change has become a part of who I think I am; I'm looking at other trans people, too, seeing how we've continually shaped and reinvented ourselves, and I can't see anything but hope in that.[66]

Without veering into the fallacy of a good Anthropocene, climate arrhythmias may realign or sharpen solidarities. I hope, along with Angus, that the Global North gains "an awareness that this is not the first time whole societies have been forced to adapt to change they didn't want, and a willingness to listen to those communities with much more respect than we have in the past."[67]

SEASONAL JUSTICE

In Detroit, maple tapping recently resumed in Rouge Park, a plot of nearly 1,200 acres. It lies roughly ten miles west of downtown and twenty-five miles south of a Mahindra Automotive manufacturing facility.[68] The park itself contains multitudes: swathes of native prairie and a marsh, the remnants of a missile control site used during the Cold War, a butterfly garden. It contains D-Town Farm, where the Detroit Black Community Food Sovereignty Network tends vegetables and herbs, but it also contains an active pistol range and bomb detonation area used by the Detroit police. At the turn of the twenty-first century, officers assigned to the city's "morality units" targeted gay men cruising in Rouge Park, arresting the men and impounding their vehicles.[69] And in 2020, as a neighborhood resident took her daily walk through the park, a strong chemical smell she posited was tear gas from police training exercises "burned her eyes, nose, and throat."[70] Inhaling tear gas can also lead to excruciating menstrual cramps and cause trans men on testosterone to bleed. In Rouge Park, these chemicals dispersed into the marsh and river, the watershed supporting the city's largest grove of sugar maples.

In 2019, Antonio Cosme, who describes himself as an "urban Native educator and organizer," envisioned tapping these maples along the Rouge River, reviving a sugar bush within city limits.[71] Cosme, a National Wildlife Federation employee, partnered with the Wikwemikong First Nations Reserve, the Detroit Black Community Food Sovereignty Network, Black to the Land, and the Sierra Club of Detroit. This coalition—a highly unusual alliance between mainstream environmental organizations and environmental justice organizations—successfully lobbied the city to allow the maples in Rouge Park to be tapped. As David Pitawanakwat, a member of the Detroit Sugarbush Project, explained on public television: "These are just huge maple groves, it's just a perfect maple tapping spot. And so we went to the city and we said, hey, this is a part of our heritage, our culture, our religious and spiritual rights to do this every season, to honor . . . the season, ourselves, and our ancestors."[72] For Cosme, the season of sap flow offered an opening, a chance "to engage young Detroiters in those late winter months" and build "important connections between the Indigenous and African-American communities" of Detroit.[73] Lugging dozens of orange plastic buckets from Home Depot to collect sap, members of the Detroit Sugarbush Project tramped through the snow and toward the trees. Resuming this seasonal rhythm swayed the city toward environmental reclamation. It allowed people with disparate histories of dispossession and inflicted pain to align in late winter, building solidarities across chronologies, all within the pulse of Detroit's maples.

However, during the revived sugar bush's third season, as roughly twenty sap collectors gathered on the evening of February 18, 2022, around a small bonfire in Rouge Park, a Michigan State Police helicopter whirred overhead. The headlights of police cars—reminiscent of the movement-activated security lights that track Biidaaban in Strong's film—approached through the trees. Seven police cars, along with officers outfitted in military tactical gear, descended on the late winter gathering, alleging that the group was trespassing in the park after daylight hours and demanding to inspect their permit from the Detroit Fire Department. "We tried to tell them about our sovereignty," Rosebud Bear-Schneider, a citizen of the Lac Courte Oreilles Band of Lake Superior Ojibwe, explained.[74] But a video of the confrontation taken by Hadassah GreenSky, a member of the Little Traverse Bay Bands of Odawa Indians, captures one of the officers insisting that "the sovereign stuff is not valid" when shown a federal tribal identification card.[75] For tapping maple trees, for resisting the experience of arrhythmia and keeping time even as it splinters, for attending to late winter and to each other, the members of the Detroit Sugarbush Project were threatened with arrest. This outsized response is obscenely familiar—an echo of law enforcement's brutality during the Black Lives Matter uprisings and the artillery sent to Standing Rock—but it is worth noting as a moment when seasonal practice provoked systems of colonial and anti-Black power.

As arrhythmias increase, I expect that both environmental justice movements and militarized repression will unfold in relation to seasonal time, intensifying during its interruptions or renewals. The Detroit Sugarbush Project was in the process of renewing their memorandum of understanding with the city—extending the paperwork for another season of tapping—when the sap began to flow. In that year—2022, one of the warmest years on record—maple sap began to flow at the early end of the season. "The maple syrup doesn't run on our time and our clocks and our schedules," Cosme insists, foregrounding the clash between seasonal rhythms and bureaucratic deadlines. "The police should expect us there February and March of every year."[76] But as the globe heats over the course of the twenty-first century, the ecologist David Lutz projects that maple tapping season in the United States "will shrink and will get closer to a December date."[77] Unstable phenology will make it increasingly difficult to anticipate when to procure paperwork. I think, too, of the characters in "Plight" and *Biidaaban*, who distribute a flyer during late fall to alert property owners of their upcoming sap collection: "We are collecting sap from this Maple Tree next year from March 21-23. We will be by to collect it once a day, and we will pick up the bucket lid and spigot on March 23. Thank you for your support in our urban sugar making adventure. FWP Collective." Intended to increase the safety of Indigenous maple tappers procuring sap in colonized neighborhoods, the information on this flyer is useless if sap runs months ahead of time. Under the conditions of a changed climate, paperwork drawn up to prevent charges of trespassing is associated with incorrect dates, leaving sap collectors exposed to state and settler vigilante violence. Far from being an emblem of reassurance, seasonality practiced in arrhythmic times will be on the front lines of struggles over inequality and power. Environmental and climate justice struggles will unfold not only along the axes of where and who but also in relation to when—certain times of the year, certain seasons will become politicized.

Who has the right to a season? What is the value of maintaining seasonal practices and rituals even as environmental time frays in a warming world? As seasonal practices are disrupted—by environmental, economic, and political forces—maintaining these practices is an inherently resistant act. I think again about form, how rhythms and repetitions exert force in a climatically altered world. As Sarah Schulman writes, reflecting on the AIDS crisis, "I believe that in long, hard struggles there is a value to what Gary Indiana calls 'the politics of repetition.' Even if it takes all of our energy, I still intend to do everything I can to at least keep these issues alive."[78] There is meaning in repetition itself, in the persistence of seasonal practice even in the face of intensifying climate change. In this sense, to keep time is also to safeguard, protect, and defend.[79]

THE ARTS OF ADAPTATION

Embedded within her influential critique of the Anthropocene, the anthropologist Zoe Todd recounts how the gentrification of Canadian urban spaces splintered her sense of herself as a creative person and urban Indigenous resident:

> When I was a little girl in the 1990s, my dad, Métis artist Gary Todd, used to take my little sister and me to his painting studio in Edmonton. It was a basement warehouse space in the inner city, a dusty and creaky building used by artists and theatre troupes and photographers and others to *make things*. . . . he taught me about cross-hatching and shading, dimensions and perspective, how to mix colors, and how to view the world as a series of pigments mixed together in shadow and light. . . . Fifteen years later I walked into the warehouse where my Dad used to paint, only now it was a high-end condominium and I was there to attend a poetry reading in a private residence. The cognitive dissonance of entering space that I had known so intimately as a child, that had loomed so large in my *making* as an artist and as an urban Indigenous person, only to find it

finished with ten-foot ceilings, burnished metal and tasteful art, was jarring.... When our gritty, dusty, poor lives were erased to make way for shiny condos, so too had my belief that I could participate in the world of *making* as it is defined by a persistently white, Eurocentric academy and art world.[80]

The personal history that Todd offers here thuds with the forces of capitalist real estate and colonial occupation, and I am struck by Todd's italicization, the import and salience of *making* within environmental crisis and economic precarity. She uses the gerund—*making*—to stress practice and craft, emphasizing the activity of creation itself rather than the commodity or product. Todd's emphasis on *making* echoes Leanne Betasamosake Simpson's short story "The Gift is in the Making," one of the pieces that Strong drew on as she filmed *Biidaaban*. In Simpson's tale, Nanabush teaches the Nishnaabeg to tap maple trees and boil syrup: he "took them to the south side of the tree, put his semaa down, and showed them how to tap the trees and collect the sap.... how to boil that sweet water down into sweet sugar."[81] In a hasty interpretation of this story, the gift is either the knowledge of this process or the syrup itself. But the Nishnaabeg know that maple products are not the gift: "They listen for the heartbeat of their mother as that ziisbaakdaaboo falls into their pails.... they know that ziinzibaakwad wasn't the real gift. They know that the real gift was in the making."[82] Here, as in Todd's story, the value inheres in the collaborative labor and practice, not the material outcome. In light of these two stories, I close this chapter by turning to the *making* of Strong's film rather than the film itself, attending to artistic practice and the arts of adaptation.

The creation of *Biidaaban (The Dawn Comes)* required a remarkable amount of labor. Each puppet entailed sculpting; their cell phones and pails and drills required assembly. Maple trees were crafted, the furrows of their bark textured, lichens attached. The vinyl siding of houses snapped together; shingles formed for the roofs. "It was a full two years, full-time," Strong explains. "I would say we spent almost a year building everything. The two main puppets—they're being made simultaneously because we have a team, but they took about six months each. . . . And it was between five and six months of shooting. Full-time, long days, alone—just to get the footage. There were definitely over 100 shoot days. . . . A lot of feature films can be shot in like 20."[83] This artistic method resembles the work portrayed within the film itself: as Matthew Harrison Tedford argues, both syrup making and stop-motion animation are labor-intensive, embodied practices.[84] They are projects that demand both time and energy. I think about how Biidaaban's fingerless gloves had to be knit, their pants patched to indicate layers of mending, and the material repairs required by those surviving on the margins of capitalist destruction. Strong and her team made those repairs too, the salvage work and environmental practices of the story flowing into the labor of the filmmakers.

Thinking about what it means to tend to time during climate disruptions, there is much to be learned from stop-motion animation, the practice that Amanda Strong employed in filming *Biidaaban*. Stop-motion animation is much like time-lapse film, but in between each photograph the filmmaker adjusts the poses of the puppets, rearranges the leaves, accumulates or diminishes the snow piled on the abandoned lawn chair. It is a rhythmic photographic practice. There is a particular tending of a world that happens between shots, an attention to the gradations of time and seasons, an accounting of what has passed, what remains, and what emerges. The thousands of individual pictures that Strong and her team took of Biidaaban and Sabe's maple tapping, adjusting their hands and their glances between camera flashes, build into a flow—played one after the other, they generate a sense of something ongoing. It is a labor to realize continuance, particularly when climate change bends toward the arrhythmic, but these labors suggest that it remains possible to craft something ongoing from what is fractured. In Strong's stop-motion practice, continuance is composed not through the grand sweep of history or the distant undulations of geological time, but instead through tending to small-scale time, marking the slight shifts that suggest a passage from one moment to the next. To keep on is to continue, to keep going, to enable continuance.

Biidaaban is an adaptation of Simpson's writing, but conversations about climate change and adaptation tend toward the environmental rather than the artistic. Increasingly, as political will crumbles and the wealthy turn opportunistic, discussions of the climatic future turn bleak. The *New York Times* reports that "the United States will drill for more oil and gas in 2030 than at any point in its history.... So will Russia and Saudia Arabia. In fact, almost all of the top 20 fossil fuel-producing countries plan to produce more oil, gas and coal in 2030 than they do today. If those projections hold, the world would overshoot the amount of fossil fuels consistent with limiting warming to 2 degrees Celsius."[85] In this context, mitigation—by which I mean curtailment of the production and consumption of fossil fuels—is more necessary than ever. At the same time, failing to design and implement adaptation measures will leave the globe's most vulnerable communities exposed. Climate adaptation—which the IPCC defines as "reducing climate risks and vulnerability mostly via adjustment of existing systems"—includes efforts to restore wetlands in anticipation of increased flooding, installing early warning systems to prepare for storms, planting a variety of heat and drought-resistant crops, and relocating from high-risk areas.[86] Climate adaptations geared toward the reduction of suffering are crucial environmental priorities and will only grow more necessary in the decades to come. Climate adaptation requires a degree of change—an openness to new ways of laboring, eating, traveling, and living. It requires revision and retailoring.

During these discussions of climate adaptation, I think often of literary and artistic adaptation. Despite their shared nomenclature, the two fields have yet to speak to each other. In her foundational theory of literary adaptation, the scholar Linda Hutcheon's description of the practice resonates profoundly with environmental adaptations. She describes adaptation as "cultural recycling," an artistic "salvaging."[87] Moreover she writes:

> To think of narrative adaptation in terms of a story's fit and its process of mutation or adjustment, through adaptation, to a particular cultural environment is something I find suggestive. Stories also evolve by adaptation and are not immutable over time. Sometimes, like biological adaptation, cultural adaptation involves migration to favorable conditions: stories travel to different cultures and different media. In short, stories adapt just as they are adapted.[88]

Following Hutcheon's description, adaptation of a literary text—as a retelling, a film, or another medium—is linked to continuance. The arts of adaptation are about crafting a culturally habitable future from the literary past. They are a storehouse of knowledge for those of us trying to envision how to create a habitable world from the bruised forms we live within.

In adaptations, rhythm and adjusted timing play a central role. "In the process of adaptation," Hutcheon notes, "pacing can be transformed, time compressed or expanded."[89] As Strong adapted Simpson's writing to film, the plotline of "Plight" continued past its textual ending, expanding onward and flowing into Simpson's poem and other writings. The daytime maple tapping project of the page—carried out in full sunlight—shifted to a nighttime venture on screen. The story is recognizable but retimed. "Part of the pleasure," Hutcheon argues, "comes simply from repetition with variation.... Recognition and remembrance are part of the pleasure (and risk) of experiencing an adaptation; so too is change."[90] The arts of literary adaptation depend on generating a newly habitable world as timelines and expectations are shuffled or realigned, of crafting new ways of being even as the echo of previous forms beat on.

On the page or the screen, out on the boulevards and within the city's back lots, so many of us are waiting for sugars to move through the sapwood, for the world to thaw and freeze and thaw again. Waiting for a drip of sap to emerge from the spile, and then another and another and another:

    Beat. Beat.
        Beat. Beat.
            Beat. Beat.
                Beat.[91]

EPILOGUE

More Habits Than Dreams

Watching the documentary *The Hottest August* while revising this manuscript, I am startled to hear a voice-over excerpt of Zadie Smith's "Elegy for a Country's Seasons." As the footage charts a blisteringly hot rush hour on the New York City subway—people descending on an escalator into the station, packed shoulder to shoulder on a C train, listening to something on headphones or checking their cells, nodding off until the train reaches the Nostrand stop—Smith's essay is read aloud:

> There is the scientific and ideological language for what is happening to the weather, but there are hardly any intimate words. Is that surprising? People in mourning tend to use euphemism.... The most melancholy of all euphemisms: "The new normal." "It's the new normal" ... as a beloved pear tree, half-drowned, loses its grip on the earth and falls over. The train line to Cornwall washes away—the new normal. We can't even say the word "abnormal to each other out loud: it reminds us of what came before ... the way season followed season.... What "used to be" is painful to remember.... Chilly April showers ... July weddings that could trust in fine weather.... At least, we say to each other, at least August is still reliably ablaze.[1]

The documentary has adjusted Smith's prose, removing a phrase here and there to transpose it from an elegy for the English seasons into an elegy for the seasons of the New York metropolitan area. The erasures allow the washed-out train track to Cornwall in southeast England to transform into a washed-out section of the Metro North line to Cornwall, New York. Colonial repetitions of place names, along with widespread flooding, facilitate this geographic blur. The edited excerpt leaves viewers familiar with Smith's work with a sense of eerie porosity.

Shot in New York City in August of 2017 by the geographer and filmmaker Brett Story, *The Hottest August* set out to capture a portrait of the megacity during the warmest August on record in the Northern Hemisphere. As it would turn out, August of 2017 was slightly cooler than the year before, but the heat in the city is palpable nonetheless: a fan spins on the ceiling of a home dance studio, a school bus driver and a housekeeper wilt in beach chairs beside the Atlantic, a Mister Softee truck glistens with condensation. Window air conditioners whir. Amid this searing heat, *The Hottest August* reprises a landmark work of cinema-verité, *Chronicle of a Summer*, directed by Jean Rouch and Edgar Morin. During the summer of 1960, Rouch and Morin conducted interviews across Paris, asking immigrants, factory workers, and students the same question: "Are you happy?" In 2017, Brett Story asked people across the five boroughs of New York City: "How do you feel about the future?" In the heat, her seemingly open-ended question is covertly rhetorical, inclining toward apprehension. It recurs throughout the film, building its own sort of rhythm: "How do you feel about the future? How do you feel about the future?"

As Story constructs this cinematic ethnography, she delves into the character of the summer, charting not the timings of budburst but the tempos of people's anxieties and dreams. As interview follows interview, vignette following vignette on the screen, *The*

Hottest August reminds me of all the repetitions that unfold over the course of this book. I think of Sara Elizabeth Jones, monitoring prairie bloomings in Wisconsin; of Nityanand Jayaraman and S. Palayam, tracking currents and winds on Besant Nagar Beach; of Christina Seely, photographing her own photograph to document a shift in snowfall; of all the members of the Detroit Sugarbush Project, listening for the repeated drip of maple sap into their plastic buckets. How do you feel about the future? How do you feel about the future?

In a month of extreme—if not record-breaking—heat, Story's question is weighted by its environmental context, by the conditions of the overheated city. And yet, as Smith notes in her essay—"we can't even say the word . . . to each other out loud"—the dozens of people that Story interviews talk around the climate. In the entire film, only one person utters the phrase "climate change." On the one hand, climate is present in the film's temporal framing, if not its overt content. The answers that New Yorkers offer up to Story's camera lens are given during a potentially record-breaking month of heat, and this temporal emphasis allows answers seemingly unrelated to the climate crisis to acquire environmental resonance. After attending a bystander training, a young white woman in a plaid shirt recounts how she witnessed the harassment of a woman in hijab in Greenpoint. "The worst part, to me, is that I kept walking," she admits. "It's just crazy to me, because it doesn't take very much, but you have to do *something*." Her voice catches, on the verge of tears. And because this footage was shot during the heat, in response to a question about how she feels about the future, her discussion of ethnic violence in her neighborhood acquires climatic overtones. Cameras, like thermometers, can measure boiling points.

But, on the other hand, climate change is present in the content of people's answers even if they avoid the phrase, even if it is not at the forefront of their minds as they respond. Two middle-aged Black women, sitting in lawn chairs on a sidewalk as dusk settles over the city, complain that their neighbors stay inside now, not mingling on porches and sidewalks like folks once did. "Don't want to mingle, don't want to meet people . . . I don't know," one of the women laments. Perhaps it is the heat, perhaps it is social isolation. Perhaps heat and social isolation cannot be separated. Later, a young man sitting in the passenger seat of a parked box truck explains that he is "looking for a room now . . . I have five appointments tomorrow morning, looking for a room. Like, I have to move out of my apartment by tomorrow." Traffic moves past on the dark street, the headlights glancing off the windshield of his spray-painted vehicle. *The Hottest August* offers this crisis to viewers without commentary, asking us to draw the connections. What does eviction feel like in extreme heat? How do exposures to capitalism's inequities coincide with exposure to the elements? How many people feel displaced? Is it possible to interpret this young man's upheaval without accounting for the sweat of lugging boxes up and down stairs in dangerously high temperatures? Story set out to portray climate change without disentangling it "from other pressing questions, such as how power is distributed in society, who capitalism serves and disserves, why scapegoating others is a dangerous distraction from the need to build a truly collective, intersectional movement against the exploitation of the planet's resources and for economic and racial justice."[2] When I ask myself how I feel about the future of climate scholarship, I hope we all hold as tightly to those questions as possible.

Near the close of *The Hottest August*, a voice-over argues that Story's interviews revealed "more habits than dreams," suggesting that people in New York during the summer of 2017 lacked a vision of the future. "The strongest case *The Hottest August* makes is for the importance of being able to imagine a future at all," one reviewer argues, caught off guard by people's lackluster sense of anticipation, their inability to forecast the coming years.[3] But expectation is shaped by the environmental and literary forms that we reside within. In these arrhythmic years, as the future proves difficult to anticipate, as train rails wash away and the seasons go haywire, the rhythms that matter most may be those crafted between ourselves. The strongest rhythm in Story's film is relational, a repeated reaching out to neighbors, to strangers that she passes on the street, to anyone willing to talk. This gesture is the kind of habit that builds a sense of the perennial even as environmental time frays. How do you feel about the future? How do you feel about the future?

ACKNOWLEDGMENTS

More thanks are due than I can possibly express here, but briefly—

This research began at the University of Wisconsin-Madison, where I was mentored by an exceptional team of environmental literary critics. Rob Nixon taught me, through our conversations and through his own writing, that literary criticism is a vital instrument in chambers of environmental thought. Lynn Keller modeled how scholarship flourishes within community. Monique Allewaert challenged my ideas when they needed to be rethought and then helped me untangle my conceptual knots. I was also fortunate to land in Madison alongside a brilliant cohort of environmental thinkers—profound thanks to everyone at the Center for Culture, History, and Environment for shaping these pages.

I will always be grateful for the two years that I spent at the Alice Kaplan Institute for the Humanities at Northwestern University, where I began to conceive of this project as a book. Harris Feinsod was the best postdoctoral mentor anyone could imagine. Kaneesha Parsard and Michelle Huang continually proved that sharp intellects do not preclude kindness or exuberance. A bevy of other friends and colleagues strengthened my writing and my spirits during those years: thanks to Andrew Britt, Dassia Posner, Elizabeth Schwall,

Hi'ilei Hobart, Jayme Collins, Jessica Winegar, Jill Manor, Keith Woodhouse, Kelly Wisecup, Megan Skord, Michelle Guittar, Ryan Jobson, Sara Černe, Tom Burke, Tristram Wolff, and Wendy Wall. Extra special gratitude goes to Corey Byrnes for years of extraordinary conversations and for taking me to the beaches, both in Andersonville and along the coast of the Atlantic. After years away, I am glad to be returning to Northwestern's faculty just as this book reaches shelves.

As an assistant professor at Lafayette College and then Harvard University, colleagues and fellow scholars offered guidance and camaraderie. Thanks to Alison Glassie, Andrea Armstrong, Anna Wilson, Annabel Kim, Annette Damayanti Lienau, Ben Cohen, Beth Blum, Bruno Carvalho, Dana Cuomo, Daniel Donoghue, David Atherton, Derek Miller, Emily Miller, Eric Hupe, Ian Miller, James Engell, Jason de Lara Molesky, Jordan Kinder, Joe Whitson, Joyce Chaplin, Karen Thornber, Kelly Rich, Kira Lawrence, Larry Buell, Lauren Bimmler, Megan Fernandes, Mikael Awake, Naomi Weiss, Nicholas Watson, Randi Gill-Sadler, Rebecca Hogue, Saul Zaritt, Sol Kim-Bentley, Tara Menon, and Vidyan Ravinthiran. I am lucky to be working in the field of the environmental humanities with a cadre of wonderful minds that pushed my ideas forward at conferences and workshops, including Alex Menrisky, Angela Hume, April Anson, Ben Stanley, Estraven Lupino-Smith, Heidi Amin-Hong, Lisa Han, Martin Premoli, Matt Hooley, Michelle Bastian, Nicole Seymour, Rebecca Oh, Samia Rahimtoola, Sara Grossman, Sarah Ensor, Sarah Wald, and Stephanie Bernhard.

For shifting and fortifying the ideas threaded throughout these chapters, I want to thank audiences at the University of Delaware, the University of Edinburgh, the Collège de France, Harvard University, the Harwood Museum of Art, Lafayette College, the Lyceum at Pied Beauty Farm (where Josh and Kerstin Mabie let me camp beneath the stars), the University of Minnesota, Northwestern University, the University of Notre Dame, the University of Stavanger, and the University of Wisconsin-Madison. Discussions with colleagues at the Colby Summer Institute in Environmental Humanities were formative; I am particularly grateful to Elizabeth DeLoughrey and Sunil Amrith for their advice and to Chris Walker and Kerill O'Neill for their organizing acumen.

For generously making time to speak with me, I want to thank Alexis Wright, A.R. Venkatachalapathy, Barbara Frey, Christina Seely, Geetha Ramaswami, Karen Coelho, Nityanand Jayaraman, Parvathi Nayar, Ramakrishnan Thyagarajan, Richard Primack, S. Palayam, Sayee Girdhari, Sekhar Raghavan, and Suhirtha Muhil. M. Ravi helped me locate the village of Kumundimoolai in Cuddalore District and brought me to the Pillaiyar Kovil Kulam.

For shepherding this manuscript into text, a hearty thanks to the incomparable Philip Leventhal and the staff of Columbia University Press including Kathryn Jorge and Emily Simon. Lis Pearson's copyedits polished this manuscript and Fred Leise devised the index. I am indebted to two reviewers—Heather Houser and Jesse Oak Taylor—who offered feedback and encouragement on this manuscript. Additional suggestions from Allison Carruth, Jennifer Wenzel, Karen Thornber, and Stephanie LeMenager during a manuscript workshop proved vital: their ideas enlivened and expanded my work. Consultations with Michelle Niemann provided insightful feedback and intellectual fellowship during an isolating pandemic. Jen Rose Smith valiantly read versions of every chapter here; I will always think of our first books as kin.

I appreciate permission from Oxford University Press to print an expanded and altered version of my article "Disordered Environmental Time: Phenology, Climate Change, and Seasonal Form in Henry David Thoreau and Aldo Leopold," *ISLE: Interdisciplinary Studies in Literature and Environment* 25, no. 4 (2018): 700–21. Similarly, I am grateful to the Board of Regents of the University of Wisconsin System for permission to rework and augment my article "The

Poetry of Climatic Witness: Slam Poets at United Nations Climate Summits," originally published in *Contemporary Literature* 62, no. 4 (2022): 558–89. The Nobel Foundation generously granted permission to use a quote from Derek Walcott's 1992 Nobel lecture as the epigraph to this book. I gratefully acknowledge support from the Andrew Mellon Foundation; the Aldo Leopold Foundation; the Center for Culture, History, and Environment at the University of Wisconsin-Madison; and the Greenhouse at the University of Stavanger.

I am endlessly grateful to my family—Cahrene and Dan, Andy and Paul, Kimbra and Bridgette, Etta and James and Maisie, my Nana and Bestefar—for their stability and love. And to my dear friends the world over—including Ana Lincoln, Andy Davey, Brandon Menke, Catherine DeRose, Chloe Wardropper, Elsbeth Pancrazi, Francisco Robles, Ida Ulleberg Jensen, Jamie Corey, Jason Baker, Jayanti Owens, Jenny Whitacre, Josh Keating, Julia Rice, Kahstoserakwathe Paulette Moore, Laura Johnson, Lindsay Renick-Mayer, Miranda Keating, Naomi Salmon, Peter Boger, Rachel Boothby, Sean Berger, and Tasha Kimmet—who are family in their own way.

Finally, this book is for all the students who have read and thought with me. Your questions and ideas inflect these pages. As the world warms, remember to tend to those close to you, to build solidarity with those far away, and to keep working toward livable times.

NOTES

INTRODUCTION: CLIMATE ARRHYTHMIAS

1. Lisa Sun-Hee Park and David Naguib Pellow, *The Slums of Aspen: Immigrants vs. the Environment in America's Eden* (New York: NYU Press, 2011), 3.
2. Harriet Rix, "The Acorn Harvest in Iraqi Kurdistan," *London Review of Books*, December 9, 2022.
3. Jonathan Blitzer, "How Climate Change Is Fueling the U.S. Border Crisis," *New Yorker*, April 3, 2019.
4. Derek Walcott, "The Muse of History," in *What the Twilight Says: Essays* (New York: Farrar, Straus and Giroux, 1998), 62.
5. A. E. Stallings, "Halcyon Days in the Saronic Gulf," *London Review of Books*, January 13, 2023.
6. "phenology, n.," OED Online, September 2022.
7. Julio L. Betancourt, foreword to *Phenology: An Integrative Environmental Science*, 2nd ed., ed. Mark D. Schwartz (Dordrecht: Springer, 2013), vi.
8. Marcela Zalamea and Grizelle González, "Leaffall Phenology in a Subtropical Wet Forest in Puerto Rico: From Species to Community Patterns," *Biotropica: The Journal of Tropical Biology and Conservation* 40, no. 3 (2008): 296.
9. Ivan Maggini et al., "Recent Phenological Shifts of Migratory Birds at a Mediterranean Spring Stopover Site: Species Wintering in the Sahel Advance Passage More Than Tropical Winterers," *PLoS ONE* 15, no. 9 (2020), https://journals.plos.org/plosone/article?id=10.1371/journal.pone.0239489.
10. Bismark Ofosu-Bamfo, "African Phenology Network: Working Towards Coordinated Phenology Monitoring in Africa," presentation, Phenomenal Time Series, organized by Michelle Bastian (Edinburgh, February 3, 2022).
11. R. Ashton Macfarlane, "Wild Laboratories of Climate Change: Plants, Phenology, and Global Warming, 1955–1980," *Journal of the History of Biology* 54 (2021): 312.

12. Michelle Bastian and Rowan Bayliss Hawitt, "Multi-Species, Ecological and Climate Change Temporalities: Opening a Dialogue with Phenology," *Environment and Planning E: Nature and Space* (2022): 15.
13. Nikolaos Christidis, Yasuyuki Aono, and Peter A. Stott, "Human Influence Increases the Likelihood of Extremely Early Cherry Tree Flowering in Kyoto," *Environmental Research Letters* 17 (2022): 1–2.
14. Caitlin McDonough MacKenzie et al., "Advancing Leaf-Out and Flowering Phenology is Not Matched by Migratory Bird Arrivals Recorded in Hunting Guide's Journal in Aroostook County, Maine," *Northeastern Naturalist* 26, no. 3 (2019): 561–79.
15. Tanisha M. Williams, Carl D. Schlichtung, and Kent E. Holsinger, "Herbarium Records Demonstrate Changes in Flowering Phenology Associated with Climate Change Over the Past Century Within the Cape Floristic Region, South Africa," *Climate Change Ecology* 1 (2021), https://doi.org/10.1016/j.ecochg.2021.100006.
16. Christos S. Zerefos et al., "Atmospheric Effects of Volcanic Eruptions as Seen by Famous Artists and Depicted in Their Paintings," *Atmospheric Chemistry and Physics* 7 (2007): 4028.
17. Yachen Liu et al., "Could Phenological Records from Chinese Poems of the Tang and Song Dynasties (618–1279 CE) Be Reliable Evidence of Past Climate Changes?," *Climate of the Past* 17 (2021): 933.
18. For a discussion of this poem, see Ronald C. Egan, "Poems on Paintings: Su Shih and Huang T'ing-chien," *Harvard Journal of Asiatic Studies* 43, no. 2 (1983): 413–51.
19. Emily Raboteau, "This Is How We Live Now: A Year's Diary of Reckoning with Climate Anxiety, Conversation by Conversation," *The Cut*, January 9, 2020.
20. Raboteau, "This Is How We Live Now."
21. Emily Raboteau, "How Do We Bring More Urgency to the Climate Crisis? Emma Sloley and Emily Raboteau in Conversation," interview by Emma Sloley, *Literary Hub*, November 7, 2019.
22. Min Hyoung Song, *Climate Lyricism* (Durham, NC: Duke University Press, 2022), 29. Indeed, Raboteau's conversations are an example of what Song, drawing on Andrew Epstein's work, calls an "every-day life project that revolves around climate change." Song, *Climate Lyricism*, 93.
23. Emily Raboteau, "How Do We Bring More Urgency to the Climate Crisis?"
24. Raboteau, "This Is How We Live Now."
25. Raboteau, "This Is How We Live Now."
26. Raboteau, "This Is How We Live Now."
27. Raboteau, "This Is How We Live Now."
28. Rob Emmett, *Cultivating Environmental Justice: A Literary History of U.S. Garden Writing* (Amherst: University of Massachusetts Press, 2016), 195–96.

29. My understanding of form is inflected by Caroline Levine, who defines form as "an arrangement of elements—an ordering, patterning, or shaping." Levine, *Forms: Whole, Rhythm, Hierarchy, Network* (Princeton, NJ: Princeton University Press, 2015), 2.
30. Anna Lowenhaupt Tsing, *The Mushroom at the End of the World: On the Possibility of Life in Capitalist Ruins* (Princeton, NJ: Princeton University Press, 2015), 21.
31. Tsing, *The Mushroom at the End of the World*, 24.
32. Elaine Gan, "Timing Rice: An Inquiry into More-Than-Human Temporalities," *New Formations: A Journal of Culture/Theory/Politics* 92, no. 6 (2017): 90–91.
33. Nathan K. Hensley and Philip Steer, "Introduction: Ecological Formalism; or, Love Among the Ruins," in *Ecological Form: System and Aesthetics in the Age of Empire*, ed. Nathan K. Hensley and Philip Steer (New York: Fordham University Press, 2019), 5.
34. Mike Hulme, *Weathered: Cultures of Climate* (Los Angeles: Sage, 2017), xv.
35. Paul Fussell, *Poetic Meter and Poetic Form* (New York: Random House, 1965), 164.
36. Kenneth Burke, *Counter Statement* (Los Altos, CA: Hermes Publications, 1953), 130.
37. Ranu Mukherjee and Alicia Escott, "Shadowtime," *The Bureau of Linguistical Reality*, ed. Heidi Quante and Alicia Escott, 2015, bureauoflinguisticalreality.com/portfolio/shadowtime.
38. T. V. F. Brogan, quoted in Jonathan Culler, "Why Rhythm?," in *Critical Rhythm: The Poetics of a Literary Life Form*, ed. Ben Glaser and Jonathan Culler (New York, Fordham University Press, 2019), 27.
39. Kamau Brathwaite, "History of the Voice 1979/1981," in *Roots* (Ann Arbor: University of Michigan Press, 1993), 263–65.
40. Levine, *Forms*, 2.
41. Anil Agarwal and Sunita Narain, "Global Warming in an Unequal World" (New Delhi: Centre for Science and Environment, 1991).
42. Ursula Heise, *Sense of Place and Sense of Planet: The Environmental Imagination of the Global* (Oxford: Oxford University Press, 2008), 210.
43. Karen Thornber, *Ecoambiguity: Environmental Crises and East Asian Literatures* (Ann Arbor: University of Michigan Press, 2012), 435.
44. Jennifer Wenzel, *The Disposition of Nature: Environmental Crisis and World Literature* (New York: Fordham University Press, 2020), 8.
45. Elizabeth DeLoughrey, Jill Didur, and Anthony Carrigan, eds., *Global Ecologies and the Environmental Humanities: Postcolonial Approaches* (New York: Routledge, 2015), 2.
46. Wenzel, *The Disposition of Nature*, 89.
47. Raboteau, "This Is How We Live Now."
48. Heise, *Sense of Place and Sense of Planet*, 33.

49. Rob Nixon, *Slow Violence and the Environmentalism of the Poor* (Cambridge, MA: Harvard University Press, 2011), 13.
50. Northrop Frye, *The Anatomy of Criticism: Four Essays*, revised edition (Princeton, NJ: Princeton University Press, 2000), 104–5.
51. Frye, *The Anatomy of Criticism*, 103.
52. Frye, *The Anatomy of Criticism*, 101; Lawrence Buell, *The Environmental Imagination: Thoreau, Nature Writing, and the Formation of American Culture* (Cambridge, MA: Harvard University Press, 1995), 220.
53. Buell, *The Environmental Imagination*, 250, 239.
54. Tess Somervell, "The Seasons," in *Climate and Literature*, ed. Adeline Johns-Putra (Cambridge: Cambridge University Press, 2019), 53.
55. Tobias Menely, *Climate and the Making of Worlds: Towards a Geohistorical Poetics* (Chicago: University of Chicago Press, 2021), 112.
56. Anne-Lise François, "Fire, Water, Moon: Supplemental Seasons in a Time Without Season," in *Climate Realism: The Aesthetics of Weather and Atmosphere in the Anthropocene*, ed. Lynn Badia et al. (New York: Routledge, 2020), 47.
57. Mary Annaïse Heglar, "Climate Change Isn't the First Existential Threat," *Medium*, February 18, 2019, https://zora.medium.com/sorry-yall-but-climate-change-ain-t-the-first-existential-threat-b3c999267aa0.
58. Kyle Whyte, "Indigenous Climate Change Studies: Indigenizing Futures, Decolonizing the Anthropocene," *English Language Notes* 55, nos. 1–2 (2017): 154.
59. Kyle Powys Whyte, "Time as Kinship," in *The Cambridge Companion to the Environmental Humanities*, ed. Jeffrey Jerome Cohen and Stephanie Foote (Cambridge: Cambridge University Press, 2021), 40–49.
60. Lynn Keller, *Recomposing Ecopoetics: North American Poetry of the Self-Conscious Anthropocene* (Charlottesville: University of Virginia Press, 2018), 1.
61. Mbozi Haimbe, "Shelter," in *Disruption: New Short Fiction from Africa*, ed. Karina Szczurek, Jason Mykl Snyman, and Rachel Zadok (Short Story Day South Africa, 2021), 132.
62. Alexis Wright, *The Swan Book* (New York: Atria Books, 2016), 5.
63. Justin McCurry, "Japan's Haiku Poets Lost for Words as Climate Crisis Disrupts Seasons," *The Guardian*, November 13, 2023.
64. Callum Angus, *A Natural History of Transition* (Montreal: Metonymy Press, 2021), 33.
65. Evie Shockley, *Semiautomatic* (Middletown, CT: Wesleyan University Press, 2017), 5.
66. Callum Angus, "The Climate of Gender," *Catapult*, May 3, 2021.

1. PHENOLOGICAL WRITING AND THE COMPOSITE YEAR

1. Sara Elizabeth Jones to Aldo Leopold, January 7, 1946, box 1, folder 23, Aldo Leopold Papers, University of Wisconsin-Madison Archives.

1. PHENOLOGICAL WRITING AND THE COMPOSITE YEAR ◦❧ 243

2. Sara Elizabeth Jones to Aldo Leopold, January 18, 1946, box 1, folder 23, Aldo Leopold Papers, University of Wisconsin-Madison Archives.
3. Aldo Leopold and Sara Elizabeth Jones, "A Phenological Record for Sauk and Dane Counties, Wisconsin, 1935–1945," *Ecological Monographs* 17, no. 1 (1947): 83.
4. Michael Kammen, *A Time to Every Purpose: The Four Seasons in American Culture* (Chapel Hill: The University of North Carolina Press, 2004), 3.
5. A few of Jones's documents use the spelling Sarah or her nickname, Libby. Upon her marriage in 1948, Jones changed her last name to Frey.
6. Since scholarship surrounding Jones's role in the 1947 phenology study is frustratingly sparse and frequently inaccurate, I want to rectify a set of common errors. Jones was not a botany student: she obtained an MA in zoology from Smith College in 1943 and a PhD in zoology from the University of Wisconsin-Madison in 1947. During her doctoral studies, she took a course in wildlife ecology taught by Aldo Leopold, but her dissertation was advised by Dr. Arthur Hasler. By the time the phenology study was published, Jones was teaching zoology at Duke University. Mary Keck, "Obituary: Sarah Elizabeth Frey, 94," *The Herald-Times* (Bloomington, Indiana), November 10, 2013.
7. Sara J. Grossman, *Immeasurable Weather: Meteorological Data and Settler Colonialism From 1820 to Hurricane Sandy* (Durham, NC: Duke University Press, 2023).
8. The complete set of letters is now deposited in the University of Wisconsin-Madison Archives, and both environmental and literary history are indebted to Barbara Frey for her labor and extraordinary generosity.
9. Richard B. Primack, *Walden Warming: Climate Change Comes to Thoreau's Woods* (Chicago: University of Chicago Press, 2014), 49–50.
10. Elizabeth R. Ellwood et al., "Record-Breaking Early Flowering in the Eastern United States," *PLoS ONE* 8, no. 1 (2013): 2.
11. Henry David Thoreau, *Walden and Resistance to Civil Government*, 2nd edition, ed. William Rossi (New York: W.W. Norton, 1992), 61.
12. Henry David Thoreau, *The Writings of Henry D. Thoreau: Journal* (Princeton, NJ: Princeton University Press, 1984), 2:156.
13. Bradley Dean, Introduction to *Wild Fruits: Thoreau's Rediscovered Last Manuscript* (New York: W.W. Norton, 2000), ix–xvii.
14. Thoreau, *The Journal of Henry David Thoreau*, 9:158.
15. Henry David Thoreau, "Nature Notes, Charts and Tables: Autograph Manuscripts," 1851–60, Manuscript 610, Pierpont Morgan Library, New York.
16. Stephanie LeMenager, "Nineteenth-Century American Literature Without Nature? Rethinking Environmental Criticism," in *The Oxford Handbook of Nineteenth-Century American Literature*, ed. Russ Castronovo (New York: Oxford University Press, 2012), 396.
17. Thoreau, *The Journal of Henry David Thoreau*, 9:174.

18. H. Daniel Peck, *Thoreau's Morning Work: Memory and Perception in a Week on the Concord and Merrimack Rivers, the Journal, and Walden* (New Haven, CT: Yale University Press, 1994), 102.
19. Grossman, *Immeasurable Weather*, 15.
20. Thoreau, *The Writings of Henry D. Thoreau: Journal*, 8:245–46.
21. Robert D. Richardson Jr., "Thoreau's Broken Task," Introduction to *Faith in A Seed: The Dispersion of Seeds and Other Late Natural History Writings*, by Henry David Thoreau, ed. Bradley P. Dean (Washington, D.C.: Island Press, 1996), 5.
22. Kristen Case, "Phenology," in *Henry David Thoreau in Context*, ed. James S. Finley (Cambridge: Cambridge University Press, 2017), 266.
23. Dean, Introduction to *Wild Fruits*, xi.
24. Thoreau, *The Writings of Henry D. Thoreau: Journal*, 5:174.
25. Thoreau, *Walden and Resistance to Civil Government*, 11.
26. Daegan Miller, *This Radical Land: A Natural History of American Dissent* (Chicago: University of Chicago Press, 2018), 39.
27. Aldo Leopold, *A Sand County Almanac* (New York: Ballantine Books, 1966), 50.
28. Leopold, *A Sand County Almanac*, 47.
29. Leopold and Jones, "A Phenological Record for Sauk and Dane Counties, Wisconsin, 1935–1945," 101.
30. Joe Alexander to Aldo Leopold, August 7, 1945, box 8, folder 1, Aldo Leopold Papers, University of Wisconsin-Madison Archives.
31. I believe these notes were taken by Ethelyn Koehler, the wife of Arthur Koehler, Leopold's colleague at the Forest Products Laboratory.
32. Aldo Leopold to Sara Elizabeth Jones, October 9, 1946, Aldo Leopold Papers, University of Wisconsin-Madison Archives. The enclosed article was Stanley Edgar Hyman's "Henry Thoreau in Our Time," *Atlantic Monthly*, November 1946, 138.
33. Sara Elizabeth Jones to Aldo Leopold, September 29, 1946, box 8, folder 1, Aldo Leopold Papers, University of Wisconsin-Madison Archives.
34. Lawrence Buell, *The Environmental Imagination: Thoreau, Nature Writing, and the Formation of American Culture* (Cambridge, MA: Belknap Press, 1995), 485.
35. Thoreau, *The Writings of Henry D. Thoreau: Journal*, 4:4–5. For analyses of Thoreau's evolving sense of seasonality, see Ken Hiltner, "Ripeness: Thoreau's Critique of Technological Modernity," *Concord Saunterer* 12/13 (2004/2005): 330; and Peck, *Thoreau's Morning Work*, 92.
36. Laura Dassow Walls, *Seeing New Worlds: Henry David Thoreau and Nineteenth-Century Natural Science* (Madison: University of Wisconsin Press, 1995), 242.
37. Thoreau, *The Journal of Henry David Thoreau*, 8:298.
38. Thoreau, *The Writings of Henry D. Thoreau: Journal*, 6:83.
39. Thoreau, *The Journal of Henry David Thoreau*, 8:102–3.

1. PHENOLOGICAL WRITING AND THE COMPOSITE YEAR ᏻ 245

40. Thoreau, *Walden and Resistance to Civil Government*, 201.
41. Thoreau, *Walden and Resistance to Civil Government*, 200.
42. Nina L. Bradley et al., "Phenological Changes Reflect Climate Change in Wisconsin," *Proceedings of the National Academy of Sciences of the United States of America* 96, no. 17 (1999): 9701.
43. Leopold and Jones, "A Phenological Record for Sauk and Dane Counties, Wisconsin, 1935–1945," 83.
44. Thoreau, *Walden and Resistance to Civil Government*, 202.
45. Thoreau, *Walden and Resistance to Civil Government*, 201.
46. Primack, *Walden Warming*, 10.
47. Henry David Thoreau, *Walden: A Fluid-Text Edition*, Digital Thoreau, http://digitalthoreau.org/fluid-text-toc, Versions A and D, paragraph 4.
48. Tristram Wolff, *Against the Uprooted Word: Giving Language Time in Transatlantic Romanticism* (Stanford, CA: Stanford University Press, 2022), 196.
49. J. Lyndon Shanley, *The Making of Walden* (Chicago: University of Chicago Press, 1957), 66–67.
50. Robert Sattelmeyer, "The Remaking of Walden," in *Walden and Resistance to Civil Government*, 2nd ed., ed. William Rossi (New York: W.W. Norton, 1992), 434.
51. Buell, *The Environmental Imagination*, 239.
52. Clinton Simpson to Aldo Leopold, April 29, 1946, box 5, folder 1, Aldo Leopold Papers, University of Wisconsin-Madison Archives.
53. Helen Clapesattle to Virginia Kiesel, January 31, 1946, box 5, folder 1, Aldo Leopold Papers, University of Wisconsin-Madison Archives.
54. Leopold, *A Sand County Almanac*, xviii.
55. Buell, *The Environmental Imagination*, 232.
56. Aldo Leopold to William Sloane, December 19, 1947, box 5, folder 1, Aldo Leopold Papers, University of Wisconsin-Madison Archives.
57. Dennis Ribbens, "The Making of a Sand County Almanac," in *Companion to A Sand County Almanac: Interpretive and Critical Essays*, ed. J. Baird Callicott (Madison: University of Wisconsin Press, 1987), 101.
58. Aldo Leopold to Charlie Schwartz, September 17, 1947, box 5, folder 1, Aldo Leopold Papers, University of Wisconsin-Madison Archives.
59. Leopold, *A Sand County Almanac*, 3. Leopold shifted the phenological study's phrase "there comes a thawy night" to "a night of thaw" as he revised this paragraph for literary publication.
60. Scholarship on Thoreau's study of natural phenomena is undergoing a renaissance. See especially Walls, *Seeing New Worlds*; and Kristin Case, "Thoreau's Radical Empiricism: The Calendar, Pragmatism, and Science," in *Thoreauvian Modernities: Transatlantic Conversations on an American Icon*, ed. François Specq et al. (Athens: University of Georgia Press, 2013), 187–99. To my knowledge, my article on Jones and Leopold's phenological study was the first consideration of Leopold's phenology within literary studies.

See Sarah Dimick, "Disordered Environmental Time: Phenology, Climate Change, and Seasonal Form in the Work of Henry David Thoreau and Aldo Leopold," *ISLE* 25, no. 4 (2018): 700–21.
61. Caroline Levine, *Forms: Whole, Rhythm, Hierarchy, Network* (Princeton, NJ: Princeton University Press, 2015), 3.
62. Tobias Menely, "'The Present Obfuscation': Cowper's Task and the Time of Climate Change," *PMLA* 127, no. 3 (May 2012): 479.
63. Thoreau, *The Journal of Henry David Thoreau*, 10:127.
64. Leopold and Jones, "A Phenological Record for Sauk and Dane Counties, Wisconsin, 1935–1945," 83.
65. Cleanth Brooks, "The Formalist Critics," *The Kenyon Review* 13, no. 1 (1951): 72.
66. Kenneth Burke, *Counter Statement* (Los Altos, CA: Hermes Publications, 1953), 124.
67. Burke, *Counter Statement*, 130.
68. Paul Fussell, *Poetic Meter and Poetic Form* (New York: Random House, 1965), 164.
69. Lauren Berlant, *Cruel Optimism* (Durham, NC: Duke University Press, 2011), 6.
70. Heather Houser, *Ecosickness in Contemporary U.S. Fiction: Environment and Affect* (New York: Columbia University Press, 2014), 38.
71. Thoreau, *Walden and Resistance to Civil Government*, 169.
72. Thoreau, *The Writings of Henry D. Thoreau: Journal*, 8:209.
73. Thoreau, *The Writings of Henry D. Thoreau: Journal*, 4:96. William Miller, a nineteenth-century Baptist minister, believed that the Book of Daniel contained textual evidence that the end of the world was near.
74. Thoreau, *The Writings of Henry D. Thoreau: Journal*, 4:450.
75. Thoreau, *The Writings of Henry D. Thoreau: Journal*, 5:343.
76. Robert M. Thorson, *Walden's Shore: Henry David Thoreau and Nineteenth-Century Science* (Cambridge, MA: Harvard University Press, 2014), 33.
77. Henry David Thoreau, "Extracts, Mostly Upon Natural History. A Commonplace Book." 1830–1862. Henry W. and Albert A. Berg Collection of English and American Literature, The New York Public Library.
78. Thoreau, *The Writings of Henry D. Thoreau: Journal*, 3:252.
79. Leopold and Jones, "A Phenological Record for Sauk and Dane Counties, Wisconsin, 1935–1945," 121.
80. Leopold and Jones, "A Phenological Record for Sauk and Dane Counties, Wisconsin, 1935–1945," 121.
81. Aldo Leopold to Sara Elizabeth Jones, April 8, 1948, box 1, folder 23, Aldo Leopold Papers, University of Wisconsin-Madison Archives.
82. Leopold, *A Sand County Almanac*, 10.
83. Leopold and Jones, "A Phenological Record for Sauk and Dane Counties, Wisconsin, 1935–1945," 83.

1. PHENOLOGICAL WRITING AND THE COMPOSITE YEAR ❧ 247

84. J. Baird Callicott, "'The Arboretum and the University:' The Speech and the Essay," *Transactions of the Wisconsin Academy of Sciences, Arts and Letters* 87 (1999): 18.
85. Naomi Oreskes, "The Scientific Consensus on Climate Change: How Do We Know We're Not Wrong?" in *Climate Change: What It Means for Us, Our Children, and Our Grandchildren*, second edition, ed. Joseph F. C. DiMento and Pamela Doughman (Boston: MIT Press, 2014), 138; Dipesh Chakrabarty, "The Climate of History: Four Theses," *Critical Inquiry* 35 (2009): 206.
86. Gary Paul Nabhan, "Learning the Language of Fields and Forests," foreword to Henry David Thoreau, *Faith in a Seed*, xvi.
87. Thoreau, *The Journal of Henry David Thoreau*, 13:279.
88. Leopold and Jones, "A Phenological Record for Sauk and Dane Counties, Wisconsin, 1935–1945," 84.
89. Leopold and Jones, "A Phenological Record for Sauk and Dane Counties, Wisconsin, 1935–1945," 114.
90. "Climate," Appendix I-Glossary, Working Group 1: The Scientific Basis, ed. A. P. M. Baede, *Intergovernmental Panel on Climate Change*.
91. Mike Hulme, "Climate," *Environmental Humanities* 6 (2015): 177.
92. The composite year is by no means a recent literary device—James Thomson's eighteenth-century poem cycle *The Seasons* comes immediately to mind, preceded by Edmund Spenser's *The Shepheardes Calendar*, a poetic almanac. In nonfiction works that condense and compress multiple years into one—including Rachel Carson's *Under the Sea Wind* and Linda LeGarde Grover's *Onigamiising: Seasons of an Ojibwe Year*—the beats and pulses of an environment are seen as exemplary. They function as an annual template formed through narratological averaging. Other texts—including Edward Abbey's *Desert Solitaire*, John Muir's *My First Summer in the Sierra*, and J. A. Baker's *The Hill of Summer*—perform a related move, condensing multiple iterations of a season into the narrative space of a single season.
93. Thoreau, *Walden and Resistance to Civil Government*, 212–13.
94. Buell, *The Environmental Imagination*, 281.
95. Elizabeth M. Wolkovich et al., "Temporal Ecology in the Anthropocene," *Ecology Letters* 17 (2014): 1356.
96. Wolkovich et al., "Temporal Ecology in the Anthropocene," 1356.
97. I owe Annette Damayanti Lienau thanks for this insight. She notes that the modern Arabic for climate change is *taghiir al-munakh*.
98. Alison A. Chapman, "Marking Time: Astrology, Almanacs, and English Protestantism," *Renaissance Quarterly* 60 (2007); 1270.
99. Leopold, *A Sand County Almanac*, 49.
100. Sarah D. Wright and Nina Leopold Bradley, "Thinking Like a Flower: Phenology and Climate Change at the Leopold Shack," in *The Vanishing Present: Wisconsin's Changing Lands, Waters, and Wildlife*, ed. Donald M. Waller and Thomas P. Rooney (Chicago: University of Chicago Press, 2008), 46.

101. Alastair Fowler, "The Life and Death of Literary Forms," *New Literary History* 2, no. 2 (1971): 204.
102. Fussell, *Poetic Meter and Poetic Form*, 33.
103. Fussell, *Poetic Meter and Poetic Form*, 17.
104. Primack, *Walden Warming*, 212.
105. Primack, *Walden Warming*, 39.
106. Robert Macfarlane, "The Burning Question," *The Guardian*, September 23, 2005.
107. Macfarlane, "The Burning Question."
108. Primack, *Walden Warming*, ix.
109. John R. Harris, *Returning North with the Spring* (Gainesville: University Press of Florida, 2016), 4.
110. Amy Seidl, *Early Spring: An Ecologist and Her Children Wake to a Warming World* (Boston: Beacon, 2009), 18–19.
111. Hayden V. White, *The Content of the Form: Narrative Discourse and Historical Representation* (Baltimore, MD: Johns Hopkins University Press, 1987), 5.
112. Wai Chee Dimock, *Weak Planet: Literature and Assisted Survival* (Chicago: University of Chicago Press, 2020), 48.
113. Walls, *Seeing New Worlds*, 182.
114. White, *The Content of the Form*, 23, 14.
115. White, *The Content of the Form*, 24.

2. REPEAT PHOTOGRAPHY DURING THE GREAT ACCELERATION

1. As Seely notes, this photograph within a photograph is an homage to Kenneth Josephson's conceptual photography.
2. Calia E. Kucheravy et al., "Extreme Climate Event Promotes Phenological Mismatch Between Sexes in Hibernating Ground Squirrels," *Scientific Reports* 11 (2021).
3. Livia Albeck-Ripka and Brad Plumer, "5 Plants and Animals Utterly Confused by Climate Change," *New York Times*, April 4, 2018.
4. Christina Seely, "Markers of Time/DEFLUO Animals, Vulpes Lagopus," https://www.christinaseely.com/defluo-animalis.
5. L. Scott Mills et al., "Camouflage Mismatch in Seasonal Coat Color Due to Decreased Snow Duration," *PNAS* 110, no. 18 (2013): 7360–65.
6. Seely, "Markers of Time/DEFLUO Animals, Vulpes Lagopus."
7. Jen Rose Smith, *Icy Matters: Race, Indigeneity, and Coloniality in Ice-Geographies* (forthcoming).
8. The phrase "climate culture industry"—referring to the wave of books, photographs, films, and music that address anthropogenic climate change—is one that I encountered through Daegan Miller's work. See Daegan Miller,

2. PHOTOGRAPHY DURING THE GREAT ACCELERATION ◈ 249

Twitter post, November 28, 2022, 8:15 a.m., https://twitter.com/Daegan Miller/status/1597217714942095360.
9. Lisa Bloom, *Climate Change and the New Polar Aesthetics: Artists Reimagine the Arctic and Antarctic* (Durham, NC: Duke University Press, 2022), 7.
10. Jen Rose Smith pointed out these proportions to me. I am grateful for her careful attention to this book, here and throughout.
11. Elizabeth Kolbert, *Field Notes from a Catastrophe: Man, Nature, and Climate Change* (New York: Bloomsbury, 2006), 49–50.
12. Nancy Campbell, *The Library of Ice: Readings from a Cold Climate* (New York: Scribner, 2018), 26.
13. Anne McClintock, "Monster: A Fugue in Fire and Ice," *E-Flux Architecture*, June 2020.
14. Marcia Bjornerud, *Timefulness: How Thinking Like a Geologist Can Help Save the World* (Princeton, NJ: Princeton University Press, 2018), 141, 16–17.
15. Kathryn Yusoff, *A Billion Black Anthropocenes or None* (Minneapolis: University of Minnesota Press, 2018), xiii.
16. Bathsheba Demuth, *Floating Coast: An Environmental History of the Bering Strait* (New York: W.W. Norton, 2019), 199.
17. Jen Rose Smith, "Cryogenics," *Edge Effects*, February 6, 2020, https://edgeeffects.net/cryogenics/.
18. Stephanie Krzywonos, "Coyolxauhqui: Time, Mexihcah, Antarctica," *Ofrenda Magazine*, 9.
19. Dani Inkpen, *Capturing Glaciers: A History of Repeat Photography and Global Warming* (Seattle: University of Washington Press, 2023), 162.
20. Robert H. Webb et al., "Introduction: A Brief History of Repeat Photography," in *Repeat Photography: Methods and Applications in the Natural Sciences*, ed. Robert H. Webb et al. (Washington, D.C.: Island Press, 2010), 4.
21. Crucial predecessors to Finsterwalder's work include photographic studies conducted by Charles and Francis Darwin during their research for *The Power of Movement in Plants* and Eadweard Muybridge's chronophotography projects. See Oliver Gaycken, "Early Cinema and Evolution," in *Evolution and Victorian Culture*, ed. Bernard Lightman and Bennett Zon (Cambridge: Cambridge University Press, 2014), 94–120; and Rebecca Solnit, *River of Shadows: Eadweard Muybridge and the Technological Wild West* (New York: Penguin Books, 2003).
22. Tim B. Brown et al., "Using Phenocams to Monitor Our Changing Earth: Toward a Global Phenocam Network," *Frontiers in Ecology and the Environment* 14, no. 2 (2016): 85.
23. Dawna L. Cerney, "The Use of Repeat Photography in Geomorphic Studies: An Evolving Approach to Understanding Landscape Change," *Geography Compass* 4, no. 9 (2010): 1341.
24. Melissa Miles, "Rephotography and the Era of Witness," *Photographies* 9, no. 1 (2016): 54.

25. Christopher Andrews et al., "Assessment of Biological and Environmental Phenology at a Landscape Level from 30 Years of Fixed-Date Repeat Photography in Northern Sweden," *Ambio* 40, no. 6 (2011): 607.
26. Elaine Gan, "Diagrams: Making Multispecies Temporalities Visible," in *Experimenting with Ethnography: A Companion to Analysis*, ed. Andrea Ballestero and Brit Ross Winthereik (Durham, NC: Duke University Press, 2021), 108–9.
27. Gary McLeod, "Rephotograph (v)," *Philosophy of Photography* 10, no. 1 (2019): 89.
28. Isabelle Gapp, "Galvanizing Glaciology: Thoughts on An Ecocritical Art History," *Environmental History Now*, January 20, 2022.
29. Allison N. Curley et al., "Glacier Changes Over the Past 144 Years at Alexandra Fiord, Ellesmere Island, Canada," *Journal of Glaciology* 67, no. 262 (2021): 511.
30. Rodney Garrard and Mark Carey, "Beyond Images of Melting Ice: Hidden Histories of People, Place, and Time in Repeat Photography of Glaciers," in *Before and After Photography: Histories and Contexts*, ed. Jordan Bear and Kate Palmer Albers (London: Bloomsbury, 2017), 103.
31. Isla H. Myers-Smith et al., "Expansion of Canopy-Forming Willows Over the Twentieth Century on Herschel Island, Yukon Territory, Canada," *Ambio* 40 (2011): 610–23.
32. Melody Jue, *Wild Blue Media: Thinking Through Seawater* (Durham, NC: Duke University Press, 2020), 21.
33. Ken Tape et al., "The Evidence for Shrub Expansion in Northern Alaska and the Pan-Arctic," *Global Change Biology* 12 (2006): 688.
34. Tape et al., "The Evidence for Shrub Expansion," 688.
35. Cerney, "The Use of Repeat Photography in Geomorphic Studies," 1352. For an analysis of the Department of Defense, see Neta C. Crawford, "Pentagon Fuel Use, Climate Change, and the Costs of War," Watson Institute, Brown University, November 13, 2019, https://watson.brown.edu/costsofwar/papers/ClimateChangeandCostofWar.
36. Sudeep Chandra et al., "Phenocam Observed Flowering Anomaly of *Rhododendron Arboreum* Sm. in Himalaya: A Climate Change Impact Perspective," *Environmental Monitoring and Assessment* 194, no. 877 (2022): 877.
37. Heather Houser, *Infowhelm: Environmental Art and Media in an Age of Data* (New York: Columbia University Press, 2020), 177.
38. Elizabeth Rush, *Rising: Dispatches from the New American Shore* (Minneapolis: Milkweed Editions, 2018), 75–76.
39. Rush, *Rising*, 75.
40. Allison Carruth and Robert P. Marzec, "Environmental Visualization in the Anthropocene: Technologies, Aesthetics, Ethics," *Public Culture* 26, no. 2 (2014): 205–7.

2. PHOTOGRAPHY DURING THE GREAT ACCELERATION ☙ 251

41. Mark Carey, "The History of Ice: How Glaciers Became an Endangered Species," *Environmental History* 12, no. 3 (2007): 498.
42. Quoted in Gaycken, "Early Cinema and Evolution," 108.
43. Quoted in Gaycken, "Early Cinema and Evolution," 108.
44. Jole Shackelford, "Wilhelm Pfeffer and the Roots of Twentieth-Century Biological Rhythms Research," *Transactions of the American Philosophical Society* 103, no. 2 (2013): 12.
45. Gaycken, "Early Cinema and Evolution," 56–57.
46. Arthur C. Pillsbury, *Picturing Miracles of Plant and Animal Life* (Philadelphia: J.B. Lippincott, 1937), 21–22.
47. Pillsbury, *Picturing Miracles of Plant and Animal Life*, 22.
48. Pillsbury, *Picturing Miracles of Plant and Animal Life*, 25.
49. Pillsbury, *Picturing Miracles of Plant and Animal Life*, 26.
50. Dave Denison, "Soul on Ice," *Boston College Magazine* (Summer 2013).
51. Extreme Ice Survey, "IL-05 Sólheimajökull," *Vimeo*, May 26, 2016.
52. John R. McNeill and Peter Engelke, *The Great Acceleration: An Environmental History of the Anthropocene Since 1945* (Cambridge, MA: Harvard University Press, 2014), 65–66.
53. McNeill and Engelke, *The Great Acceleration*, 69.
54. Mika Rantanen et al., "The Arctic Has Warmed Nearly Four Times Faster Than the Globe Since 1970," *Communications Earth & Environment* 3, no. 1 (2022): 6.
55. Rantanen et al., "The Arctic Has Warmed Nearly Four Times Faster Than the Globe Since 1970," 5.
56. See Jimena Canales, "Clock/Lived," in *Time: A Vocabulary of the Present* (New York NYU Press, 2016), 124.
57. David Lavery, "Poetry as Time-Lapse Photography," *Essays in Arts and Science* 17, no. 1 (1988): 7.
58. Damian Carrington, "2016 Will Be the Hottest Year on Record, UN Says," *The Guardian*, November 14, 2016.
59. Jennifer Chu, " 'Storm of the Century?' Try 'Storm of the Decade,' " *MIT News: On Campus and Around the World*, February 13, 2012.
60. Charles M. Tung, "Time Machines and Timelapse Aesthetics in Anthropocenic Modernism," in *Timescales: Thinking Across Ecological Temporalities*, ed. Bethany Wiggin et al. (Minneapolis: University of Minnesota Press, 2020), 84.
61. Allan Cameron and Richard Misek, "Time Lapse and the Projected Body," *Moving Image Review and Art Journal* 3, no. 1 (2014): 39–40.
62. James Card, *Seductive Cinema: The Art of Silent Film* (New York: Knopf, 1994), 54.
63. Card, *Seductive Cinema*, 54.
64. Alison L. Beamish et al., "Phenology and Vegetation Change Measurements from True Colour Digital Photography in High Arctic Tundra," *Arctic Science* 2 (2016): 38.

65. Beamish et al., "Phenology and Vegetation Change Measurements," 45.
66. Robert A. E. Fosbury and Glen Jeffrey, "Reindeer Eyes Seasonally Adapt to Ozone-Blue Arctic Twilight by Tuning a Photonic Tapetum Lucidum," *Proceedings of the Royal Society B* 289, no. 1977 (2022).
67. Katherine J. Wu, "Twice A Year, Reindeer Eyes Pull Off a Wonderful Magic Trick," *The Atlantic*, June 28, 2022.
68. Mary Caswell Stoddard, "Inside the Colorful World of Birds and Their Eggs," YouTube, May 5, 2022, https://www.youtube.com/watch?v=KuPqaDEiw5g&t=1s.
69. Jue, *Wild Blue Media*, 10.
70. Stoddard, "Inside the Colorful World of Birds and Their Eggs."
71. Stoddard, "Inside the Colorful World of Birds and Their Eggs."
72. Allison Carruth, "The Digital Cloud and the Micropolitics of Energy," *Public Culture* 26, no. 2 (2014): 352.
73. Heather Houser, "Human/Planetary," in *Time: A Vocabulary of the Present*, ed. Joel Burgess and Amy J. Elias (New York: NYU Press, 2020), 147–48.
74. Stoddard, "Inside the Colorful World of Birds and Their Eggs."
75. Naomi Klein, *On Fire: The (Burning) Case for a Green New Deal* (New York: Simon & Schuster, 2019), 120–21.
76. Jean-Robert Wells et al., "Carbon Footprint Assessment of a Paperback Book: Can Planned Integration of Deinked Market Pulp Be Detrimental to Climate?," *Journal of Industrial Ecology* 16, no. 2 (2012): 212–22. For an assessment of the climate impact of a particular academic book, see Stephanie LeMenager, *Living Oil: Petroleum Culture in the American Century* (Oxford: Oxford University Press, 2014), 197–209.

3. URBAN PHENOLOGY AND MONSOON REALISM

1. Abundant thanks to S. Palayam and Nityanand Jayaraman for allowing me to join one of their predawn conversations. I owe additional gratitude to Jayaraman for carefully translating Palayam's Tamil into English. As Jayaraman notes, Palayam speaks vadakathu kadalmozhi, a Tamil dialect used in Chennai's coastal fishing enclaves.
2. Nityanand Jayaraman and S. Palayam, "Reading Trash, Telling Seasons," Science of the Seas, *The Wire*, March 21, 2022, https://science.thewire.in/science-of-the-seas/.
3. Jayaraman and Palayam, "Reading Trash, Telling Seasons."
4. A. K. Ramanujan, *The Interior Landscape: Classical Tamil Love Poems* (New York: New York Review of Books, 1967), 49.
5. Nityanand Jayaraman and S. Palayam, "Hunting Anchovies in a Night Sea," Science of the Seas, *The Wire*, October 14, 2021, https://science.thewire.in/science-of-the-seas/.

3. URBAN PHENOLOGY AND MONSOON REALISM ○✃ 253

6. Nityanand Jayaraman and S. Palayam, "Sea Changed; Therefore Climate Change," Science of the Seas, *The Wire*, January 30, 2023, https://science.thewire.in/science-of-the-seas/.
7. *Seaspeaker*, dir. Parvathi Nayar. Film, commissioned by Dakshina Chitra for the exhibition "The Living Ocean." 2024.
8. *Seaspeaker*, dir. Parvathi Nayar.
9. Nityanand Jayaraman and S. Palayam, "Saved by the Wind: Why Chennai's Air May Be Cleaner This Bhogi," Science of the Seas, *The Wire*, December 1, 2022, https://science.thewire.in/science-of-the-seas/.
10. Sekhar Raghavan in discussion with the author, September 24, 2022.
11. Nityanand Jayaraman, "Welcome to 'Science of the Seas,'" *The Wire*, https://science.thewire.in/science-of-the-seas/.
12. Jayaraman, "Welcome to 'Science of the Seas.'"
13. Jayaraman and Palayam, "Sea Changed; Therefore Climate Change."
14. Jayaraman and Palayam, "Sea Changed; Therefore Climate Change."
15. Somini Sengupta, "Life in a City Without Water: Anxious, Exhausting and Sweaty," *New York Times*, July 11, 2019.
16. Lakshmi Holmström, introduction to *Water*, viii.
17. Sunil Amrith, *Unruly Waters: How Rains, Rivers, Coasts, and Seas Have Shaped Asia's History* (New York: Basic Books, 2018), 230.
18. Ashokamitran, *Water*, trans. Lakshmi Holmström (Oxford: Heinemann, 1993), 20. I refer to the city as Chennai when referencing contemporary events and as Madras when referencing Ashokamitran's novella, which is set in 1969.
19. Ashokamitran, *Water*, 17.
20. Ashokamitran, *Water*, 1.
21. Ramachandra Guha and Joan Martínez Alier, *Varieties of Environmentalism: Essays North and South* (London: Earthscan, 1997), xxi.
22. Karen Coelho, "Urban Waterlines: Socio-Natural Productions of Indifference in an Indian City," *International Journal of Urban and Regional Research* 46, no. 2 (2022): 161.
23. Ashokamitran, *Water*, 20–21.
24. Naomi Klein, *On Fire: The (Burning) Case for a Green New Deal* (New York: Simon & Schuster, 2019), 124.
25. Ashokamitran, *Water*, 17.
26. Gérard Genette, "Time and Narrative in *A La Recherche Du Temps Perdu*," in *Aspects of Narrative: Selected Papers from the English Institute*, ed. J. Hillis Miller (New York: Columbia University Press, 1971), 93–118.
27. Ashokamitran, *Water*, 76.
28. Ashokamitran, *Water*, 76.
29. Ashokamitran, *Water*, 76.
30. V. G. Prasad Rao, "Drought Affects Tamil Nadu: Food Crisis Feared," *Times of India*, March 20, 1969.

31. "Ground Water Sources Dry Up In Tamil Nadu," *Times of India*, April 4, 1969.
32. See Jamie Linton and Jessica Budds, "The Hydrosocial Cycle: Defining and Mobilizing a Relational-Dialectical Approach to Water," *Geoforum* 57 (2014): 170–80.
33. Ravishankar Thyagarajan, Ashokamitran's other son, is inclined to place the story one neighborhood to the east, in T. Nagar.
34. Ashokamitran, *Water*, 31.
35. Coelho, "Urban Waterlines," 176.
36. Coelho, "Urban Waterlines," 177.
37. Like Walden Pond for Thoreau, the tail-end is both the central image of Ashokamitran's text and a phenological device.
38. Pamila Gupta, "Ways of Seeing Wetness," *Wasafiri* 36, no. 2 (2021): 40.
39. Ashokamitran, *Water*, 2.
40. Linton and Budds, "The Hydrosocial Cycle," 172–73.
41. Ramanujan, *The Interior Landscape*, 26.
42. Sunil Amrith, "When the Monsoon Goes Away," *Aeon*, March 4, 2019, https://aeon.co/essays/the-life-and-possible-death-of-the-great-asian-monsoon.
43. Ramanujan, *The Interior Landscape*, 90–101.
44. Ramanujan, *The Interior Landscape*, 101.
45. Ramanujan, *The Interior Landscape*, 49.
46. Ramanujan, *The Interior Landscape*, 48.
47. Ramanujan, *The Interior Landscape*, 101.
48. Geetha Ramaswami and Suhel Quader, "The Case of the Confusing Kanikonna Trees," *The Wire*, June 26, 2018, https://science.thewire.in/environment/the-case-of-the-confusing-kanikonna-trees/.
49. Ramaswami and Quader, "The Case of the Confusing Kanikonna Trees."
50. Deepa Soman. "Vishu Is Almost Here but Where Do We Get the Konna for the Kani?," *Times of India*, April 12, 2017, https://timesofindia.indiatimes.com/city/kochi/vishu-is-almost-here-but-where-do-we-get-the-konna-for-the-kani/articleshow/58127647.cms.
51. Deepa Soman, "Vishu Is Almost Here But Where Do We Get the Konna for the Kani?"
52. Ashokamitran, "Landscape in Literature: A Tamil Perception," *Literary Criterion* 18, no. 4 (1983): 25.
53. M. Vinothkumar and V. Peruvalluthi, "Sere Life in Ashokamitran's Novel 'Water:' An Eco-Critical Study," *Smart Moves Journal IJELLH* 8, no. 1 (2020): 3.
54. Ashokamitran, *Water*, 31.
55. Lakshmi Holmström, "The Modern Tamil Novel: Changing Identities and Transformations," in *Indian Literature and the World: Multilingualism, Translation, and the Public Sphere*, ed. Rosella Ciocca and Neelam Srivastava (London: Palgrave Macmillan, 2017), 138.
56. Ashokamitran, *Water*, 20.

57. Ashokamitran, *Water*, 95.
58. Ashokamitran, *Water*, 25.
59. Anjana Shekhar, "Revisiting 'Thanneer,' Ashokamitran's Insightful Tamil Novel on Water Scarcity," *The News Minute*, August 11, 2019, https://www.thenewsminute.com/article/revisiting-thanneer-ashokamitrans-insightful-tamil-novel-water-scarcity-107043.
60. A. R. Venkatachalapathy, *Tamil Characters: Personalities, Politics, Culture* (New Delhi: Pan Macmillan India, 2018), 172–73.
61. Chittaroopa Palit, "Monsoon Risings: Mega-Dam Resistance in the Narmada Valley," *New Left Review* 21 (2003), https://newleftreview.org/issues/ii21/articles/chittaroopa-palit-monsoon-risings.
62. Khushwant Singh, "The Indian Monsoon in Literature," in *Monsoons*, ed. Jay S. Fein and Pamela L. Stephens (New York: John Wiley & Sons, 1987), 35.
63. Amrith, *Unruly Waters*, 22.
64. Singh, "The Indian Monsoon in Literature," 38.
65. Gupta, "Ways of Seeing Wetness," 37, 41.
66. Singh, "The Indian Monsoon in Literature," 37.
67. Deepti Singh, "Tug of War on Rainfall Changes," *Nature Climate Change* 6 (2016): 22.
68. Stephen Smith, "India: Delivering Water by Hand," *American Public Media Reports*, May 12, 2016, https://www.apmreports.org/episode/2016/05/22/india-carrying-water-by-hand.
69. Beth Cullen, "Fieldwork Encounters with Monsoon Time," in *Monsoon as Method: Assembling Monsoonal Multiplicities*, ed. Lindsay Bremner (New York: Actar Publishing, 2022), 216–17.
70. Cullen, "Fieldwork Encounters with Monsoon Time," 213.
71. Khushwant Singh, "For Three Years the Great Rains Failed," *New York Times*, August 26, 1973.
72. Amitav Ghosh, *The Great Derangement: Climate Change and the Unthinkable* (Chicago: University of Chicago Press, 2016), 23, 17. While Ghosh uses the terms "serious fiction" or "literary fiction," I use the term "realist fiction" since it seems to more aptly describe the texts that Ghosh engages.
73. Ghosh, *The Great Derangement*, 24.
74. Roland Barthes, "An Introduction to the Structural Analysis of Narrative," trans. Lionel Duisit, *New Literary History* 6, no. 2 (1975): 247–48.
75. Barthes, "An Introduction to the Structural Analysis of Narrative," 247.
76. Frederic Jameson. *The Antimonies of Realism* (New York: Verso, 2013), 109.
77. Franco Moretti, "Serious Century," in *The Novel: Volume 1, History, Geography, and Culture* (Princeton, NJ: Princeton University Press, 2006), 381. I choose not to cite Moretti by name in the body of this chapter in light of the multiple accusations of sexual assault that blight his scholarly legacy.
78. Ghosh, *The Great Derangement*, 7.

79. Ghosh, *The Great Derangement*, 9.
80. Prema Nandakumar, review of *Water*, by Ashokamitran, translated by Lakshmi Holmström, *World Literature Today* 68, no. 3 (1994): 635.
81. Ashokamitran, "The Pre-Occupations in Tamil Short Story Today," *Indian Literature* 37, no. 3 (1994): 182.
82. Aravind Adiga, "The Boss Will See You Now," *Outlook* (February 2022), https://www.outlookindia.com/magazine/story/the-boss-will-see-you-now/285083; Venkatachalapathy, *Tamil Characters*, 171.
83. Lakshmi Holmström, introduction to *Water*, viii.
84. Holmström, "The Modern Tamil Novel," 138.
85. Holmström, Introduction to *Water*, viii.
86. Ashokamitran, *My Years with Boss: At Gemini Studios* (New Delhi: Orient Longman, 2002), 20.
87. Ashokamitran, *My Years with Boss*, 1–2. R. K. Narayan's brother worked as a film editor at Gemini Studios.
88. Anand Pandian, *Reel World: An Anthropology of Creation* (Durham, NC: Duke University Press, 2015), 212.
89. Ashokamitran, *Water*, 53–54.
90. Holmström, "The Modern Tamil Novel," 138.
91. Ashokamitran, *Water*, 41.
92. In lieu of a citation for his time and expertise, M. Ravi requested that I include his contact information in this book. If you require transportation within or beyond the borders of Chennai, he can be reached at: +91 9444888540. He reassures me that his phone number will not change.
93. "Mahindra Gives $10M for Humanities Center," *Harvard Gazette*, October 4, 2010.
94. Colleen Walsh, "Gift of Opportunity," *Harvard Gazette*, April 26, 2011; Arundhati Roy, *Capitalism: A Ghost Story* (Chicago: Haymarket Books, 2014), 17.
95. Padmapriya Baskaran, "Connected by Water for Life," *Madras Musings* 31, no. 13 (2021).
96. Baskaran, "Connected by Water for Life."
97. Corey Byrnes, *Fixing Landscape: A Techno-Poetic History of China's Three Gorges* (New York: Columbia University Press, 2019), 5.
98. Victoria Saramago, *Fictional Environments: Mimesis, Deforestation, and Development in Latin America* (Evanston, IL: Northwestern University Press, 2021), 8.
99. Kevin Nguyen, "Fires in NSW Partly Caused by Delayed Monsoons in India, Experts Say," *ABC News*, November 8, 2019.

4. CLIMATE FICTION AND THE UNPRECEDENTED

1. Alexis Wright, "We All Smell the Smoke, We All Feel the Heat. This Environmental Catastrophe Is Global," *The Guardian*, May 17, 2019.

4. CLIMATE FICTION AND THE UNPRECEDENTED ⚘ 257

2. Alexis Wright, *The Swan Book* (New York: Atria Books, 2016), 298.
3. Wright, *The Swan Book*, 297.
4. See Martín Premoli, "Global Anthropocene Fiction and the Politics of Climate Disaster," PhD diss. (University of Pennsylvania, 2020); Ben Holgate, "Unsettling Narratives: Re-Evaluating Magical Realism as Postcolonial Discourse Through Alexis Wright's *Carpentaria* and *The Swan Book*," *Journal of Postcolonial Writing* 51, no. 6 (2015); Laura Singeot, "The Swamp and Desert Tropes in Post-Apocalyptic Australian Indigenous Fiction: *The Swan Book* (2013) by Alexis Wright and *Terra Nullius* (2018) by Claire Coleman," *Commonwealth Essays and Studies* 43, no. 2 (2021).
5. Emmett Stinson and Beth Driscoll, "Difficult Literature on Goodreads: Reading Alexis Wright's *The Swan Book*," *Textual Practice* 36, no. 1 (2022): 94–95.
6. Wright, *The Swan Book*, 5.
7. Frank Krause, "Seasons as Rhythms on the Kemi River in Finnish Lapland," *Ethnos* 78, no. 1 (2013): 26–30.
8. Alexis Wright, in conversation with the author, May 6, 2021.
9. Deborah Rose, "Rhythms, Patterns, Connectivities: Indigenous Concepts of Seasons and Change," in *A Change in the Weather: Climate and Culture in Australia*, ed. Tim Sherratt et al. (Canberra: National Museum of Australia Press, 2005), 40.
10. Wright, "We All Smell the Smoke."
11. Calla Wahlquist, "Australian Bushfires: The Story So Far in Each State," *The Guardian*, December 23, 2019.
12. Matthias M. Boer et al., "Unprecedented Burn Area of Australian Mega Forest Fires," *Nature Climate Change* 10 (2020): 171–72.
13. Kyle Whyte, "Against Crisis Epistemology," in *Routledge Handbook of Critical Indigenous Studies*, ed. Brendan Hokowhitu (New York: Routledge, 2020): 55.
14. Kyle Powys Whyte, "Time as Kinship," in *The Cambridge Companion to the Environmental Humanities*, ed. Jeffrey Cohen and Stephanie Foote (Cambridge: Cambridge University Press, 2021), 39.
15. Kyle Powys Whyte, "Against Crisis Epistemology," in *Routledge Handbook of Critical Indigenous Studies*, ed. Brendan Hokowhitu (New York: Routledge, 2020), 59.
16. Lorena Allam, "Grave Fears Held for Hundreds of Important NSW South Coast Indigenous Sites," *The Guardian*, January 15, 2020.
17. Lauren Berlant, "Genre Flailing, *Capacious: Journal for Emerging Affect Inquiry* 1, no. 2 (2018): 156.
18. Read through a historicist lens, Oblivia's rape and subsequent disappearance allude to Australia's 2007 Northern Territory National Emergency Response, colloquially known as "The Intervention." In response to allegations of rampant child sexual abuse and neglect in Aboriginal communities, a federal investigation dramatically increased law enforcement

presence in the Northern Territory. Wright observes that the Intervention, in practice, was an effort "to bring about the end of Aboriginal rights to land—the big unsettled business of occupation." This land grab reprised the conquest of the continent and the child abductions that occurred during earlier phases of colonial rule. Wright explains, "In our family, my great-great-grandmother was stolen from her family. As a little girl my grandmother used to tell the story of her mother and another little girl who were found up in a tree by a pastoralist at that particular time, towards the end of the 19th century." See Alexis Wright, "A Weapon of Poetry," *Overland* 193 (2008): 20; Alexis Wright, interview by Jean-François Vernay, *Antipodes* 18, no. 2 (2004): 119.
19. Wright, *The Swan Book*, 78.
20. Notably, western swamp tortoises are the first vertebrate species to undergo assisted colonization due to climate change. Their natural habitat in western Australia's Swan Valley no longer receives sufficient rain to sustain them, so scientists relocated surviving tortoises to Meerup and Moore River National Park. See Calla Wahlquist, "Australia's Rarest Tortoises Get New Home to Save Them from Climate Change," *The Guardian*, August 16, 2016; Saskia Main, "Desert Frogs Resurface After Months—and Sometimes Years—Underground Waiting for Rain," *Australian Broadcasting Corporation*, March 21, 2020.
21. Alexis Pauline Gumbs, *Undrowned: Black Feminist Lessons from Marine Mammals* (Chico, CA: AK Press, 2020), 2.
22. Wright, *The Swan Book*, 73.
23. Wright, *The Swan Book*, 9.
24. Wright, *The Swan Book*, 72.
25. Wright, *The Swan Book*, 73.
26. This sense of linguistic materiality appears throughout *The Swan Book*. As Jane Gleeson-White observes, quoting several sections from Wright's novel, "Here a story can extrude a real world effect: 'Something dropped into the water. Plop! Was this a fact that had slipped from her hypothetical love stories?' And words have a quasi-material dimension: 'You could almost reach out and grab each word with your hand.'" See Jane Gleeson-White, "Going Viral," *Sydney Review of Books*, August 23, 2013.
27. I am of course drawing on Gerald Vizenor's work here. See *Survivance: Narratives of Native Presence*, ed. Gerald Vizenor (Lincoln: University of Nebraska Press, 2008).
28. Francis X. Whalen et al., "Inhaled Anesthetics: An Historical Overview," *Best Practice & Research Clinical Anesthesiology* 19, no. 3 (2005): 325; Raymond J. Clausen, "Ethylene Anaesthesia," *Proceedings of the Royal Society of Medicine* 23, no. 9 (1930): 1259–62.
29. Maria Takolander, "Magical Realism and Indigenous Survivance in Australia: The Fiction of Alexis Wright," in *The Palgrave Handbook of Magical*

Realism in the Twenty-First Century, ed. Richard Perez and Victoria A. Chevalier (Cham: Springer International Publishing, 2020), 173–95; Holgate, "Unsettling Narratives," 634–47.
30. Wright, *The Swan Book*, 243.
31. Wright, *The Swan Book*, 6.
32. Alison Ravenscroft, "Dreaming of Others: *Carpentaria* and Its Critics," *Cultural Studies Review* 16, no. 2 (2010): 196.
33. Jennifer Wenzel, *The Disposition of Nature: Environmental Crisis and World Literature* (New York: Fordham University Press, 2020), 122.
34. Michael McCormack, interview by Eliza Edwards, *Sky News*, December 18, 2019.
35. Wright, *The Swan Book*, 7, 11.
36. Wright, *The Swan Book*, 242.
37. Wright, *The Swan Book*, 6.
38. Jessica Machado, "What It's Like to Live Through the Australian Bushfires," *Vox*, January 24, 2020.
39. Maani Truu, "Coming to Age in Climate Change," *ABC News*, November 5, 2021.
40. Lorena Allam and Nick Evershed, "Too Hot for Humans? First Nations People Fear Becoming Australia's First Climate Refugees," *The Guardian*, December 17, 2019.
41. Alexis Wright, "The Future of Swans," interview by Arnold Zable, *Overland* 213 (2013): 30.
42. Wright, *The Swan Book*, 13–14.
43. Wright, *The Swan Book*, 57.
44. Juvenal, *The Sixteen Satires*, 3rd ed., trans. Peter Green (London: Penguin Books, 1998), 39.
45. Wright, *The Swan Book*, 71.
46. Nassim Nicholas Taleb, *The Black Swan: The Impact of the Highly Improbable* (New York: Random House, 2007), xvii.
47. Taleb, *The Black Swan*, xviii.
48. Taleb, *The Black Swan*, xix.
49. IPCC, "Summary for Policymakers," in *Climate Change 2021: The Physical Science Basis. Contribution of Working Group I to the Sixth Assessment Report of the Intergovernmental Panel on Climate Change* (2021), 27.
50. Calla Wahlquist, "Australia Had More Supersized Bushfires Creating Their Own Storms Last Summer Than in Previous 30 Years," *The Guardian*, June 16, 2020.
51. Wright, *The Swan Book*, 41.
52. Wright, *The Swan Book*, 5–6.
53. Wright, *The Swan Book*, 15–23.
54. Wright, *The Swan Book*, 274.
55. Wright, *The Swan Book*, 276.

56. Wright, *The Swan Book*, 277.
57. Wright, *The Swan Book*, 280.
58. Wright, *The Swan Book*, 27–28, 72–75.
59. Maria Takolander, "Theorizing Irony and Trauma in Magical Realism: Junot Díaz's *The Brief Wondrous Life of Oscar Wao* and Alexis Wright's *The Swan Book*," *Ariel: A Review of International English Literature* 47, no. 3 (2016): 114–15.
60. Wright, *The Swan Book*, 30, 20.
61. Wright, *The Swan Book*, 26.
62. Alexis Wright, "The Inward Migration in Apocalyptic Times," *Emergence Magazine*, October 26, 2022.
63. Wright, *The Swan Book*, 28.
64. Wright, *The Swan Book*, 57.
65. Philip Steer, "The Climates of the Victorian Novel: Seasonality, Weather, and Regional Fiction in Britain and Australia," *PMLA* 136, no. 3 (2021): 372.
66. Libby Robin, "Uncertain Seasons in the El Niño Continent: Local and Global Views," *Anglica: An International Journal of English Studies* 28, no. 3 (2019): 9.
67. Libby Robin, *How a Continent Created a Nation* (Sydney: University of New South Wales Press, 2007), 3.
68. Robin, *How a Continent Created a Nation*, 4.
69. Robin, "Uncertain Seasons in the El Niño Continent," 8.
70. Steer, "The Climates of the Victorian Novel," 377.
71. Robin, "Uncertain Seasons in the El Niño Continent," 8.
72. Wright, *The Swan Book*, 194.
73. Yuriko Furuhata, *Climatic Media: Transpacific Experiments in Atmospheric Control* (Durham, NC: Duke University Press, 2022), 19.
74. Wright, *The Swan Book*, 189–90.
75. Wright, *The Swan Book*, 189.
76. Wright, *The Swan Book*, 192.
77. Wright, *The Swan Book*, 195.
78. Brigid Rooney, *Suburban Space, the Novel, and Australian Modernity* (London: Anthem Press, 2018), 186.
79. Wright, *The Swan Book*, 193.
80. Wright, *The Swan Book*, 196.
81. Wright, *The Swan Book*, 195.
82. Wright, *The Swan Book*, 196.
83. Wright, *The Swan Book*, 196.
84. Wright, *The Swan Book*, 197.
85. Wright, *The Swan Book*, 215–16.
86. Wright, *The Swan Book*, 243.
87. Wright, *The Swan Book*, 275.
88. Wright, *The Swan Book*, 273.

89. Wright, *The Swan Book*, 29.
90. Shelley Streeby, *Imagining the Future of Climate Change: World-Making Through Science Fiction and Activism* (Oakland: University of California Press, 2018), 4.
91. Alex Trexler, *Anthropocene Fictions: The Novel in a Time of Climate Change* (Charlottesville: University of Virginia Press, 2015), 7–9; Rebecca Evans, "Fantastic Futures?: Cli-fi, Climate Justice, and Queer Futurity," *Resilience* 4, nos. 2–3 (2017): 95.
92. Axel Goodbody and Adeline Johns-Putra, *Cli-Fi: A Companion* (Oxford: Peter Lang, 2019), 1–2.
93. See Nishant Batsha, "Why All Fiction Is Climate Fiction Now," *Lit Hub*, June 7, 2022; James Bradley, "Writing on the Precipice," *Sydney Review of Books*, February 21, 2017.
94. Ralph Cohen, "History and Genre," *New Literary History* 17, no. 2 (1986): 204, 210.
95. Bruce Robbins, "Afterword," *PMLA* 122, no. 5 (2007): 1650.
96. Jenny Offill, *Weather* (New York: Knopf, 2020), 17–18.
97. See Alastair Fowler, *Kinds of Literature: An Introduction to the Theory of Genres and Modes* (Cambridge, MA: Harvard University Press, 1982), 41.
98. Robin, "Uncertain Seasons in the El Niño Continent," 9.
99. Rachael Scarborough King, "The Scale of Genre," *New Literary History* 52, no. 2 (2021): 261.
100. Caroline Levine, *Forms: Whole, Rhythm, Hierarchy, Network* (Princeton, NJ: Princeton University Press, 2015), 13.
101. Martin Puchner, *Literature for A Changing Planet* (Princeton, NJ: Princeton University Press, 2022), 36.
102. Taleb, *The Black Swan*, xviii.
103. Stephanie LeMenager, "Climate Change and the Struggle for Genre," in *Anthropocene Reading: Literary History in Geologic Times*, ed. Tobias Menely and Jesse Oak Taylor (University Park: Penn State University Press, 2017), 222.
104. Jesse Oak Taylor, "A Great Fire Somewhere? Synchronous Living in Epochal Times," *PMLA* 136, no. 3 (2021): 425.
105. Subhankar Banerjee, "An Unknowable Tragedy: Sundarbans After Cyclone Amphan," *Species in Peril* 1, no. 2 (2020).
106. Isabel Hofmeyr, "B-Sides: Bessie Head's 'The Collector of Treasures,'" *Public Books*, August 12, 2012.
107. Hofmeyr, "B-Sides: Bessie Head's 'The Collector of Treasures.'"
108. Min Hyoung Song, *Climate Lyricism* (Durham, NC: Duke University Press, 2022), 183.
109. Song, *Climate Lyricism*, 183.
110. Song, *Climate Lyricism*, 183.
111. Toshi Reagon, *Octavia's Parables*, Chapter 1, June 22, 2020.
112. adrienne maree brown, *Octavia's Parables*, Chapter 24, December 7, 2020.

113. adrienne maree brown, *Octavia's Parables*, Chapter 14, September 21, 2020.
114. Wright, *The Swan Book*, 51.
115. Wright, *The Swan Book*, 57.
116. Berlant, "Genre Flailing," 161.
117. Alexis Wright, "The Future of Swans," interview by Arnold Zable, *Overland* 213 (Summer 2013).

5. OCCASIONAL POETRY IN STRESSED TIMES

1. Kathy Jetñil-Kijiner, *Iep Jāltok: Poems from a Marshallese Daughter* (Tucson: University of Arizona Press, 2017), 70.
2. See Paul Fussell, *Poetic Meter and Poetic Form* (New York: Random House, 1965), 9.
3. Hilda Heine, "We Are on the Front Line of Climate Change, Marshall Islands President Says," interview by Rachel Martin, *Morning Edition*, National Public Radio, September 24, 2019.
4. "Paris Agreement," *United Nations Framework Convention on Climate Change* (2015): 3, unfccc.int/sites/default/files/english_paris_agreement.pdf.
5. Global Call for Climate Action, "Competition: Spoken Word for the World," October 19, 2015.
6. The panel selecting the four poets who would travel to Paris bridged the environmental and the literary: judges included members of the climate activism organization 350.org, the international media campaign Avaaz, and Button Poetry, a prominent publisher of performance poems with an influential YouTube channel.
7. Sahra Vang Nguyen, "Pacific Islander Poets Use Art, Stories to Urge Climate Action at UN Conference," *NBC News*, December 9, 2015, www.nbcnews.com/news/asian-america/pacific-islander-poets-use-art-stories-urge-climate-action-un-n476486.
8. See Javon Johnson, *Killing Poetry: Blackness and the Making of Slam and Spoken Word Communities* (New Brunswick, NJ: Rutgers University Press, 2017), 14–18; Urayoán Noel, *In Visible Movement: Nuyorican Poetry from the Sixties to Slam* (Iowa City: University of Iowa Press, 2014), 123–63; and Susan Somers-Willett, *The Cultural Politics of Slam Poetry: Race, Identity, and the Performance of Popular Verse in America* (Ann Arbor: University of Michigan Press, 2009), 57–65.
9. Cristin O'Keefe Aptowicz, *Words in Your Face: A Guided Tour Through Twenty Years of the New York City Poetry Slam* (New York: Soft Skull Press, 2008), 44–49.
10. D. Keali'i MacKenzie, "In Words There Is Life: Kanaka 'Ōiwi Participation in Slam Poetry" (PhD diss., University of Hawai'i at Mānoa, 2016), 12. Thanks to Craig Santos Perez for pointing me toward MacKenzie's dissertation.
11. Rob Wilson, "Towards an Ecopoetics of Oceania: Worlding the Asia-Pacific Region as Space-Time Ecumene," in *American Studies as Transnational Practice: Turning Toward the Transpacific*, ed. Yuan Shu and Donald E. Pease

5. OCCASIONAL POETRY IN STRESSED TIMES 263

(Hanover, NH: Dartmouth College Press, 2015), 214; Hsinya Huang, "Toward Transpacific Ecopoetics: Three Indigenous Texts," *Comparative Literature Studies* 50, no. 1 (2013): 121.

12. "Pacific Tongues," accessed August 24, 2020, http://pacifictongues.weebly.com/about.html.
13. Hi'ilei Julia Hobart, "On Oceanic Fugitivity," *Items*, September 9, 2020, https://items.ssrc.org/ways-of-water/on-oceanic-fugitivity.
14. Jules Boykoff and Kaia Sand, "Ocean Leveling the Land: Kathy Jetñil-Kijiner, Global Warming, & the Marshall Islands," *Jacket 2*, September 3, 2011, https://jacket2.org/commentary/ocean-leveling-land-0.
15. TINTA-UP Cebu, *Facebook*, April 21, 2015, it-it.facebook.com/uptinta/photos/slam!-slam!-do-you-hear/1095544960460683/.
16. Lacee A. C. Martinez, " 'Island Haze' Earns Guam Poet Performances in Paris," *USA Today*, December 3, 2015.
17. Eunice Andrada, interview by Tiegan Dakin, *Cahoodaloodaling* 20 (2016): 23.
18. Roger Harrabin, "UN Seeks 'Malala' On Climate Change," *BBC News*, August 29, 2014, www.bbc.com/news/science-environment-28958227.
19. Spoken Word for the World, "Thank You to All the Spoken Word for the World Contestants," *Facebook*, October 30, 2015.
20. Susanna Sacks, "Moving Forms: Individuals, Institutions, and the Production of Slam Poetry Networks in Southern Africa," *ASAP Journal* 5, no. 1 (2020): 175.
21. Craig Santos Perez, "Wayreading Chamorro Literature from Guam" (PhD diss., University of California Berkeley, 2015), 127, and "Signs of Being: Chamoru Poetry and the Work of Cecilia C.T. Perez," *Jacket2*, April 2, 2011, jacket2.org/article/signs-being.
22. Kathy Jetñil-Kijiner, "Iep Jāltok: A History of Marshallese Literature" (MA thesis, University of Hawai'i at Manoa, 2014), 117.
23. MacKenzie, "In Words There Is Life," 17.
24. Albert Wendt, ed., *Nuanua: Pacific Writing in English Since 1980* (Honolulu: University of Hawai'i' Press, 1995), 3.
25. Selina Tusitala Marsh, "Slow Walking, Fast Talking," in *Anglo-American Imperialism and the Pacific: Discourses of Encounter*, ed. Michelle Known et al. (New York: Routledge, 2018), 69.
26. Jetñil-Kijiner, "Iep Jāltok: A History of Marshallese Literature," 52. For the full legend, see the video of Jetñil-Kijiner's performance at the United Nations in 2014.
27. "Statement and Poem by Kathy Jetñil-Kijiner, Climate Summit 2014—Opening Ceremony," *YouTube*, https://www.youtube.com/watch?v=mc_IgE7TBSY.
28. Jetñil-Kijiner, "Iep Jāltok: A History of Marshallese Literature," 72–75.
29. Jessica Schwartz, "Making Waves: Marshallese Youth Culture, 'Minor Songs,' and Major Challenges," in *Reppin:' Pacific Islander Youth and Native*

Justice, ed. Keith Camacho (Seattle: University of Washington Press, 2021), 169; Jetñil-Kijiner, *Iep Jāltok: Poems from a Marshallese Daughter*, 70.
30. Angela Robinson, "Of Monsters and Mothers: Affective Climates and Human-Nonhuman Sociality in Kathy Jetñil-Kijiner's 'Dear Matabele Peinam,' " *The Contemporary Pacific* 32, no. 2 (2020): 312.
31. Robinson, "Of Monsters and Mothers," 323.
32. Terisa Tinei Siagatonu, "Layers," *YouTube*, uploaded by Global Call for Climate Action, December 1, 2015, www.youtube.com/watch?v=XgXYP6zqzJk. In a personal email, Siagatonu approved the choices made in this transcription regarding capitalization, punctuation, and lineation. For accuracy, she requested that the word "hurricane" in the original performance be replaced with "tsunami" in this chapter.
33. Siagatonu, "Layers."
34. Robinson, "Of Monsters and Mothers," 322.
35. Robinson, "Of Monsters and Mothers," 322.
36. Rebecca H. Hogue and Anaïs Maurer, "Pacific Women's Anti-Nuclear Poetry: Centring Indigenous Knowledges," *International Affairs* 98, no. 4 (2022): 1267–88
37. Siagatonu, "Layers"; Maria Damon, "Was That 'Different,' 'Dissident' or 'Dissonant?' Poetry (n) the Public Spear: Slams, Open Readings, and Dissident Traditions," in *Close Listening: Poetry and the Performed Word*, ed. Charles Bernstein (Oxford: Oxford University Press, 1998), 329.
38. Ron Silliman, "Who Speaks: Ventriloquism and the Self in Poetry Reading," in *Close Listening: Poetry and the Performed Word*, 362.
39. Carolyn Forché, Introduction to *Against Forgetting: Twentieth Century Poetry of Witness* (New York: Norton, 1993), 30.
40. John "Meta" Sarmiento, "Island Haze," *YouTube*, uploaded by Meta Sarmiento, November 24, 2015, www.youtube.com/watch?v=iekYyIToIro.
41. Nguyen, "Pacific Islander Poets Use Art, Stories to Urge Climate Action at UN Conference."
42. Johnson, *Killing Poetry*, 20.
43. Somers-Willett, *The Cultural Politics of Slam Poetry*, 35.
44. Jesse Lichtenstein, "How Poetry Came to Matter Again," *The Atlantic*, September 2018, 93.
45. "Tell Them" was also performed in London in 2012. See *Iep Jāltok: Poems from a Marshallese Daughter*, 64–67.
46. Elizabeth DeLoughrey, *Allegories of the Anthropocene* (Durham, NC: Duke University Press, 2019), 3. For DeLoughrey's extended analysis of "Tell Them," see *Allegories of the Anthropocene*, 1–4, 192–96.
47. DeLoughrey, *Allegories of the Anthropocene*, 4.
48. Isabella Borgeson, "Yolanda Winds," *YouTube*, uploaded by Global Call for Climate Action, December 1, 2015. www.youtube.com/watch?v=w4d8uM1H7pI.

49. Borgeson, "Yolanda Winds."
50. Nguyen, "Pacific Islander Poets Use Art, Stories to Urge Climate Action at UN Conference."
51. Borgeson, "Yolanda Winds."
52. Samuel H. Monk, "Introduction to John Dryden," in *The Norton Anthology of English Literature, Vol. 1*, 7th ed., ed. M. H. Abrams and Stephen Greenblatt (New York: Norton, 2000), 2071.
53. J. L. Austin, *How to Do Things with Words*, 2nd ed., ed. J. O. Urmson and Marina Sbisà (Cambridge, MA: Harvard University Press, 1962), 12.
54. *Oxford English Dictionary Online*, s.v. "occasion," accessed August 24, 2020.
55. Joshua P. Howe, "This Is Nature; This Is Un-Nature: Reading the Keeling Curve," *Environmental History* 20 (2015): 291.
56. Howe, "This Is Nature; This Is Un-Nature," 290.
57. Howe, "This Is Nature; This Is Un-Nature," 289.
58. "Paris Agreement," 3.
59. Eunice Andrada, "Pacific Salt," *YouTube*, uploaded by Global Call for Climate Action, December 1, 2015, www.youtube.com/watch?v=T4C2g-PHE4Q.
60. For accounts of the Pacific Proving Grounds in literary scholarship, see Aimee Bahng, "The Pacific Proving Grounds and the Proliferation of Settler Environmentalism," *Journal of Transnational American Studies* 11, no. 2 (2020); Elizabeth DeLoughrey, "Radiation Ecologies and the Wars of Light," *Modern Fiction Studies* 55, no. 3 (2009); Rebecca Hogue, "Oceans, Radiations, and Monsters," *Critical Ethnic Studies* 7, no. 2 (2022); and Michelle Keown, "Children of Israel: US Military Imperialism and Marshallese Migration in the Poetry of Kathy Jetñil-Kijiner," *Interventions* 19, no. 7 (2017).
61. DeLoughrey, "Radiation Ecologies and the Wars of Light," 469.
62. Karl Mathiesen, "Losing Paradise: The People Displaced by Atomic Bombs, and Now Climate Change," *The Guardian*, March 9, 2015.
63. Julianne Walsh and Hilda Heine, *Etto ñan Raan Kein: A Marshall Island History* (Honolulu, HI: Bess Press, 2012), 304–5.
64. Keith Leonard, "Rising to the Occasion," *American Periodicals* 25 (2015): 182.
65. Stephen Wilson, "Poetry and Its Occasions: 'Undoing the Folded Lie,'" in *A Companion to Poetic Genre*, 1st ed., ed. Erik Martiny (Hoboken, NJ: John Wiley & Sons, 2012), 492.
66. Giovanna DiChiro, "Environmental Justice," in *Keywords for Environmental Studies*, ed. Joni Adamson et al. (New York: NYU Press, 2016), 103.
67. Andrada, "Pacific Salt."
68. Jetñil-Kijiner, "Statement and Poem by Kathy Jetñil-Kijiner, Climate Summit 2014—Opening Ceremony."
69. Sophie Yeo, "Marshall Islands Poet Says Youth Must Lead Climate Fight," *Climate Home News*, October 22, 2014, www.climatechangenews.com/2014/10/22/marshall-islands-poet-says-youth-must-lead-climate-fight.

70. Rob Nixon, "The Anthropocene: The Promises and Pitfalls of an Epochal Idea," *Edge Effects*, November 6, 2014.
71. Jetñil-Kijiner, *Iep Jāltok: Poems from a Marshallese Daughter*, 71.
72. Jetñil-Kijiner, *Iep Jāltok: Poems from a Marshallese Daughter*, 71.
73. Barbara Johnson, "Thresholds of Difference: Structures of Address in Zora Neale Hurston," *Critical Inquiry* 12, no. 1 (1985): 284.
74. Johnson, "Thresholds of Difference," 285.
75. Jetñil-Kijiner, *Iep Jāltok: Poems from a Marshallese Daughter*, 71.
76. Andrada, "Pacific Salt."
77. Andrada, "Pacific Salt."
78. Andrada, "Pacific Salt."
79. Barbara Johnson, "Apostrophe, Animation, and Abortion," *Diacritics* 16, no. 1 (1986): 30.
80. Jetñil-Kijiner, *Iep Jāltok: Poems from a Marshallese Daughter*, 73.
81. Suzuki is commenting on Jetñil-Kijiner's videopoem "Butterfly Thief." The fact that we see this interlocutionary strategy being used in multiple poems suggests that it is a recurring feature of Jetñil-Kijiner's work, a structure of address shaped by her rhetorical position within the climate crisis. See Erin Suzuki, *Ocean Passages: Navigating Pacific Islander and Asian American Literatures* (Philadelphia: Temple University Press, 2021), 76.
82. Johnson, "Apostrophe, Animation, and Abortion," 31.
83. Jetñil-Kijiner, *Iep Jāltok: Poems from a Marshallese Daughter*, 72.
84. Anjali Vaidya, "COP21 Diary: A Ray of Sunshine, A Song of Despair," *The Wire*, December 1, 2015.
85. *Oxford English Dictionary Online*, s.v. "urgency," accessed August 24, 2020.
86. *Oxford English Dictionary Online*, s.v. "urgency,"
87. Andrada, "Pacific Salt."
88. Schwartz, "Making Waves," 169.
89. Jetñil-Kijiner, *Iep Jāltok: Poems from a Marshallese Daughter*, 72.
90. Andrada, "Pacific Salt."
91. Michelle Yonetani, "Global Estimates 2014: People Displaced by Disasters," *Norwegian Refugee Council*, September 2014.
92. Borgeson, "Yolanda Winds."
93. Borgeson, "Yolanda Winds."

6. KEEPING TIME

1. Jesse A. Randall, "Maple Syrup Production," *Iowa State University Forestry Extension*, Publication F-337A (2010).
2. Callum Angus, "The Climate of Gender," *Catapult*, May 3, 2021, https://catapult.co/stories/the-climate-of-gender-callum-angus-climate-change-transitioning-maple-syrup-gender.
3. City of Toronto, *Toronto Municipal Code, Chapter 813: Trees*, May 12, 2022.

4. City of Detroit, Michigan, *Code of Ordinances*, Code 1964, § 64-1-3; Code 1984, § 57-2-3, https://library.municode.com/mi/detroit/codes/code_of_ordinances.
5. Leanne Betasamosake Simpson, *This Accident of Being Lost: Songs and Stories* (Toronto: House of Anansi, 2017), 6.
6. James Chaarani, "Sugarbush Tree Tappers Get to Work a Month Earlier Than in the Past," *Canadian Broadcasting Corporation News*, March 1, 2022, https://www.cbc.ca/news/canada/london/sugarbush-tree-tappers-get-to-work-a-month-earlier-than-in-the-past-1.6367990; Kristen Giesting, "Maple Syrup," *USDA Forest Service Climate Change Resource Center*, 2020, https://www.fs.usda.gov/ccrc/topics/maple-syrup; Simon Legault et al., "Perceptions of U.S. and Canadian Maple Syrup Producers Toward Climate Change, Its Impacts, and Potential Adaptation Measures," *PLoS ONE* 14, no. 4 (2019).
7. Leanne Betasamosake Simpson, "Land as Pedagogy: Nishnaabeg Intelligence and Rebellious Transformation," *Decolonization: Indignity, Education & Society* 3, no. 3 (2014): 2.
8. Leah Collins. " 'Live Action Could Never Have Created These Worlds:' Amanda Strong on Her Latest Film, *Biidaaban*." *CBC Arts*, June 15, 2019, https://www.cbc.ca/arts/live-action-could-never-have-created-these-worlds-amanda-strong-on-her-latest-film-biidaaban-1.4821934.
9. Collins, " 'Live Action Could Never Have Created These Worlds.' "
10. Grace Dillon, *Walking the Clouds: An Anthology of Indigenous Science Fiction* (Tucson: University of Arizona Press, 2012), 3–4.
11. Michael Kammen, *A Time to Every Purpose: The Four Seasons in American Culture* (Chapel Hill: The University of North Carolina Press, 2004), 119.
12. Kammen, *A Time to Every Purpose*, 108.
13. Simpson, *This Accident of Being Lost*, 5.
14. Simpson, *This Accident of Being Lost*, 7.
15. Simpson, *This Accident of Being Lost*, 33.
16. Simpson, *This Accident of Being Lost*, 7.
17. Kristen Simmons, "Settler Atmospherics," *Cultural Anthropology*, November 2017, https://culanth.org/fieldsights/settler-atmospherics.
18. Simpson, *This Accident of Being Lost*, 33.
19. Alexis Wright, *The Swan Book* (New York: Atria Books, 2016), 5.
20. Cameron Awkward-Rich, *Dispatch* (New York: Persea Books, 2019).
21. For more on tenderness, see Zoe Todd, "Tenderness Manifesto," 2016, https://zoestodd.com/tenderness-manifesto/.
22. "keep, v.," OED Online, September 2022.
23. Angus, "The Climate of Gender." Also see "The World's Only Reserve of Maple Syrup," PPAQ, October 19, 2020, https://ppaq.ca/en/sale-purchase-maple-syrup/worlds-only-reserve-maple-syrup/.
24. "The World's Only Reserve of Maple Syrup." *PPAQ*, October 19, 2020.

25. Michael Moynihan, "Inside Quebec's Maple Syrup Cartel," *Vice*, April 19, 2017, https://www.vice.com/en/article/ywnjkv/inside-quebecs-maple-syrup-black-market.
26. Anne-Lise François, "Fire, Water, Moon: Supplemental Seasons in a Time Without Season," in *Climate Realism: The Aesthetics of Weather and Atmosphere in the Anthropocene*, ed. Lynn Badia et al. (New York: Routledge, 2020), 50.
27. "keep, v." OED Online. September 2022.
28. Stephanie LeMenager, "Skilling Up for the Anthropocene," *Feminist Queer Anticolonial Propositions for Hacking the Anthropocene: Archive*, ed. Jennifer Mae Hamilton et al. (London: One Humanities Press, 2021), 212.
29. LeMenager, "Skilling Up for the Anthropocene," 210.
30. Simpson, *This Accident of Being Lost*, 33–34.
31. Chris Fox, "Looking to Rent One-Bedroom Apartment in Toronto? New Report Suggests You'll Pay More Than $2,500 a Month," *CTV News Toronto*, March 14, 2023.
32. Simpson, *This Accident of Being Lost*, 5.
33. Lisa Sun-Hee Park and David Naguib Pellow, *The Slums of Aspen: Immigrants vs. the Environment in America's Eden* (New York: NYU Press, 2011), 3.
34. Simpson, *This Accident of Being Lost*, 7.
35. Simpson, *This Accident of Being Lost*, 6; Justin Mann, "What's Your Emergency? White Women and the Policing of Public Space," *Feminist Studies* 44, no. 3 (2018): 768–69.
36. Simpson, *This Accident of Being Lost*, 7.
37. Suzannah Clark generously directed my attention toward the film's score.
38. "Firm Stole Indian Oil, Panel Told: $31 Million Owed, Investigators Tell Senate Committee," *Los Angeles Times*, May 9, 1989.
39. Christopher Leonard, "How an Oil Theft Investigation Laid the Groundwork for the Koch Playbook," *Politico*, July 22, 2019.
40. Christopher Leonard, *Kochland: The Secret History of Koch Industries and Corporate Power in America* (New York: Simon & Schuster, 2019), 12.
41. Hilary Plum and Lucy Biederman, "Literature, Capital, Catapult, and the Kochs: A Dialogue," *Fence*, https://fenceportal.org/literature-capital-catapult-and-the-kochs-a-dialogue/.
42. Jennifer Wenzel, *The Disposition of Nature: Environmental Crisis and World Literature* (New York: Fordham University Press, 2019), 55.
43. Arundhati Roy, *Capitalism: A Ghost Story* (Chicago: Haymarket Books, 2014).
44. Eli Clare, *Brilliant Imperfection: Grappling with Cure* (Durham, NC: Duke University Press, 2017), 33.
45. Eli Clare, *Brilliant Imperfection*, 173.
46. Zadie Smith, "Elegy for a Country's Seasons," *New York Review of Books*, April 3, 2014.

47. Elizabeth Freeman, *Time Binds: Queer Temporalities, Queer Histories* (Durham, NC: Duke University Press, 2010), 3.
48. Freeman, *Time Binds*, 19.
49. Jack Halberstam, *Queer Time and Place: Transgender Bodies, Subcultural Lives* (New York: NYU Press, 2005), 6.
50. Kadji Amin, "Temporality," *Transgender Studies Quarterly* 1, nos. 1–2 (2014): 220.
51. "Theorizing Queer Temporalities: A Roundtable Discussion," *GLQ: A Journal of Lesbian and Gay Studies* 13, nos. 2–3 (2007): 191.
52. Callum Angus interview by David Naimon, "Between the Covers: Callum Angus Interview," *Tin House*.
53. Angus, "The Climate of Gender."
54. "keep, v." OED Online. September 2022.
55. Callum Angus, *A Natural History of Transition* (Montreal: Metonymy Press, 2021), 2.
56. Angus, *A Natural History of Transition*, 40.
57. Angus, *A Natural History of Transition*, 53.
58. Angus, *A Natural History of Transition*, 42–43.
59. Angus, *A Natural History of Transition*, 45.
60. Nicole Seymour, *Strange Natures: Futurity, Empathy, and the Queer Ecological Imagination* (Urbana: University of Illinois Press, 2013), 30.
61. Angus, *A Natural History of Transition*, 32.
62. Angus, "The Climate of Gender."
63. Angus, "The Climate of Gender."
64. Angus, "The Climate of Gender."
65. Smith, "Elegy for a Country's Seasons."
66. Angus, "The Climate of Gender."
67. Angus, "The Climate of Gender."
68. See chapter 3 of this book for a discussion of how Mahindra Automotive, an Indian corporation, funds humanities research.
69. ACLU of Michigan, "Detroit Settles ACLU Lawsuit Challenging Police Sting Operation Against Gay Men," July 23, 2022, https://www.aclu.org/press-releases/detroit-settles-aclu-lawsuit-challenging-police-sting-operation-against-gay-men.
70. Jena Brooker and Bryce Huffman, "Can the Police and the Public Coexist at Rouge Park?," *Planet Detroit*, August 16, 2022, https://planetdetroit.org/2022/08/can-the-police-and-public-coexist-at-rouge-park.
71. Antonio Cosme, "Special Sauce: The Detroit Sugarbush Project," *National Wildlife Federation Blog*, May 10, 2021, https://blog.nwf.org/2021/05/special-sauce-the-detroit-sugarbush-project/#:~:text=with%20Indigenous%20experts.-,A%20unique%20partnership%20between%20the%20National%20Wildlife%20Federation%2C%20the%20city,tradition%20of%20making%20maple%20syrup.

72. AJ Walker, "Tapping into Their Roots: Detroit Sugarbush Project Collects Sap from Rouge Park," *One Detroit*, April 25, 2022, https://www.onedetroitpbs.org/one-detroit/tapping-into-their-roots-detroit-sugarbush-project-begins-collecting-sap-from-rouge-park.
73. Cosme, "Special Sauce: The Detroit Sugarbush Project."
74. Russ McNamara, "'A Beautiful Process:' Work Continues for Detroit Sugarbush Project," *WDET*, February 25, 2022, https://wdet.org/2022/02/25/a-beautiful-process-work-continues-for-detroit-sugarbush-project.
75. Elissa Welle, "Detroit Police Break Up Native Sugarbush Ceremony, Saying 'Sovereign Stuff Is Not Valid,'" *Detroit Free Press*, February 19, 2022, https://www.freep.com/story/news/local/michigan/detroit/2022/02/19/detroit-police-break-up-native-ceremony/6861547001.
76. Chris Aadland, "Detroit Police Break Up Indigenous Sugarbush, Later Apologize," *Indian Country Today*, February 25, 2022, https://indiancountrytoday.com/news/detroit-police-break-up-indigenous-sugarbush-later-apologize.
77. "Climate Change Study Finds That Maple Syrup Season May Come Earlier," *Dartmouth News*, September 20, 2019, https://home.dartmouth.edu/news/2019/09/climate-change-study-finds-maple-syrup-season-may-come-earlier.
78. Sarah Schulman, *My American History: Lesbian and Gay Life During the Reagan and Bush Years* (New York: Routledge, 2018).
79. "keep, v." OED Online. September 2022.
80. Zoe Todd, "Indigenizing the Anthropocene," in *Art in the Anthropocene: Encounters Among Aesthetics, Politics, Environments and Epistemologies*, ed. Heather Davis and Etienne Turpin (London: Open Humanities Press, 2015), 241–43.
81. Leanne Betasamosake Simpson, *The Gift Is in the Making: Anishinaabeg Stories* (Winnipeg, Canada: Highwater Press, 2013), 93.
82. Simpson, *The Gift Is in the Making*, 93.
83. Collins. "'Live Action Could Never Have Created These Worlds.'"
84. Matthew Harrison Tedford, "Is a Non-Capitalist World Imaginable? Embodied Practices and Slipstream Potentials in Amanda Strong's Biidaaban," *Feminist Media Histories* 8, no. 1 (2022): 47.
85. David Gelles and Manuela Andreoni, "Coming Soon: More Oil, Gas and Coal," Climate Forward Newsletter, *New York Times*, November 9, 2023.
86. IPCC, "2022: Summary for Policymakers," in *Climate Change 2022: Impacts, Adaptation and Vulnerability. Contribution of Working Group II to the Sixth Assessment Report of the Intergovernmental Panel on Climate Change*, ed. H.-O. Pörtner, D. C. Roberts, M. Tignor, E. S. Poloczanska, K. Mintenbeck, A. Alegría, M. Craig, S. Langsdorf, S. Löschke, V. Möller, A. Okem, B. Rama (Cambridge: Cambridge University Press, 3–33, doi:10.1017/9781009325844.001.

87. Linda Hutcheon, *A Theory of Adaptation* (New York: Routledge, 2012), 3, 20.
88. Hutcheon, *A Theory of Adaptation*, 31.
89. Hutcheon, *A Theory of Adaptation*, 11.
90. Hutcheon, *A Theory of Adaptation*, 4.
91. Simpson, *The Gift Is in the Making*, 89.

EPILOGUE: MORE HABITS THAN DREAMS

1. Zadie Smith, "Elegy for a Country's Seasons," *New York Review of Books*, April 3, 2014.
2. Craig Philips, "Filmmaker Asks New Yorkers, What Does the Future Look Like?," *PBS.org*, April 16, 2020.
3. Mallory Andrews, "More Habits Than Dreams: *The Hottest August*," *Cleo: A Journal of Film and Feminism* (2019).

BIBLIOGRAPHY

Aadland, Chris. "Detroit Police Break Up Indigenous Sugarbush, Later Apologize." *Indian Country Today*, February 25, 2022. https://indiancountrytoday.com/news/detroit-police-break-up-indigenous-sugarbush-later-apologize.

ACLU of Michigan. "Detroit Settles ACLU Lawsuit Challenging Police Sting Operation Against Gay Men." July 23, 2022. https://www.aclu.org/press-releases/detroit-settles-aclu-lawsuit-challenging-police-sting-operation-against-gay-men.

Adiga, Aravind. "The Boss Will See You Now." *Outlook* (February 2022). https://www.outlookindia.com/magazine/story/the-boss-will-see-you-now/285083.

Agarwal, Anil, and Sunita Narain. "Global Warming in an Unequal World." New Delhi: Centre for Science and Environment, 1991.

Albeck-Ripka, Livia, and Brad Plumer. "5 Plants and Animals Utterly Confused by Climate Change." *New York Times*, April 4, 2018.

Alexander, Joe. Joe Alexander to Aldo Leopold, August 7, 1945. Box 8, folder 1. Aldo Leopold Papers, University of Wisconsin-Madison Archives.

Allam, Lorena. "Grave Fears Held for Hundreds of Important NSW South Coast Indigenous Sites." *The Guardian*, January 15, 2020.

Allam, Lorena, and Nick Evershed. "Too Hot for Humans? First Nations People Fear Becoming Australia's First Climate Refugees." *The Guardian*, December 17, 2019.

Amin, Kadji. "Temporality." *Transgender Studies Quarterly* 1, nos. 1–2 (2014): 220.

Amrith, Sunil. *Unruly Waters: How Rains, Rivers, Coasts, and Seas Have Shaped Asia's History*. New York: Basic Books, 2018.

———. "When the Monsoon Goes Away." *Aeon*, March 4, 2019.

Andrada, Eunice. Interview by Tiegan Dakin. *Cahoodaloodaling* 20 (2016): 23–24.

———. "Pacific Salt." *YouTube*, uploaded by Global Call for Climate Action, December 1, 2015. www.youtube.com/watch?v=T4C2g-PHE4Q.

Andrews, Christopher, Jan Dick, Christer Jonasson, and Terry Callaghan. "Assessment of Biological and Environmental Phenology at a Landscape Level from 30 Years of Fixed-Date Repeat Photography in Northern Sweden." *Ambio* 40, no. 6 (2011): 600–9.

Andrews, Mallory. "More Habits Than Dreams: *The Hottest August.*" *Cleo: A Journal of Film and Feminism* (2019).

Angus, Callum. *A Natural History of Transition*. Montreal: Metonymy Press, 2021.

———. "The Climate of Gender." *Catapult*, May 3, 2021. https://catapult.co/stories/the-climate-of-gender-callum-angus-climate-change-transitioning-maple-syrup-gender.

———. Interview by David Naimon. "Between the Covers: Callum Angus Interview." *Tin House.*

Aptowicz, Cristin O'Keefe. *Words in Your Face: A Guided Tour Through Twenty Years of the New York City Poetry Slam*. New York: Soft Skull Press, 2008.

Armbruster, Karla. "Nature Writing." In *Keyword for Environmental Studies*, ed. Joni Adamson, William A. Gleason, and David N. Pellow, 156–58. New York: NYU Press, 2016.

Ashokamitran. "Landscape in Literature: A Tamil Perception." *Literary Criterion* 18, no. 4 (1983): 25–30.

———. *My Years With Boss: At Gemini Studios*. New Delhi: Orient Longman, 2002.

———. "The Pre-Occupations in Tamil Short Story Today." *Indian Literature* 37, no. 3 (1994): 180–83.

———. *Water*. Trans. Lakshmi Holmström. Oxford: Heinemann, 1993.

Austin, J. L. *How to Do Things with Words*, 2nd ed. Ed. J. O. Urmson and Marina Sbisà. Cambridge, MA: Harvard University Press, 1962.

Awkward-Rich, Cameron. *Dispatch*. New York: Persea Books, 2019.

Bahng, Aimee. "The Pacific Proving Grounds and the Proliferation of Settler Environmentalism." *Journal of Transnational American Studies* 11, no. 2 (2020).

Banerjee, Subhankar. "An Unknowable Tragedy: Sundarbans After Cyclone Amphan." *Species in Peril* 1, no. 2 (2020).

Barboza, Tony. "Study: Rockies' Wildflower Season 35 Days Longer from Climate Change." *Los Angeles Times*, March 17, 2014.

Baskaran, Padmapriya. "Connected by Water for Life." *Madras Musings* 31, no. 13 (2021).

Barthes, Roland. "An Introduction to the Structural Analysis of Narrative." Trans. Lionel Duisit. *New Literary History* 6, no. 2 (1975): 237–72.

Bastian, Michelle, and Rowan Bayliss Hawitt. "Multi-Species, Ecological and Climate Change Temporalities: Opening a Dialogue with Phenology." *Environment and Planning E: Nature and Space* (2022): 1–24.

Batsha, Nishant. "Why All Fiction Is Climate Fiction Now." *Lit Hub*, June 7, 2022.

Beamish, Alison L., Wiebe Nijland, Marc Edwards, Nicholas C. Coops, and Greg H.R. Henry. "Phenology and Vegetation Change Measurements from True Colour Digital Photography in High Arctic Tundra." *Arctic Science* 2 (2016): 33–49.

Berlant, Lauren. *Cruel Optimism*. Durham, NC: Duke University Press, 2011.
——. "Genre Flailing." *Capacious: Journal for Emerging Affect Inquiry* 1, no. 2 (2018): 156–62.
Betancourt, Julio L. Foreword to *Phenology: An Integrative Environmental Science*, 2nd ed. Ed. Mark D. Schwartz. Dordrecht: Springer, 2013.
Bjornerud, Marcia. *Timefulness: How Thinking Like a Geologist Can Help Save the World*. Princeton, NJ: Princeton University Press, 2018.
Blitzer, Jonathan. "How Climate Change Is Fueling the U.S. Border Crisis." *New Yorker*, April 3, 2019.
Bloom, Harold. "The Man in the Back Row Has a Question VI." *Paris Review* 40, no. 154 (2000): 370–402.
Bloom, Lisa. *Climate Change and the New Polar Aesthetics: Artists Reimagine the Arctic and Antarctic*. Durham, NC: Duke University Press, 2022.
Boer, Matthias M., Victor Resco de Dios, and Ross A. Bradstock. "Unprecedented Burn Area of Australian Mega Forest Fires." *Nature Climate Change* 10 (2020): 171–72.
Borgeson, Isabella. "Yolanda Winds." *YouTube*, uploaded by Global Call for Climate Action, December 1, 2015. www.youtube.com/watch?v=w4d8uM1H7pI.
Boykoff, Jules, and Kaia Sand. "Ocean Leveling the Land: Kathy Jetñil-Kijiner, Global Warming, & the Marshall Islands." *Jacket 2*, September 3, 2011. https://jacket2.org/commentary/ocean-leveling-land-0.
Bradley, Nina L., A. Carl Leopold, John Ross, and Wellington Huffaker. "Phenological Changes Reflect Climate Change in Wisconsin." *Proceedings of the National Academy of Sciences of the United States of America* 96, no. 17 (1999): 9701–704.
Bradley, James. "Writing on the Precipice." *Sydney Review of Books*, February 21, 2017.
Brathwaite, Kamau. *Roots*. Ann Arbor: University of Michigan Press, 1993.
Brooker, Jena, and Bryce Huffman. "Can the Police and the Public Coexist at Rouge Park?" *Planet Detroit*. August 16, 2022. https://planetdetroit.org/2022/08/can-the-police-and-public-coexist-at-rouge-park.
Brooks, Cleanth. "The Formalist Critics." *Kenyon Review* 13, no. 1 (1951): 72–81.
brown, adrienne maree, and Toshi Reagon. *Octavia's Parables*. www.readingoctavia.com.
Brown, Tim B., Kevin R. Hultine, Heidi Steltzer, Ellen G. Denny, Michael W. Denslow, Joel Granados, Sandra Henderson, David Moore, Shin Nagai, Michael SanClements, Arturo Sánchez-Azofeifa, Oliver Sonnentag, David Tazik, and Andrew D. Richardson. "Using Phenocams to Monitor Our Changing Earth: Toward a Global Phenocam Network." *Frontiers in Ecology and the Environment* 14, no. 2 (2016): 84–93.
Buell, Lawrence. *The Environmental Imagination: Thoreau, Nature Writing, and the Formation of American Culture*. Cambridge, MA: Belknap Press, 1995.
Burke, Kenneth. *Counter Statement*. Los Altos, CA: Hermes Publications, 1953.

Byrnes, Corey. *Fixing Landscape: A Techno-Poetic History of China's Three Gorges.* New York: Columbia University Press, 2019.

Callicott, J. Baird. "'The Arboretum and the University:' The Speech and the Essay." *Transactions of the Wisconsin Academy of Sciences, Arts and Letters* 87 (1999): 5–21.

Cameron, Allan, and Richard Misek. "Time Lapse and the Projected Body." *Moving Image Review and Art Journal* 3, no. 1 (2014): 38–51.

Campbell, Nancy. *The Library of Ice: Readings from a Cold Climate.* New York: Scribner, 2018.

Canales, Jimena. "Clock/Lived." In *Time: A Vocabulary of the Present*, ed. Joel Burges and Amy Elias, 7. New York: NYU Press, 2016.

Card, James. *Seductive Cinema: The Art of Silent Film.* New York: Knopf, 1994.

Carey, Mark. "The History of Ice: How Glaciers Became an Endangered Species." *Environmental History* 12, no. 3 (2007): 497–527.

Carrington, Damian. "2016 Will Be the Hottest Year on Record, UN Says." *The Guardian*, November 14, 2016.

Carruth, Allison. "The Digital Cloud and the Micropolitics of Energy." *Public Culture* 26, no. 2 (2014): 339–64.

Carruth, Allison, and Robert P. Marzec. "Environmental Visualization in the Anthropocene: Technologies, Aesthetics, Ethics." *Public Culture* 26, no. 2 (2014): 205–11.

Case, Kristen. "Phenology." In *Henry David Thoreau in Context*, ed. James S. Finley, 259–68. Cambridge: Cambridge University Press, 2017.

——. "Thoreau's Radical Empiricism: The Calendar, Pragmatism, and Science." In *Thoreauvian Modernities: Transatlantic Conversations on an American Icon*, ed. François Specq, Laura Dassow Walls, and Michel Granger, 187–99. Athens: University of Georgia Press, 2013.

Cerney, Dawna L. "The Use of Repeat Photography in Geomorphic Studies: An Evolving Approach to Understanding Landscape Change." *Geography Compass* 4, no. 9 (2010): 1339–57.

Chaarani, James. "Sugarbush Tree Tappers Get to Work a Month Earlier Than in the Past." *Canadian Broadcasting Corporation News*, March 1, 2022. https://www.cbc.ca/news/canada/london/sugarbush-tree-tappers-get-to-work-a-month-earlier-than-in-the-past-1.6367990.

Chakrabarty, Dipesh. "The Climate of History: Four Theses." *Critical Inquiry* 35 (2009): 197–222.

Chandra, Sudeep, Ankit Singh, Jincy Rachel Mathew, C.P. Singh, Mehul R. Pandya, Bimal K. Bhattacharya, Hitesh Solanki, M.C. Nautiyal, and Rajesh Joshi. "Phenocam Observed Flowering Anomaly of *Rhododendron Arboreum* Sm. in Himalaya: A Climate Change Impact Perspective." *Environmental Monitoring and Assessment* 194, no. 877 (2022): 876–77.

Chapman, Alison A. "Marking Time: Astrology, Almanacs, and English Protestantism." *Renaissance Quarterly* 60 (2007): 1257–90.

Christidis, Nikolaos, Yasuyuki Aono, and Peter A. Stott. "Human Influence Increases the Likelihood of Extremely Early Cherry Tree Flowering in Kyoto." *Environmental Research Letters* 17 (2022): 054051.

Chu, Jennifer. " 'Storm of the Century?' Try 'Storm of the Decade.' " *MIT News: On Campus and Around the World*, February 13, 2012.

City of Detroit, Michigan. *Code of Ordinances*. Code 1964, § 64-1-3; Code 1984, § 57-2-3, https://library.municode.com/mi/detroit/codes/code_of_ordinances.

City of Toronto. *Toronto Municipal Code, Chapter 813: Trees*, May 12, 2022.

Clapesattle, Helen. Helen Clapesattle to Virginia Kiesel, January 31, 1946. Box 5, folder 1. Aldo Leopold Papers, University of Wisconsin-Madison Archives.

Clare, Eli. *Brilliant Imperfection: Grappling with Cure*. Durham, NC: Duke University Press, 2017.

Clausen, Raymond J. "Ethylene Anaesthesia." *Proceedings of the Royal Society of Medicine* 23, no. 9 (1930): 1259–62.

"Climate." Appendix I-Glossary, Working Group 1: The Scientific Basis. Ed. A. P. M. Baede. *Intergovernmental Panel on Climate Change*.

"Climate Change Study Finds That Maple Syrup Season May Come Earlier." *Dartmouth News*. September 20, 2019. https://home.dartmouth.edu/news/2019/09/climate-change-study-finds-maple-syrup-season-may-come-earlier.

Coelho, Karen. "Urban Waterlines: Socio-Natural Productions of Indifference in an Indian City." *International Journal of Urban and Regional Research* 46, no. 2 (2022), 160–81.

Cohen, Ralph. "History and Genre." *New Literary History* 17, no. 2 (1986): 203–18.

Collins, Leah. " 'Live Action Could Never Have Created These Worlds:' Amanda Strong on Her Latest Film, *Biidaaban*." *CBC Arts*. June 15, 2019. https://www.cbc.ca/arts/live-action-could-never-have-created-these-worlds-amanda-strong-on-her-latest-film-biidaaban-1.4821934.

Cosme, Antonio. "Special Sauce: The Detroit Sugarbush Project." *National Wildlife Federation Blog*, May 10, 2021. https://blog.nwf.org/2021/05/special-sauce-the-detroit-sugarbush-project/#:~:text=with%20Indigenous%20experts.-,A%20unique%20partnership%20between%20the%20National%20Wildlife%20Federation%2C%20the%20city,tradition%20of%20making%20maple%20syrup.

Crawford, Neta C. "Pentagon Fuel Use, Climate Change, and the Costs of War." Watson Institute. Brown University. November 13, 2019. https://watson.brown.edu/costsofwar/papers/ClimateChangeandCostofWar.

Cullen, Beth. "Fieldwork Encounters with Monsoon Time." In *Monsoon as Method: Assembling Monsoonal Multiplicities*, ed. Lindsay Bremner, 210–17. New York: Actar Publishing, 2022.

Culler, Jonathan. "Why Rhythm?" In *Critical Rhythm: The Poetics of a Literary Life Form*, ed. Ben Glaser and Jonathan Culler, 21–39. New York: Fordham University Press, 2019.

Curley, Allison N., William H. Kochtitzky, Benjamin R. Edwards, and Luke Copland. "Glacier Changes Over the Past 144 Years at Alexandra Fiord, Ellesmere Island, Canada." *Journal of Glaciology* 67, no. 262 (2021): 511–22.

Damon, Maria. "Was That 'Different,' 'Dissident' or 'Dissonant?' Poetry (n) the Public Spear: Slams, Open Readings, and Dissident Traditions." In *Close Listening: Poetry and the Performed Word*, ed. Charles Bernstein, 324–42. Oxford: Oxford University Press, 1998.

Dean, Bradley. Introduction to *Wild Fruits: Thoreau's Rediscovered Last Manuscript*. New York: Norton, 2000.

Dean, Cornelia. "Thoreau Is Rediscovered as a Climatologist." *New York Times*, October 27, 2008.

de León, Concepción. "The Early Days of the Nuyorican Poets Cafe." *New York Times*, December 6, 2018.

DeLoughrey, Elizabeth. *Allegories of the Anthropocene*. Durham, NC: Duke University Press, 2019.

———. "Radiation Ecologies and the Wars of Light." *Modern Fiction Studies* 55, no. 2 (2009): 468–98.

DeLoughrey, Elizabeth, Jill Didur, and Anthony Carrigan. Introduction to *Global Ecologies and the Environmental Humanities: Postcolonial Approaches*. Ed. Elizabeth DeLoughrey, Jill Didur, and Anthony Carrigan. New York: Routledge, 2015.

Demuth, Bathsheba. *Floating Coast: An Environmental History of the Bering Strait*. New York: Norton, 2019.

Denison, Dave. "Soul On Ice." *Boston College Magazine* (Summer 2013).

Dewey, Edward R. Edward R. Dewey to Aldo Leopold, October 7, 1949. Box 6, folder 4. Aldo Leopold Papers, University of Wisconsin-Madison Archives.

Dhar, Shobita. "Now, Slam Poets Are Speaking in India's Many Languages." *Times of India*, July 10, 2017.

DiChiro, Giovanna. "Environmental Justice." In *Keywords for Environmental Studies*, ed. Joni Adamson, William A. Gleason, and David N. Pellow, 100–105. New York: NYU Press, 2016.

Dillon, Grace. *Walking the Clouds: An Anthology of Indigenous Science Fiction*. Tucson: University of Arizona Press, 2012.

Dimick, Sarah. "Disordered Environmental Time: Phenology, Climate Change, and Seasonal Form in the Work of Henry David Thoreau and Aldo Leopold." *ISLE* 25, no. 4 (2018): 700–21.

Dimock, Wai Chee. *Weak Planet: Literature and Assisted Survival*. Chicago: University of Chicago Press, 2020.

Egan, Ronald C. "Poems on Paintings: Su Shih and Huang T'ing-chien." *Harvard Journal of Asiatic Studies* 43, no. 2 (1983): 413–51.

Ellwood, Elizabeth R., Stanley A. Temple, Richard B. Primack, Nina L. Bradley, and Charles C. Davis. "Record-Breaking Early Flowering in the Eastern United States." *PLoS ONE* 8, no. 1 (2013): 1–9.

Emmett, Rob. *Cultivating Environmental Justice: A Literary History of U.S. Garden Writing*. Amherst: University of Massachusetts Press, 2016.
Evans, Rebecca. "Fantastic Futures?: Cli-fi, Climate Justice, and Queer Futurity." *Resilience* 4, nos. 2–3 (2017): 94–110.
Extreme Ice Survey. "IL-05 Sólheimajökull." *Vimeo*, May 26, 2016.
"Firm Stole Indian Oil, Panel Told: $31 Million Owed, Investigators Tell Senate Committee." *Los Angeles Times*, May 9, 1989.
Flood, Alison. "Scientists Use Thoreau's Journal Notes to Track Climate Change." *The Guardian*, March 14, 2012.
Forché, Carolyn. Introduction to *Against Forgetting: Twentieth Century Poetry of Witness*. New York: Norton, 1993.
Fosbury, Robert A. E., and Glen Jeffrey. "Reindeer Eyes Seasonally Adapt to Ozone-Blue Arctic Twilight by Tuning a Photonic Tapetum Lucidum." *Proceedings of the Royal Society B* 289, no. 1977 (2022): 1–9.
Fowler, Alastair. *Kinds of Literature: An Introduction to the Theory of Genres and Modes*. Cambridge, MA: Harvard University Press, 1982.
———. "The Life and Death of Literary Forms." *New Literary History* 2, no. 2 (1971): 199–216.
Fox, Chris. "Looking to Rent One-Bedroom Apartment in Toronto? New Report Suggests You'll Pay More Than $2,500 a Month." *CTV News Toronto*. March 14, 2023.
François, Anne-Lise. "Fire, Water, Moon: Supplemental Seasons in a Time Without Season." In *Climate Realism: The Aesthetics of Weather and Atmosphere in the Anthropocene*, ed. Lynn Badia, Marija Cetinić, and Jeff Diamanti, 47–65. New York: Routledge, 2020.
Freeman, Elizabeth. *Time Binds: Queer Temporalities, Queer Histories*. Durham, NC: Duke University Press, 2010.
Frye, Northrop. *The Anatomy of Criticism: Four Essays*, rev. ed. Princeton, NJ: Princeton University Press, 2000.
Furuhata, Yuriko. *Climatic Media: Transpacific Experiments in Atmospheric Control*. Durham, NC: Duke University Press, 2022.
Fussell, Paul. *Poetic Meter and Poetic Form*. New York: Random House, 1965.
Gapp, Isabelle. "Galvanizing Glaciology: Thoughts on An Ecocritical Art History." *Environmental History Now*. January 20, 2022.
Gan, Elaine. "Diagrams: Making Multispecies Temporalities Visible." In *Experimenting with Ethnography: A Companion to Analysis*, ed. Andrea Ballestero and Brit Ross Winthereik, 106–20. Durham, NC: Duke University Press, 2021.
———. "Timing Rice: An Inquiry into More-Than-Human Temporalities." *New Formations: A Journal of Culture/Theory/Politics* 92, no. 6 (2017): 87–101.
Garrard, Rodney, and Mark Carey. "Beyond Images of Melting Ice: Hidden Histories of People, Place, and Time in Repeat Photography of Glaciers." In *Before and After Photography: Histories and Contexts*, ed. Jordan Bear and Kate Palmer Albers, 101-22. London: Bloomsbury, 2017.

Gaycken, Oliver. "Early Cinema and Evolution." In *Evolution and Victorian Culture*, ed. Bernard Lightman and Bennett Zon, 94–120. Cambridge: Cambridge University Press, 2014.

Gelles, David, and Manuela Andreoni. "Coming Soon: More Oil, Gas and Coal." Climate Forward Newsletter. *New York Times*, November 9, 2023.

Genette, Gérard. "Time and Narrative in *A La Recherche Du Temps Perdu*." *Aspects of Narrative: Selected Papers from the English Institute*, ed. J. Hillis Miller, 93–118. New York: Columbia University Press, 1971.

Ghosh, Amitav. *The Great Derangement: Climate Change and the Unthinkable*. Chicago: University of Chicago Press, 2016.

Giesting, Kristen. "Maple Syrup." *USDA Forest Service Climate Change Resource Center*, 2020. https://www.fs.usda.gov/ccrc/topics/maple-syrup.

Gleeson-White, Jane. "Going Viral." *Sydney Review of Books*, August 23, 2013.

Goodbody, Axel, and Adeline Johns-Putra. *Cli-Fi: A Companion*. Oxford: Peter Lang, 2019.

Gowanloch, J. N. "Natural Cycles—A Mystery of Life." *Louisiana Conservation Review*, October 1931. Box 6, folder 4. Aldo Leopold Papers, University of Wisconsin-Madison Archives.

Griffiths, Devin. "The Ecology of Form." *Critical Inquiry* 48, no. 1 (2021): 68–93.

Grossman, Sara J. *Immeasurable Weather: Meteorological Data and Settler Colonialism From 1820 to Hurricane Sandy*. Durham, NC: Duke University Press, 2023.

"Ground Water Sources Dry Up In Tamil Nadu." *Times of India*, April 4, 1969.

Guha, Ramachandra, and Joan Martínez Alier. *Varieties of Environmentalism: Essays North and South*. London: Earthscan, 1997.

Gumbs, Alexis Pauline. *Undrowned: Black Feminist Lessons from Marine Mammals*. Chico, CA: AK Press, 2020.

Gupta, Pamila. "Ways of Seeing Wetness." *Wasafiri* 36, no. 2 (2021): 37–47.

Haimbe, Mbozi. "Shelter." In *Disruption: New Short Fiction from Africa*, ed. Karina Szczurek, Jason Mykl Snyman, and Rachel Zadok, 132. Short Story Day South Africa, 2021.

Halberstam, Jack. *Queer Time and Place: Transgender Bodies, Subcultural Lives*. New York: NYU Press, 2005.

Harrabin, Roger. "UN Seeks 'Malala' On Climate Change." *BBC News*, August 29, 2014. www.bbc.com/news/science-environment-28958227.

Harris, John R. *Returning North with the Spring*. Gainesville: University Press of Florida, 2016.

Heglar, Mary Annaïse. "Climate Change Isn't the First Existential Threat." *Medium*, February 18, 2019.

Heine, Hilda. "We Are on the Front Line of Climate Change, Marshall Islands President Says." Interview by Rachel Martin. *Morning Edition*. National Public Radio, September 24, 2019.

Heise, Ursula. *Sense of Place and Sense of Planet: The Environmental Imagination of the Global*. Oxford: Oxford University Press, 2008.

Hensley, Nathan K., and Philip Steer. "Introduction: Ecological Formalism; or, Love Among the Ruins." In *Ecological Form: System and Aesthetics in the Age of Empire*, ed. Nathan K. Hensley and Philip Steer, 1–17. New York: Fordham University Press, 2019.

Hiltner, Ken. "Ripeness: Thoreau's Critique of Technological Modernity." *Concord Saunterer* 12/13 (2004/2005): 322–38.

Hobart, Hi'ilei Julia. "On Oceanic Fugitivity." *Items*, September 9, 2020. https://items.ssrc.org/ways-of-water/on-oceanic-fugitivity.

Hoffman, Tyler. *American Poetry in Performance: From Walt Whitman to Hip Hop*. Ann Arbor: University of Michigan Press, 2013.

Hogue, Rebecca H. and Anaïs Maurer. "Pacific Women's Anti-Nuclear Poetry: Centring Indigenous Knowledges." *International Affairs* 98, no. 4 (2022): 1267-88.

Hofmeyr, Isabel. "B-Sides: Bessie Head's 'The Collector of Treasures.' " *Public Books*, August 12, 2012.

Hogue, Rebecca. "Oceans, Radiations, and Monsters." *Critical Ethnic Studies* 7, no. 2 (2022).

Holgate, Ben. "Unsettling Narratives: Re-Evaluating Magical Realism as Postcolonial Discourse Through Alexis Wright's *Carpentaria* and *The Swan Book*." *Journal of Postcolonial Writing* 51, no. 6 (2015): 634–47.

Holmström, Lakshmi. Introduction to *Water*. Oxford: Heinemann, 1993.

——. "The Modern Tamil Novel: Changing Identities and Transformations." In *Indian Literature and the World: Multilingualism, Translation, and the Public Sphere*, ed. Rosella Ciocca and Neelam Srivastava, 135–51. London: Palgrave Macmillan, 2017.

Houser, Heather. *Ecosickness in Contemporary U.S. Fiction: Environment and Affect*. New York: Columbia University Press, 2014.

——. "Human/Planetary." In *Time: A Vocabulary of the Present*, ed. Joel Burgess and Amy J. Elias, 144-60. New York: NYU Press, 2020.

——. *Infowhelm: Environmental Art and Media in an Age of Data*. New York: Columbia University Press, 2020.

Howe, Joshua P. "This Is Nature; This Is Un-Nature: Reading the Keeling Curve." *Environmental History* 20 (2015): 286–93.

Huang, Hsinya. "Toward Transpacific Ecopoetics: Three Indigenous Texts." *Comparative Literature Studies* 50, no. 1 (2013): 120–47.

Hulme, Mike. "Climate." *Environmental Humanities* 6 (2015): 175–78.

——. *Weathered: Cultures of Climate*. Los Angeles: Sage, 2017.

Hutcheon, Linda. *A Theory of Adaptation*. New York: Routledge, 2012.

Hyman, Stanley Edgar. "Henry Thoreau In Our Time." *Atlantic Monthly*, November 1946.

Inkpen, Dani. *Capturing Glaciers: A History of Repeat Photography and Global Warming*. Seattle: University of Washington Press, 2023.

IPCC. "Summary for Policymakers." In *Climate Change 2021: The Physical Science Basis. Contribution of Working Group I to the Sixth Assessment Report of the Intergovernmental Panel on Climate Change* (2021).

Jameson, Frederic. *The Antinomies of Realism*. New York: Verso, 2013.

Jayaraman, Nityanand. "Welcome to 'Science of the Seas.'" *The Wire*. https://science.thewire.in/science-of-the-seas/.

Jayaraman, Nityanand and S. Palayam. "Hunting Anchovies in a Night Sea." Science of the Seas, *The Wire*, October 14, 2021. https://science.thewire.in/science-of-the-seas/.

———. "Reading Trash, Telling Seasons." Science of the Seas, *The Wire*, March 21, 2022. https://science.thewire.in/science-of-the-seas/.

———. "Saved By the Wind: Why Chennai's Air May Be Cleaner This Bhogi." Science of the Seas, *The Wire*, December 1, 2022. https://science.thewire.in/science-of-the-seas/.

———. "Sea Changed; Therefore Climate Change." Science of the Seas, *The Wire*, January 30, 2023. https://science.thewire.in/science-of-the-seas/.

Jetñil-Kijiner, Kathy. "Iep Jāltok: A History of Marshallese Literature." MA thesis. University of Hawai'i at Manoa, 2014.

———. *Iep Jāltok: Poems from a Marshallese Daughter*. Tucson: University of Arizona Press, 2017.

———. "Statement and Poem by Kathy Jetñil-Kijiner, Climate Summit 2014—Opening Ceremony." *YouTube*, uploaded by United Nations, September 23, 2014. www.youtube.com/watch?v=mc_IgE7TBSY.

Johnson, Barbara. "Apostrophe, Animation, and Abortion." *Diacritics* 16, no. 1 (1986): 28–47.

———. "Thresholds of Difference: Structures of Address in Zora Neale Hurston." *Critical Inquiry* 12, no. 1 (1985): 278–89.

Johnson, Javon. *Killing Poetry: Blackness and the Making of Slam and Spoken Word Communities*. New Brunswick, NJ: Rutgers University Press, 2017.

Jones, Sara Elizabeth. Sara Elizabeth Jones to Aldo Leopold, January 7, 1946. Box 1, folder 23. Aldo Leopold Papers, University of Wisconsin-Madison Archives.

———. Sara Elizabeth Jones to Aldo Leopold, January 18, 1946. Box 1, folder 23. Aldo Leopold Papers, University of Wisconsin-Madison Archives.

———. Sara Elizabeth Jones to Aldo Leopold, September 29, 1946. Box 8, folder 1. Aldo Leopold Papers, University of Wisconsin-Madison Archives.

Jue, Melody. *Wild Blue Media: Thinking Through Seawater*. Durham, NC: Duke University Press, 2020.

Juvenal. *The Sixteen Satires*, 3rd ed. Trans. Peter Green. London: Penguin Books, 1998.

Kammen, Michael. *A Time to Every Purpose: The Four Seasons in American Culture*. Chapel Hill: The University of North Carolina Press, 2004.

Keck, Mary. "Obituary: Sarah Elizabeth Frey, 94." *The Herald-Times*. Bloomington, Indiana, November 10, 2013.

"keep, v." OED Online. September 2022. Oxford University Press. https://doi.org/10.1093/OED/7985374782.

Keller, Lynn. *Recomposing Ecopoetics: North American Poetry of the Self-Conscious Anthropocene*. Charlottesville: University of Virginia Press, 2018.

Keown, Michelle. "Children of Israel: US Military Imperialism and Marshallese Migration in the Poetry of Kathy Jetñil-Kijiner." *Interventions* 19, no. 7 (2017): 930–47.

King, Rachael Scarborough. "The Scale of Genre." *New Literary History* 52, no. 2 (2021): 261–84.

Klein, Naomi. *On Fire: The (Burning) Case for a Green New Deal*. New York: Simon & Schuster, 2019.

Kolbert, Elizabeth. *Field Notes from a Catastrophe: Man, Nature, and Climate Change*. New York: Bloomsbury, 2006.

Krause, Frank. "Seasons as Rhythms on the Kemi River in Finnish Lapland." *Ethnos* 78, no. 1 (2013): 23–46.

Krzywonos, Stephanie. "Coyolxauhqui: Time, Mexihcah, Antarctica." *Ofrenda Magazine* 9.

Kucheravy, Calia E., Jane M. Waterman, Elaine A.C. dos Anjos, James F. Hare, Chris Enright, and Charlene N. Berkvens. "Extreme Climate Event Promotes Phenological Mismatch Between Sexes in Hibernating Ground Squirrels." *Scientific Reports* 11 (2021): 21684.

Lavery, David. "Poetry As Time-Lapse Photography." *Essays in Arts and Science* 17 (1988): 1.

Legault, Simon, Daniel Houle, Antoine Plouffe, Aitor Ameztegui, Diane Kuehn, Lisa Chase, Anne Blondlot, and Timothy D. Perkins. "Perceptions of U.S. and Canadian Maple Syrup Producers Toward Climate Change, Its Impacts, and Potential Adaptation Measures." *PLoS ONE* 14, no. 4 (2019).

LeMenager, Stephanie. "Climate Change and the Struggle for Genre." In *Anthropocene Reading: Literary History in Geologic Times*, ed. Tobias Menely and Jesse Oak Taylor, 220–38. University Park: Penn State University Press, 2017.

——. *Living Oil: Petroleum Culture in the American Century*. Oxford: Oxford University Press, 2014.

——. "Nineteenth-Century American Literature Without Nature? Rethinking Environmental Criticism." In *The Oxford Handbook of Nineteenth-Century American Literature*, ed. Russ Castronovo, 392–410. New York: Oxford University Press, 2012.

——. "Skilling Up for the Anthropocene." In *Feminist Queer Anticolonial Propositions for Hacking the Anthropocene: Archive*, ed. Jennifer Mae Hamilton, Sue Reid, Pia van Gelder, and Astrida Neimanis, 212. London: One Humanities Press, 2021.

Leonard, Christopher. "How an Oil Theft Investigation Laid the Groundwork for the Koch Playbook." *Politico*, July 22, 2019.

———. *Kochland: The Secret History of Koch Industries and Corporate Power in America.* New York: Simon & Schuster, 2019.

Leonard, Keith. "Rising to the Occasion." *American Periodicals* 25 (2015): 182–84.

Leopold, Aldo. Aldo Leopold to Charlie Schwartz, September 17, 1947. Box 5, folder 1. Aldo Leopold Papers, University of Wisconsin-Madison Archives.

———. Aldo Leopold to Keith Denis, April 16, 1948. Box 8, folder 1. Aldo Leopold Papers, University of Wisconsin-Madison Archives.

———. Aldo Leopold to Sara Elizabeth Jones, October 9, 1946. Aldo Leopold Papers, University of Wisconsin-Madison Archives.

———. Aldo Leopold to Sara Elizabeth Jones, April 8, 1948. Box 1, folder 23. Aldo Leopold Papers, University of Wisconsin-Madison Archives.

———. Aldo Leopold to William Sloane, December 19, 1947. Box 5, folder 1. Aldo Leopold Papers, University of Wisconsin-Madison Archives.

———. *Game Management.* New York: Charles Scribner's Sons, 1933.

———. *A Sand County Almanac.* New York: Ballantine Books, 1966.

Leopold, Aldo, and Sara Elizabeth Jones. "A Phenological Record for Sauk and Dane Counties, Wisconsin, 1935–1945." *Ecological Monographs* 17, no. 1 (1947): 81–122.

Levine, Caroline. *Forms: Whole, Rhythm, Hierarchy, Network.* Princeton, NJ: Princeton University Press, 2015.

Lichtenstein, Jesse. "How Poetry Came to Matter Again." *The Atlantic,* September 2018.

Linton, Jamie, and Jessica Budds. "The Hydrosocial Cycle: Defining and Mobilizing a Relational-Dialectical Approach to Water." *Geoforum* 57 (2014): 170–80.

Liu, Yachen, Xiuqi Fang, Junhu Dai, Huanjiong Wang, and Zexing Tao. "Could Phenological Records from Chinese Poems of the Tang and Song Dynasties (618–1279 CE) Be Reliable Evidence of Past Climate Changes?" *Climate of the Past* 17 (2021): 929–50.

Lyell, Charles. *Principles of Geology* 1. Chicago: University of Chicago Press, 1990.

Lyman, Don. "Can Thoreau Make Us Care About Forest Wildflowers?" *Boston Globe,* February 28, 2019.

Macfarlane, R. Ashton. "Wild Laboratories of Climate Change: Plants, Phenology, and Global Warming, 1955–1980." *Journal of the History of Biology* 54 (2021): 311–40.

Macfarlane, Robert. "The Burning Question." *The Guardian,* September 23, 2005.

Machado, Jessica. "What It's Like to Live Through the Australian Bushfires." *Vox,* January 24, 2020.

MacKenzie, Caitlin McDonough, Jason Johnston, Abraham J. Miller-Rushing, William Sheehan, Robert Pinette, and Richard Primack. "Advancing Leaf-Out and Flowering Phenology Is Not Matched by Migratory Bird Arrivals Recorded in Hunting Guide's Journal in Aroostook County, Maine." *Northeastern Naturalist* 26, no. 3 (2019): 561–79.

MacKenzie, D. Kealiʻi. "In Words There Is Life: Kanaka ʻŌiwi Participation in Slam Poetry." PhD dissertation. University of Hawaiʻi at Mānoa, 2016.

Maggini, Ivan, Massimiliano Cardinale, Jonas Hentati Sundberg, Fernando Spina, and Leonida Fusani. "Recent Phenological Shifts of Migratory Birds at a Mediterranean Spring Stopover Site: Species Wintering in the Sahel Advance Passage More Than Tropical Winterers." *PLoS ONE* 15, no. 9 (2020). https://doi.org/ 10.1371/journal.pone.0239489.

"Mahindra Gives $10M for Humanities Center." *Harvard Gazette*, October 4, 2010.

Main, Saskia. "Desert Frogs Resurface After Months—and Sometimes Years—Underground Waiting for Rain." *Australian Broadcasting Corporation*, March 21, 2020.

Mann, Justin. "What's Your Emergency? White Women and the Policing of Public Space." *Feminist Studies* 44, no. 3 (2018): 768–69.

Marsh, Selina Tusitala. "Slow Walking, Fast Talking." In *Anglo-American Imperialism and the Pacific: Discourses of Encounter*, ed. Michelle Known, Andrew Taylor, and Mandy Treagus, 68–88. New York: Routledge, 2018.

Martinez, Lacee A.C. "'Island Haze' Earns Guam Poet Performances in Paris." *USA Today*, December 3, 2015.

Mathiesen, Karl. "Losing Paradise: The People Displaced by Atomic Bombs, and Now Climate Change." *The Guardian*, March 9, 2015.

McClintock, Anne. "Monster: A Fugue in Fire and Ice." *E-Flux Architecture*, June 2020.

McCormack, Michael. Interview by Eliza Edwards. *Sky News*, December 18, 2019.

McCurry, Justin. "Japan's Haiku Poets Lost for Words as Climate Crisis Disrupts Seasons." *The Guardian*, November 13, 2023.

McLeod, Gary. "Rephotograph (v)." *Philosophy of Photography* 10, no. 1 (2019): 89–99.

McNamara, Russ. "'A Beautiful Process:' Work Continues for Detroit Sugarbush Project." *WDET*, February 25, 2022. https://wdet.org/2022/02/25/a-beautiful-process-work-continues-for-detroit-sugarbush-project.

McNeill, John R., and Peter Engelke. *The Great Acceleration: An Environmental History of the Anthropocene Since 1945.* Cambridge, MA: Harvard University Press, 2014.

Meine, Curt. *Aldo Leopold: His Life and Work.* Madison: University of Wisconsin Press, 1991.

Menely, Tobias. *Climate and the Making of Worlds: Towards a Geohistorical Poetics.* Chicago: The University of Chicago Press, 2021.

———. "'The Present Obfuscation': Cowper's Task and the Time of Climate Change." *PMLA* 127, no. 3 (2012).

Miles, Melissa. "Rephotography and the Era of Witness." *Photographies* 9, no. 1 (2016): 51–69.

Miller, Daegan. *This Radical Land: A Natural History of American Dissent.* Chicago: University of Chicago Press, 2018.

———. Twitter post, November 28, 2022, 8:15 a.m. https://twitter.com/Daegan Miller/status/1597217714942095360.

Mills, L. Scott, Marketa Zimova, Jared Tyler, Steven Running, John T. Abatzoglou, and Paul M. Lukacs. "Camouflage Mismatch in Seasonal Coat Color Due to Decreased Snow Duration." *PNAS* 110, no. 18 (2013), 7360–65.

Mitman, Gregg. "In Search of Health: Landscape and Disease in American Environmental History." *Environmental History* 10 (April 2005): 184–210.

Monk, Samuel H. "Introduction to John Dryden." In *The Norton Anthology of English Literature, Vol. 1*, 7th ed., ed. M. H. Abrams and Stephen Greenblatt, 2071–72. New York: Norton, 2000.

Moynihan, Michael. "Inside Quebec's Maple Syrup Cartel." *Vice*, April 19, 2017. https://www.vice.com/en/article/ywnjkv/inside-quebecs-maple-syrup-black-market.

Mukherjee, Ranu, and Alicia Escott. "Shadowtime." *The Bureau of Linguistic Reality*, ed. Heidi Quante and Alicia Escott, 2015. https://bureauoflinguisticreality.com/portfolio/shadowtime/.

Myers-Smith, Isla H., David S. Hik, Catherine Kennedy, Dorothy Cooley, Jill F. Johnstone, Alice J. Kenny, and Charles J. Krebs. "Expansion of Canopy-Forming Willows Over the Twentieth Century on Herschel Island, Yukon Territory, Canada." *Ambio* 40 (2011): 610–23.

Nabhan, Gary Paul. "Learning the Language of Fields and Forests." Foreword to Henry David Thoreau, *Faith in a Seed: The Dispersion of Seeds and Other Late Natural History Writings*, ed. Bradley Dean, xi–xviii. Washington D.C.: Island Press, 1996.

Nandakumar, Prema. Review of *Water*, by Ashokamitran. *World Literature Today* 68, no. 3 (1994): 635.

Nayar, Parvathi, dir. *Seaspeaker*. Film. Chennai, India: Dakshina Chitra Museum, 2024. https://www.dakshinachitra.net/art-craft-events-ecr.

Nixon, Rob. "The Anthropocene: The Promises and Pitfalls of an Epochal Idea." *Edge Effects*, November 6, 2014. edgeeffects.net/anthropocene-promise-and-pitfalls/.

——. *Slow Violence and the Environmentalism of the Poor*. Cambridge, MA: Harvard University Press, 2011.

Nguyen, Kevin. "Fires in NSW Partly Caused by Delayed Monsoons in India, Experts Say." *ABC News*, November 8, 2019.

Nguyen, Sahra Vang. "Pacific Islander Poets Use Art, Stories to Urge Climate Action at UN Conference." *NBC News*, December 9, 2015. www.nbcnews.com/news/asian-america/pacific-islander-poets-use-art-stories-urge-climate-action-un-n476486.

Noel, Urayoán. *In Visible Movement: Nuyorican Poetry from the Sixties to Slam*. Iowa City: University of Iowa Press, 2014.

Offill, Jenny. *Weather*. New York: Knopf, 2020.

Ofosu-Bamfo, Bismark. "African Phenology Network: Working Towards Coordinated Phenology Monitoring in Africa." Presentation, Phenomenal Time Series, organized by Michelle Bastian. Edinburgh, February 3, 2022.

Oh, Rebecca. "Making Time: Pacific Futures in Kiribati's Migration with Dignity, Kathy Jetñil-Kijiner's *Iep Jāltok*, and Keri Hulme's *Stonefish*." *Modern Fiction Studies* 66, no. 4 (2020): 597–619.

Onion, Rebecca. "Want to Fight Climate Change? Start by Carefully Watching Your Own Backyard." *Slate*, July 16, 2018.

Oreskes, Naomi. "The Scientific Consensus on Climate Change: How Do We Know We're Not Wrong?" In *Climate Change: What It Means for Us, Our Children, and Our Grandchildren*, 2nd ed., ed. Joseph F.C. DiMento and Pamela Doughman, 105–48. Boston: MIT Press, 2014.

"Pacific Tongues." Accessed August 24, 2020. http://pacifictongues.weebly.com/about.html.

Palit, Chittaroopa. "Monsoon Risings: Mega-Dam Resistance in the Narmada Valley." *New Left Review* 21 (2003). https://newleftreview.org/issues/ii21/articles/chittaroopa-palit-monsoon-risings.

Pandian, Anand. *Reel World: An Anthropology of Creation.* Durham, NC: Duke University Press, 2015.

"Paris Agreement." *United Nations Framework Convention on Climate Change*, 2015. unfccc.int/sites/default/files/english_paris_agreement.pdf.

Park, Lisa Sun-Hee, and David Naguib Pellow. *The Slums of Aspen: Immigrants vs. the Environment in America's Eden.* New York: NYU Press, 2011.

Parry, Wynne. "Thoreau's Notes Reveal How Spring Has Changed In 150 Years." *NBC*, March 9, 2012.

Peattie, Donald Culross. *An Almanac for Moderns.* San Antonio, TX: Trinity University Press, 2013.

Peck, H. Daniel. *Thoreau's Morning Work: Memory and Perception in a Week on the Concord and Merrimack Rivers, the Journal, and Walden.* New Haven, CT: Yale University Press, 1994.

Perez, Craig Santos. "Signs of Beibg: Chamoru Poetry and the Work of Cecilia C. T. Perez." *Jacket 2*, April 2, 2011. jacket2.org/article/signs-being.

——. "Wayreading Chamorro Literature from Guam." PhD dissertation. University of California Berkeley, 2015.

"phenology, n." OED Online. September 2022. Oxford University Press. https://www-oed-com.ezp-prod1.hul.harvard.edu/view/Entry/235540?redirectedFrom=phenology. Accessed October 16, 2022.

Philips, Craig. "Filmmaker Asks New Yorkers, What Does the Future Look Like?" *PBS.org*, April 16, 2020.

Pillsbury, Arthur C. *Picturing Miracles of Plant and Animal Life.* Philadelphia: J.B. Lippincott, 1937.

Plum, Hilary, and Lucy Biederman. "Literature, Capital, Catapult, and the Kochs: A Dialogue." *Fence*. https://fenceportal.org/literature-capital-catapult-and-the-kochs-a-dialogue/.

Poole, Sara. "'*Slambiguité?*' Youth Culture and the Positioning of 'Le Slam' in France." *Modern and Contemporary France* 15, no. 3 (2007): 339–50.

Premoli, Martín. "Global Anthropocene Fiction and the Politics of Climate Disaster." PhD dissertation. University of Pennsylvania, 2020.

Primack, Richard B. *Walden Warming: Climate Change Comes to Thoreau's Woods*. Chicago: University of Chicago Press, 2014.

Puchner, Martin. *Literature for a Changing Planet*. Princeton, NJ: Princeton University Press, 2022.

Raboteau, Emily. "How Do We Bring More Urgency to the Climate Crisis? Emma Sloley and Emily Raboteau in Conversation." Interview by Emma Sloley. *Literary Hub*, November 7, 2019.

——. "This Is How We Live Now: A Year's Diary of Reckoning with Climate Anxiety, Conversation by Conversation." *The Cut*, January 9, 2020.

Ramanujan, A.K. *The Interior Landscape: Classical Tamil Love Poems*. New York: New York Review of Books, 1967.

Ramaswami, Geetha, and Suhel Quader. "The Case of the Confusing Kanikonna Trees." *The Wire*, June 26, 2018. https://science.thewire.in/environment/the-case-of-the-confusing-kanikonna-trees/.

Randall, Jesse A. "Maple Syrup Production." *Iowa State University Forestry Extension*, Publication F-337A (2010).

Rantanen, Mika, Alexey Yu. Karpechko, Antti Lipponen, Kalle Nordling, Otto Hyvärinen, Kimmo Ruosteenoja, Timo Vihma, and Ari Laaksonen. "The Arctic Has Warmed Nearly Four Times Faster Than the Globe Since 1970." *Communications Earth & Environment* 3, no. 1 (2022): 1–10.

Rao, V. G. Prasad. "Drought Affects Tamil Nadu: Food Crisis Feared." *Times of India*, March 20, 1969.

Ravenscroft, Alison. "Dreaming of Others: *Carpentaria* and Its Critics." *Cultural Studies Review* 16, no. 2 (2010): 194–224.

Ribbens, Dennis. "The Making of a Sand County Almanac." In *Companion to A Sand County Almanac: Interpretive and Critical Essays*, ed. J. Baird Callicott, 91–109. Madison: University of Wisconsin Press, 1987.

Richardson, Robert D., Jr. "Thoreau's Broken Task." Introduction to *Faith in A Seed: The Dispersion of Seeds and Other Late Natural History Writings*, by Henry David Thoreau, ed. Bradley P. Dean, 3–22. Washington, D.C.: Island Press, 1996.

Rix, Harriet. "The Acorn Harvest in Iraqi Kurdistan." *London Review of Books*, December 9, 2022.

Robbins, Bruce. "Afterword." *PMLA* 122, no. 5 (2007): 1644–51.

Robin, Libby. *How a Continent Created a Nation*. Sydney: University of New South Wales Press, 2007.

——. "Uncertain Seasons in the El Niño Continent: Local and Global Views." *Anglica: An International Journal of English Studies* 28, no. 3 (2019): 7–19.

Robinson, Angela. "Of Monsters and Mothers: Affective Climates and Human-Nonhuman Sociality in Kathy Jetñil-Kijiner's 'Dear Matabele Peinam.'" *The Contemporary Pacific* 32, no. 2 (2020): 311–39.

Rooney, Brigid. *Suburban Space, the Novel, and Australian Modernity.* London: Anthem Press, 2018.
Rose, Deborah. "Rhythms, Patterns, Connectivities: Indigenous Concepts of Seasons and Change." In *A Change in the Weather: Climate and Culture in Australia,* ed. Tim Sherratt, Tom Griffiths, and Libby Robin, 32–41. Canberra: National Museum of Australia Press, 2005.
Roy, Arundhati. *Capitalism: A Ghost Story.* Chicago: Haymarket Books, 2014.
"Run For Your Life—Island Poets." *YouTube,* uploaded by Global Call for Climate Action. December 2, 2015. https://www.youtube.com/watch?v=MoNn2Q8MBAE&t=20s.
Rush, Elizabeth. *Rising: Dispatches from the New American Shore.* Minneapolis: Milkweed Editions, 2018.
Ryan, Finn. "Phenology." Climate Wisconsin. *PBS Wisconsin Education,* 2019.
Sacks, Susanna. "Moving Forms: Individuals, Institutions, and the Production of Slam Poetry Networks in Southern Africa." *ASAP Journal* 5, no. 1 (2020): 153–79.
Saramago, Victoria. *Fictional Environments: Mimesis, Deforestation, and Development in Latin America.* Evanston, IL: Northwestern University Press, 2021.
Sarmiento, John "Meta." "Island Haze." *YouTube,* uploaded by Meta Sarmiento, November 24, 2015. www.youtube.com/watch?v=iekYyIToIro.
Sattelmeyer, Robert. "The Remaking of Walden." In *Walden and Resistance to Civil Government,* 2nd ed., ed. William Rossi, 428–43. New York: Norton, 1992.
Schulman, Sarah. *My American History: Lesbian and Gay Life During the Reagan and Bush Years.* New York: Routledge, 2018.
Schwartz, Jessica. "Making Waves: Marshallese Youth Culture, 'Minor Songs,' and Major Challenges." In *Reppin:' Pacific Islander Youth and Native Justice,* ed. Keith Camacho, 150–73. Seattle: University of Washington Press, 2021.
Seely, Christina. "Markers of Time: DEFLUO Animalis, Vulpes Lagopus." https://www.christinaseely.com/defluo-animalis.
Seidel, Amy. *Early Spring: An Ecologist and Her Children Wake to a Warming World.* Boston: Beacon, 2009.
Sengupta, Somini. "Life in a City Without Water: Anxious, Exhausting and Sweaty." *New York Times,* July 11, 2019.
Seymour, Nicole. *Strange Natures: Futurity, Empathy, and the Queer Ecological Imagination.* Urbana: University of Illinois Press, 2013.
Shackelford, Jole. "Wilhelm Pfeffer and the Roots of Twentieth-Century Biological Rhythms Research." *Transactions of the American Philosophical Society* 103, no. 2 (2013): 9–14.
Shanley, J. Lyndon. *The Making of Walden.* Chicago: University of Chicago Press, 1957.
Shekhar, Anjana. "Revisiting 'Thanneer,' Ashokamitran's Insightful Tamil Novel on Water Scarcity." *The News Minute,* August 11, 2019. https://www

.thenewsminute.com/article/revisiting-thanneer-ashokamitrans-insightful-tamil-novel-water-scarcity-107043.

Shockley, Evie. *Semiautomatic*. Middletown, CT: Wesleyan University Press, 2017.

Shogren, Elizabeth. "Understanding Climate Change, With Help from Thoreau." All Things Considered. *NPR*, January 17, 2013.

Siagatonu, Terisa Tinei. "Layers." *YouTube*, uploaded by Global Call for Climate Action, December 1, 2015. www.youtube.com/watch?v=XgXYP6zqzJk.

Silliman, Ron. "Who Speaks: Ventriloquism and the Self in Poetry Reading." In *Close Listening: Poetry and the Performed Word*, ed. Charles Bernstein, 360–78. Oxford: Oxford University Press, 1998.

Simmons, Kristen. "Settler Atmospherics." Member Voices. *Fieldsights*, November 20, 2017. https://culanth.org/fieldsights/settler-atmospherics.

Simpson, Clinton. Clinton Simpson to Aldo Leopold, April 29, 1946. Box 5, folder 1. Aldo Leopold Papers, University of Wisconsin-Madison Archives.

Simpson, Leanne Betasamosake. *The Gift Is in the Making: Anishinaabeg Stories*. Winnipeg: Highwater Press, 2013.

——. "Land as Pedagogy: Nishnaabeg Intelligence and Rebellious Transformation." *Decolonization: Indignity, Education & Society* 3, no. 3 (2014): 1–25.

——. *This Accident of Being Lost: Songs and Stories*. Toronto: House of Anansi, 2017.

Singeot, Laura. "The Swamp and Desert Tropes in Post-Apocalyptic Australian Fiction: *The Swan Book* (2013) by Alexis Wright and *Terra Nullius* (2018) by Claire Coleman." *Commonwealth Essays and Studies* 43, no. 2 (2021).

Singh, Deepti. "Tug of War on Rainfall Changes." *Nature Climate Change* 6 (2016): 20–22.

Singh, Khushwant. "For Three Years the Great Rains Failed." *New York Times*, August 26, 1973.

——. "The Indian Monsoon in Literature." In *Monsoons*, ed. Jay S. Fein and Pamela L. Stephens, 35–49. New York: John Wiley & Sons, 1987.

Smith, Jen Rose. "Cryogenics." *Edge Effects*, February 6, 2020. https://edgeeffects.net/cryogenics/.

——. *Icy Matters: Race, Indigeneity, and Coloniality in Ice-Geographies*. Forthcoming.

Smith, Stephen. "India: Delivering Water by Hand." *American Public Media Reports*, May 12, 2016. https://www.apmreports.org/episode/2016/05/22/india-carrying-water-by-hand.

Smith, Zadie. "Elegy For a Country's Seasons." *New York Review of Books*, April 3, 2014.

Smithsonian Institution. "Registry of Periodical Phenomena." Record Unit 65, Box 1, Smithsonian Institution Archives, Washington D.C.

Solnit, Rebecca. *River of Shadows: Eadweard Muybridge and the Technological Wild West*. New York: Penguin Books, 2003.

Soman, Deepa. "Vishu Is Almost Here but Where Do We Get the Konna for the Kani?" *Times of India*, April 12, 2017.

Somers-Willett, Susan B. A. *The Cultural Politics of Slam Poetry: Race, Identity, and the Performance of Popular Verse in America*. Ann Arbor: University of Michigan Press, 2009.

Somervell, Tess. "The Seasons." In *Climate and Literature*, ed. Adeline Johns-Putra, 45-59. Cambridge: Cambridge University Press, 2019.

Song, Min Hyoung. *Climate Lyricism*. Durham, NC: Duke University Press, 2022

Sparks, Tim, Judith Garforth, and Lorienne Whittle. "A Comparison of Nature's Calendar with Gilbert White's Phenology." *British Wildlife* 31, no. 4 (2020): 271-75.

Spoken Word for the World. "Thank You to All the Spoken Word for the World Contestants." *Facebook*, October 30, 2015. Accessed July 1, 2018.

Stallings, Alicia E. "Halcyon Days in the Saronic Gulf." *London Review of Books*, January 13, 2023.

Steer, Philip. "The Climates of the Victorian Novel: Seasonality, Weather, and Regional Fiction in Britain and Australia." *PMLA* 136, no. 3 (2021): 370-85.

Stinson, Emmett, and Beth Driscoll, "Difficult Literature on Goodreads: Reading Alexis Wright's *The Swan Book*." *Textual Practice* 36, no. 1 (2022): 94-115.

Story, Brett, dir. *The Hottest August*. New York: Grasshopper Film, 2019.

Streeby, Shelley. *Imagining the Future of Climate Change: World-Making Through Science Fiction and Activism*. Oakland: University of California Press, 2018.

Stoddard, Mary Caswell. "Inside the Colorful World of Birds and Their Eggs." *YouTube*, May 5, 2022. https://www.youtube.com/watch?v=KuPqaDEiw5g&t=1s.

Suzuki, Erin. *Ocean Passages: Navigating Pacific Islander and Asian American Literatures*. Philadelphia: Temple University Press, 2021.

Taleb, Nassim Nicholas. *The Black Swan: The Impact of the Highly Improbable*. New York: Random House, 2007.

Takolander, Maria. "Magical Realism and Indigenous Survivance in Australia: The Fiction of Alexis Wright." In *The Palgrave Handbook of Magical Realism in the Twenty-First Century*, ed. Richard Perez and Victoria A. Chevalier, 173-95. Cham: Springer International Publishing, 2020.

——. "Theorizing Irony and Trauma in Magical Realism: Junot Díaz's *The Brief Wondrous Life of Oscar Wao* and Alexis Wright's *The Swan Book*." *Ariel: A Review of International English Literature* 47, no. 3 (2016): 95-122.

Tape, Ken, Matthew Sturm, and Charles Racine. "The Evidence for Shrub Expansion in Northern Alaska and the Pan-Arctic." *Global Change Biology* 12 (2006): 686-702.

Taylor, Jesse Oak. "A Great Fire Somewhere? Synchronous Living in Epochal Times." *PMLA* 136, no. 3 (2021): 424-31.

——. *The Sky of Our Manufacture: The London Fog in British Fiction from Dickens to Woolf*. Charlottesville: University of Virginia Press, 2016.

Teaiwa, Teresia. "What Remains to Be Seen: Reclaiming the Visual Roots of Pacific Literature." *PMLA* 125, no. 3 (2010): 730-36.

Tedford, Matthew Harrison. "Is a Non-Capitalist World Imaginable? Embodied Practices and Slipstream Potentials in Amanda Strong's Biidaaban." *Feminist Media Histories* 8, no. 1 (2022): 46–71.

Temple, Stanley. "Phenology and the Changing of the Seasons." Interview by Larry Meiller. *Wisconsin Public Radio*, November 24, 2021.

"Theorizing Queer Temporalities: A Roundtable Discussion." *GLQ: A Journal of Lesbian and Gay Studies* 13, nos. 2–3 (2007): 191.

Thomas, Lorenzo. "Neon Griot: The Functional Role of Poetry Readings in the Black Arts Movement." In *Close Listening: Poetry and the Performed Word*, ed. Charles Bernstein, 300–23. Oxford: Oxford University Press, 1998.

Thoreau, Henry David. "Extracts, Mostly Upon Natural History. A Commonplace Book." 1830–1862. Henry W. and Albert A. Berg Collection of English and American Literature, The New York Public Library.

——. *The Journal of Henry David Thoreau*. Boston: Houghton Mifflin, 1906.

——. "Nature Notes, Charts and Tables: Autograph Manuscripts." 1851–60. Manuscript 610, Pierpont Morgan Library, New York.

——. *Walden: A Fluid-Text Edition*. Digital Thoreau. http://digitalthoreau.org/fluid-text-toc.

——. *Walden and Resistance to Civil Government*, 2nd ed. Ed. William Rossi. New York: Norton, 1992.

——. *The Writings of Henry D. Thoreau: Journal*. Princeton, NJ: Princeton University Press, 1984.

Thornber, Karen. *Ecoambiguity: Environmental Crises and East Asian Literatures*. Ann Arbor: University of Michigan Press, 2012.

Thorson, Robert M. *Walden's Shore: Henry David Thoreau and Nineteenth-Century Science*. Cambridge, MA: Harvard University Press, 2014.

TINTA-UP Cebu. Facebook, April 21, 2015. it-it.facebook.com/uptinta/photos/slam!-slam!-do-you-hear/1095544960460683/.

Todd, Zoe. "Indigenizing the Anthropocene." In *Art in the Anthropocene: Encounters Among Aesthetics, Politics, Environments and Epistemologies*, ed. Heather Davis and Etienne Turpin, 241–43. London: Open Humanities Press, 2015.

Trexler, Alex. *Anthropocene Fictions: The Novel in a Time of Climate Change*. Charlottesville: University of Virginia Press, 2015.

Truu, Maani. "Coming To Age in Climate Change." *ABC News*, November 5, 2021.

Tsing, Anna Lowenhaupt. *The Mushroom at the End of the World: On the Possibility of Life in Capitalist Ruins*. Princeton, NJ: Princeton University Press, 2015.

Tung, Charles M. "Time Machines and Timelapse Aesthetics in Anthropocenic Modernism." In *Timescales: Thinking Across Ecological Temporalities*, ed. Bethany Wiggin, Carolyn Fornoff, and Patricia Eunji Kim, 79–93. Minneapolis: University of Minnesota Press, 2020.

Tyndall, John. *The Glaciers of the Alps*. London: John Murray, 1860.

Vaidya, Anjali. "COP21 Diary: A Ray of Sunshine, A Song of Despair." *The Wire*, December 1, 2015.

Venkatachalapathy, A.R. *Tamil Characters: Personalities, Politics, Culture*. New Delhi: Pan Macmillan India, 2018.

Vinothkumar, M., and V. Peruvalluthi. "Sere Life in Ashokamitran's Novel 'Water:' An Eco-Critical Study." *Smart Moves Journal IJELLH* 8, no. 1 (2020): 1–7.

Vizenor, Gerald. *Survivance: Narratives of Native Presence*. Ed. Gerald Vizenor. Lincoln: University of Nebraska Press, 2008.

Wahlquist, Calla. "Australia Had More Supersized Bushfires Creating Their Own Storms Last Summer Than in Previous 30 Years." *The Guardian*, June 16, 2020.

———. "Australian Bushfires: The Story So Far in Each State." *The Guardian*, December 23, 2019.

———. "Australia's Rarest Tortoises Get New Home to Save Them from Climate Change." *The Guardian*, August 16, 2016.

Walcott, Derek. *What the Twilight Says: Essays*. New York: Farrar, Straus and Giroux, 1998.

Walker, AJ. "Tapping into Their Roots: Detroit Sugarbush Project Collects Sap from Rouge Park." *One Detroit*, April 25, 2022. https://www.onedetroitpbs.org/one-detroit/tapping-into-their-roots-detroit-sugarbush-project-begins-collecting-sap-from-rouge-park.

Walls, Laura Dassow. *Seeing New Worlds: Henry David Thoreau and Nineteenth-Century Natural Science*. Madison: University of Wisconsin Press, 1995.

Walsh, Colleen. "Gift of Opportunity." *Harvard Gazette*, April 26, 2011.

Walsh, Julianne M., and Hilda C. Heine. *Etto ñan Raan Kein: A Marshall Island History*. Honolulu: Bess Press, 2012.

Webb, Robert H., Diane E. Boyer, and Raymond M. Turner. "Introduction: A Brief History of Repeat Photography." In *Repeat Photography: Methods and Applications in the Natural Sciences*, ed. Robert H. Webb, Diane E. Boyer, and Raymond M. Turner, 3–11. Washington, D.C.: Island Press, 2010.

Welle, Elissa. "Detroit Police Break Up Native Sugarbush Ceremony, Saying 'Sovereign Stuff Is Not Valid.'" *Detroit Free Press*, February 19, 2022. https://www.freep.com/story/news/local/michigan/detroit/2022/02/19/detroit-police-break-up-native-ceremony/6861547001.

Wells, Jean-Robert, Jean-François Boucher, Achille-Benjamin Laurent, and Claude Villeneuve. "Carbon Footprint Assessment of a Paperback Book: Can Planned Integration of Deinked Market Pulp Be Detrimental to Climate?" *Journal of Industrial Ecology* 16, no. 2 (2012): 212–22.

Wendt, Albert, ed. *Nuanua: Pacific Writing in English Since 1980*. Honolulu: University of Hawai'i' Press, 1995.

Wenzel, Jennifer. *The Disposition of Nature: Environmental Crisis and World Literature*. New York: Fordham University Press, 2020.

Whalen, Francis X., Douglas R. Bacon, and Hugh M. Smith. "Inhaled Anesthetics: An Historical Overview." *Best Practice & Research Clinical Anesthesiology* 19, no. 3 (2005): 323–30.

White, Hayden V. *The Content of the Form: Narrative Discourse and Historical Representation*. Baltimore, MD: Johns Hopkins University Press, 1987.

Whyte, Kyle. "Against Crisis Epistemology." In *Routledge Handbook of Critical Indigenous Studies*. Ed. Brendan Hokowhitu. New York: Routledge, 2020.

——. "Indigenous Climate Change Studies: Indigenizing Futures, Decolonizing the Anthropocene." *English Language Notes* 55, no. 1–2 (2017): 153–62.

——. "Time as Kinship." In *The Cambridge Companion to the Environmental Humanities*, ed. Jeffrey Jerome Cohen and Stephanie Foote. Cambridge: Cambridge University Press, 2021.

Williams, Tanisha M., Carl D. Schlichting, and Kent E. Holsinger. "Herbarium Records Demonstrate Changes in Flowering Phenology Associated with Climate Change Over the Past Century Within the Cape Floristic Region, South Africa." *Climate Change Ecology* 1 (2021): 100006.

Wilson, Rob. "Towards an Ecopoetics of Oceania: Worlding the Asia-Pacific Region as Space-Time Ecumene." In *American Studies as Transnational Practice: Turning Toward the Transpacific*, ed. Yuan Shu and Donald E. Pease, 213–36. Hanover, NH: Dartmouth College Press, 2015.

Wilson, Stephen. "Poetry and Its Occasions: 'Undoing the Folded Lie.'" In *A Companion to Poetic Genre*, 1st ed., ed. Erik Martiny, 490–504. Hoboken, NJ: John Wiley & Sons, 2012.

Wolff, Tristram. *Against the Uprooted Word: Giving Language Time in Transatlantic Romanticism*. Stanford, CA: Stanford University Press, 2022.

Wolkovich, Elizabeth M., Benjamin I. Cook, Kendra K. McLauchlan, and T. J. Davies. "Temporal Ecology in the Anthropocene." *Ecology Letters* 17 (2014): 1365–79.

"The World's Only Reserve of Maple Syrup." *PPAQ*, October 19, 2020. https://ppaq.ca/en/sale-purchase-maple-syrup/worlds-only-reserve-maple-syrup.

Wright, Alexis. Interview by Jean-François Vernay. *Antipodes* 18, no. 2 (2004): 119–22.

——. "The Future of Swans." Interview by Arnold Zable. *Overland* 213 (2013): 27–30.

——. "The Inward Migration in Apocalyptic Times." *Emergence Magazine*, October 26, 2022.

——. *The Swan Book*. New York: Atria Books, 2016.

——. "We All Smell the Smoke, We All Feel the Heat, This Environmental Catastrophe Is Global." *The Guardian*, May 17, 2019.

——. "A Weapon of Poetry." *Overland* 193 (2008): 19–24.

Wright, Sarah D., and Nina Leopold Bradley. "Thinking Like a Flower: Phenology and Climate Change at the Leopold Shack." In *The Vanishing Present: Wisconsin's Changing Lands, Waters, and Wildlife*, ed. Donald M. Waller and Thomas P. Rooney, 41–56. Chicago: University of Chicago Press, 2008.

Wu, Katherine J. "Twice A Year, Reindeer Eyes Pull Off a Wonderful Magic Trick." *The Atlantic*, June 28, 2022.

Yeo, Sophie. "Marshall Islands Poet Says Youth Must Lead Climate Fight." *Climate Home News*, October 22, 2014. www.climatechangenews.com/2014/10/22/marshall-islands-poet-says-youth-must-lead-climate-fight.

Yonetani, Michelle. "Global Estimates 2014: People Displaced by Disasters." *Norwegian Refugee Council*, September 2014.

Yusoff, Kathryn. *A Billion Black Anthropocenes or None*. Minneapolis: University of Minnesota Press, 2018.

Zalamea, Marcela, and Grizelle González. "Leaffall Phenology in a Subtropical Wet Forest in Puerto Rico: From Species to Community Patterns." *Biotropica: The Journal of Tropical Biology and Conservation* 40, no. 3 (2008): 295–304.

Zerefos, Christos S., V. T. Gerogiannis, D. Balis, S. C. Zerefos, and A. Kazantzidis. "Atmospheric Effects of Volcanic Eruptions as Seen by Famous Artists and Depicted in Their Paintings." *Atmospheric Chemistry and Physics* 7 (2007): 4027–42.

INDEX

Figures are indicated by "*f*" after the page number.

Abbey, Edward, 247n92
Abisko Scientific Research Station (Sweden), 74–75
Aboriginal peoples: globalization and, 144; seasonal knowledge among, 131. *See also* Indigenous peoples
acceleration, time-lapse and, 79–88
accents, in Anglophone poetry, 195–196
activism, 167
activist writing, urgency in, 192–193
adaptation, arts of, 223–228
Adiga, Aravind, 121
advocacy, poetry as, 167
aestivation, 134, 136
African Phenology Network, 6
Agarwal, Anil, 17
agriculture, colonial, 55. *See also* harvesting
Akkad, Omar El, 152–153
Alaska, summer in, 73
Alexander, Joe, 42, 43*f*
Alexandra Fiord (Ellesmere Island, Nunavut), 88
alexandrines, 194
Alice Springs, Australia, during bushfires, 138
Alier, Joan Martínez, 105
almanacs, 49–50, 59–60
Alzner, Susan, 170–171
American environmental literature, canon of, 33–36
American War (Akkad), 152–153
Amin, Kadji, 215
Amrith, Sunil, 104, 111, 112
Anatomy of Criticism, The (Frye), 20
Andrada, Eunice, 167, 170, 183, 185, 190–197
Anglophone poetry, accents in, 195–196
Angus, Callum: "The Climate of Gender," 200–201, 213, 218–219; *A Natural History of Transition*, 24, 27, 201, 216–217; on Producteurs Acéricoles du Québec, 206–207; on seasons, stability of, 28; on sugar maples, 199; on transitions, 219; on writing about gender, 215–216
annals, phenological records as, 65
Anthropocene, popularization as geologic epoch, 71–72
anthropogenic activity, 59–62
anthropogenic climate change, 55, 164, 182, 194–195

anthropogenic peripeteia, 63–66
anthropogenic time, 180–186
anti-capitalist practices, 206–213
anticipation. *See* expectation
apocalypse, phenology versus, 53
Arctic: American imperialism in, 70; Great Acceleration's impact on, 84–85
arctic fox (*vulpes lagopus*), 67–68, 68f, 70–71
Arctic reindeer, 15–16
arrhythmias: arrhythmic world, question of keeping time in, 27; audible, in *Biidaaban*, 211–212; in glaciers, 80; in *The Swan Book*, 130; at Walden Pond, 61–62. *See also* climate arrhythmias; keeping time
art, as source for phenology, 7–8
Ashokamitran (Jagadisa Thyagarajan): at Gemini Studios, 121–122; honors for, 116; on magical realism, 121; mentioned, 26; *My Years With Boss*, 122; plaque honoring, 127; *Thanneer* (*Water*), 26, 103–110, 113–116, 118, 121–125
asynchrony, 215
atmospheric carbon dioxide levels, 181–182
atomic cartography, 183
Austin, J. L., 181
Australia: bushfires in, 128, 129, 137–138 (*See also* climate fiction and the unprecedented); Northern Territory National Emergency Response, 257–258n18; Robin on climate of, 153; seasons in, 23, 130–131
averages: climatic, composite years and, 58; sequence of, 56
Awkward-Rich, Cameron, 205–206

Baker, J. A., 247n92
Balog, James, 82–83
banded stilts (Australian birds), 146
Banerjee, Subhankar, 155
Barthes, Roland, 119–120
baselines: for Bay of Bengal currents, 100–101; of climate expectations, 32; historical, seasonal rhythms as, 60
Bastian, Michelle, 7
Bay of Bengal: baseline for currents in, 100–101; mentioned, 26; seasons in, 99–100
Beamish, Alison, 25, 69, 88–89
Bear-Schneider, Rosebud, 221
Bella Donna (character in *The Swan Book*), 134–135, 139, 140, 142–145, 150
Bering Strait, seasonal dynamism of, 72
Berlant, Lauren, 51, 133, 154, 158
Besand Nagar beach (Urur Kuppam, Chennai, India), urban phenological practices in, 99–100
Biden administration, Willow Project and, 78
Biidaaban (character in *Biidaaban*), 202, 204, 206, 208–212, 211
Biidaaban (The Dawn Comes) (Strong): anti-capitalism in, 208; discussion of, 201–205, 208–210, 213, 222; film stills from, 203f, 207f; making of, 224–226; mentioned, 27, 200; soundscape of, 211
biological rhythms, variations in, 54
bird migrations, 7, 138–145
Bjornerud, Marcia, 71
Black Arts Movement, 168
black swan events, 158. *See also* the unprecedented
Black Swan: The Impact of the Highly Improbable, The (Taleb), 140–141
black swans (*Cygnus atratus*), 138–145, 150
Black to the Land, 220

Blodget, Lorin, 53
Bloom, Lisa, 70
blue vervain, 44–45
bodies, embodied experience in slam performances, 175–180
Borgeson, Isabella, 167, 170, 179–180, 196–198
Bowman, David, 141
Bradley, Nina Leopold, 63
Brathwaite, Kamau, 15
Brave New Voices, 170
Brooks, Cleanth, 51
brown, adrienne maree, 157
bud burst, premature, impact on maple sugaring, 200
Buell, Lawrence, 21, 48–49, 59
The Bureau of Linguistic Reality, 14
Burford, Angela, 131
Burke, Kenneth, 14, 51
bushfires, in Australia, 128, 129, 137–138. *See also* climate fiction and the unprecedented
Butler, Octavia, 157–158
"Butterfly Thief" (Jetñil-Kijiner), 266n81
Button Poetry, 171
bwebwenato (Marshall Island oral literature), 173, 189
Byrnes, Corey, 127

caesuras, environmental, 133–138
call and response, 172
cameras, automated, 79. *See also* photography
Cameron, Allan, 86
Campbell, Nancy, 71
Canada: phenological mismatch in, 67; urban spaces, impact of gentrification of, 223–224
Canberra, Australia, hibernation during bushfires, 137–138
canículas (dry spells), 4
Cannon, Mrs. B. E., 146

canon of American environmental literature, 33–36
canonization, pervasive power of, 34–35
capitalism: anti-capitalist practices, 206–213; climate change, relationship to, 207; impact on Indigenous peoples, 138
carbon dioxide levels, 181–182
Card, James, 87
Carey, Mark, 76
caribou, 67–68
"Caribou Ghosts & Untold Stories" (Simpson), 202, 205–206
Carrigan, Anthony, 18
Carruth, Allison, 70, 80, 91–92
Carson, Rachel, 64, 247n92
Carteret Islanders, 187–188, 196
Case, Kristen, 38
Castle Bravo nuclear test, 184
Castro, Fanai, 171–172
Catapult (literary magazine), Angus essay in, 213
cause-based advocacy, 171
Cerney, Dawna, 78
Chakrabarty, Dipesh, 55
Chamorro oral narration, 172
Chaya (character in *Water*), 114–115
Chennai, India: drought in (1969), 103; institutional meteorological observations, 100–101; monsoon's rhythm in, 117–118; as software hub, 102; water crises in, 103, 127
cherry blossoms, 7
Christmas house (location in *The Swan Book*), 147–149
Chronicle of a Summer (Rouch and Morin), 230
chronobiopolitics, 215
Clapesattle, Helen, 48
Clare, Eli, 214
class-based enclosure, 209
class consciousness, 209

classrooms, in heat waves, 11–12
cli-fi. *See* climate fiction
climate: belief in permanent, 52–55; climate adaptation, 226; climate crisis, universal representations of, 187–188; climate culture industry, 80–81, 82, 248n8; climate realism, of *Water*, 125; climate refugees, 142; climate silence, breaking of, 9; climate stress, 164; climate-related events, sources for timing of, 7; climatic witness, poetry of, 176; cultures, relationship to, 13; description of, 56; as language in Tamil literature, 113; literature, relationship to, 56, 58; seasonality versus, 17. *See also* seasons
climate arrhythmias, 1–28; description of, 1–2; form and environmental prosody, 12–16; hoarding as response to, 207; introduction to, 1–5; phenology, introduction to, 5–12; proximities, introduction to, 16–20; question of life during, 218; sources of, 61; stress and, 164–166; unseasonable literature and criticism, 20–28
climate change: in Angus's writings, 217; Australia, impact on, 149; capitalism, relationship to, 207; colonialism, relationship to, 63, 132, 141, 143–144; definition of, 59; as dysphoria, 218; impact on literary almanac, 60; nature of, 84; in realist fiction, 120; Tamil literature and, 110–116; tokenization of frontline communities and poetry, 171
climate fiction: counsel in, 157–158; as genre, question of, 133, 151–159; prescience in, 154–156; resonance in, 156–157; theorization of, 26

climate fiction and the unprecedented, 129–159; climate fiction as genre, question of, 151–159; environmental caesuras, 133–138; introduction to, 129–133; migrations and black swans, 138–145; seasonal hegemony, 145–151
climate justice: climate injustices in Chennai, 101–102; climate justice movement, 189; climate justice rhetoric, 178; forces mitigating against, 19
"Climate of Gender, The" (Angus), 200–201, 213, 218–219
climate science: colonial inheritance of, 77–78; literary canon and, 34–35; misogyny in, 33–34; unpredictability in, 140–141
Climatology of the United States (Blodget), 53
clockwork, 44–47
clouds, pyrocumulonimbus, 141
Coelho, Karen, 105, 108–109
Cohen, Ralph, 152
colonialism: climate change, relationship to, 63, 132, 141, 143–144; colonial nostalgia for white male heroism, 70; colonial surveillance, repeat photography and, 76–77; decolonial occasional performances and anthropogenic time, 180–186; decolonization, seasonal rights and, 210; environmental, 183–184; fumes of, 135; magical realism and, 136; ongoing, of fossil fuel industry, 137; in the Pacific, 168, 172; phenology as symptom of, 40–41; seasonal hegemony in, 145–151; in *The Swan Book*, 144; water distribution in Chennai and, 108–109

colors, speculative futures and, 88–92
commodity biographies, 213
composite year: description of, 25, 32; discussion of, 32–35, 55–58; disruption of, 36; as literary device, 56, 58, 62. *See also* phenological writing and composite year
ConocoPhillips, 78
continuance, 14, 225–226, 227
COP21 (United Nations Conference of the Parties), poetry performances at, 166–167, 175, 176, 178, 181–182, 185–192
corporations: fossil fuel industry, ongoing colonialism of, 137; reclamation of sap season from, 208
Cosme, Antonio, 220, 222
counsel, in climate fiction, 157–158
crisis epistemology, 132
criticism, unseasonable literature and, 20–28
Cullen, Beth, 118
culture(s): climate, relationship to, 13; cultural imperialism, 15; cultural recycling, 227; weathering of, 13
Curley, Allison, 76
cut-leaf Silphium (compass plant), 60
cyclones, 155, 156. *See also* hurricanes
Cygnus atratus (black swans), 138–145, 150

Da Poetry Lounge slam team, 170
Damon, Maria, 176
Darwin, Charles and Francis, 249n21
"Dear Matafele Peinam" (Jetñil-Kijiner), 163–164, 165*f*, 173, 186–188, 191
decolonial occasional performances, 180–186. *See also* colonialism

decolonization, seasonal rights and, 210
deep time, 69, 71–73
DeLoughrey, Elizabeth, 18, 178, 183
Demuth, Bathsheba, 70, 72
Department of Defense, entanglement in repeat photography, 78
desert frogs, 15
Desert Solitaire (Abbey), 247n92
Detroit, Michigan: maple tapping, resumption of, 219–223; trees in, 199–200, 201
Detroit Black Community Food Sovereignty Network, 219, 220
Detroit Sugarbush Project, 220–221, 231
DiChiro, Giovanna, 185
Didur, Jill, 18
differential vulnerabilities, 76
"Difluo Animalis" (Seely), 67–68, 68*f*
digital data, increase in, 91–92
Dillon, Grace, 202
Dimock, Wai Chee, 65
discord, 52
"Dispersion and Average Dates" (Leopold and Jones), 57*f*
Disposition of Nature, The (Wenzel), 18
droughts, water access of renters versus owners during, 109–110
dry spells (*canículas*), 4
D-Town Farm, 219

Early Spring (Seidl), 64
echoes, 18–19
ecocriticism, first wave of, 21
ecological formalism, 13
economic justice, seasonal rights and, 210
"Elegy for a Country's Seasons" (Smith), 1, 229–230, 231
Ellesmere Island, Nunavut: glaciers, sketches of, 76; warmed plots on, 89

Elroy, John, 212–213
emergencies, rhythm of, 192–198
emerging phenology of survival, 12
Emmett, Rob, 12
energy, literary genre and, 22
Engelke, Peter, 84
environment: environmental caesuras, 133–138; environmental change, time-lapse photography and, 83–84; environmental colonialism, 183–184; environmental condensation, 85–86; environmental extremity, connection to rhetorical pressure, 193; environmental field work, 10; environmental injustice, 184; environmental justice movements, 221; environmental literary criticism, form in, 13; environmental observation, connection with literary craft, 10; environmental privilege as term, use of, 2; environmental prosody, 12–16; environmental time, 5, 86; environmental visualizations, 80; environmentalism of Global North versus Global South, 105
Environmental Imagination, The (Buell), 21
Epstein, Andrew, 240n22
ethics, proximal, 19–20
ethnic violence, 231
ethylene, 135–136
European Alps, glacial melt in, 84
Evans, Rebecca, 151
everyday attention, 10
existential threats, 22
expectation (anticipation): form's generation of, 13, 51; of the future, problematic nature of, 66; influences on, 233; rhythms as patterns of, 61

experiential witnesses, 174–180
extraordinary events, in realist fiction, 119
Extreme Ice Survey, 80
extremity, literature of, 167

federations, reclamation of sap season from, 208
fiction, necessity of, 133
Field Notes from a Catastrophe (Kolbert), 71, 82
film, frame rates of, 85
financial precarity, 102, 113. *See also* poverty
Finsterwalder, Sebastian, 73–74
fixed-point observation. *See* repeat photography during Great Acceleration
Forché, Carolyn, 176
form(s): Brooks on, 51; chronic forms, 63; environmental prosody and, 12–16; Levine on, 50, 241n29; of *Water*, 124
fossil fuel industry, ongoing colonialism of, 137
fossil fuels, 78, 84, 134–135, 148
Foster, Warren, 132
Fourth World Collective, 210
Fowler, Alastair, 60
frame rates in photography, 85, 87
France, nuclear testing by, 183
François, Anne-Lise, 22, 207
Freeman, Elizabeth, 215
Frey, Barbara, 34, 243n8
Frye, Northrop, 20–21
Furuhata, Yuriko, 147
Fussell, Paul, 13, 51, 60–61
future, importance of imagining, 232–233

Gan, Elaine, 12, 70, 75
Gapp, Isabelle, 70, 75
Garrard, Rodney, 76

INDEX 303

gay men, in Rouge Park, Detroit, 220
GCCA (Global Call for Climate Action), 166, 169
Gemini Studios, 121–122
gender: Angus on writing about, 215–216; "The Climate of Gender," 200–201, 213, 218–219; gender fluidity, in "Winter of Men," 216–217; gender transition, phenology of, 216; gender transition and seasonality in Angus's writings, 217; organic transgenderism, 217; representation in slam poetry, 170–171. *See also* trans people
general phenomena for May (Thoreau), 39f
genre: question of climate fiction as, 133, 151–159; seasonal associations of, 21–22
Ghosh, Amitav: *The Great Derangement*, 119, 120; *The Hungry Tide*, 155–156; on realist fiction, 119, 120; on realist literature in a climatically altered world, 26
ghost neighbors (*vecinos fantasmas*), 4
"Gift is in the Making, The" (Simpson), 202, 224
glaciers and glacial regions: glacial arrhythmias, 80; glacial retreat, time-lapse photography of, 83; repeat photography of, 73–79; seasonal time in, 72–73; timescales and, 71
Glauert, Ludwig, 146
Gleeson-White, Jane, 258n26
global, use as term, 16–17
Global Call for Climate Action (GCCA), 166, 169
global literatures, climate change in: climate fiction and the unprecedented, 129–159; epilogue to, 229–233; introduction to, 1–28;

keeping time, 199–228; occasional poetry in stressed times, 163–198; phenological writing and composite year, 31–66; repeat photography during Great Acceleration, 67–95; urban phenology and monsoon realism, 99–128
Global North: anthropogenic activity in, 70; climate change, role in, 84; environmentalism of, 105; hopes for self-awareness of, 219; industrial activity of, 95
Global South: environmentalism of, 105; phenological observation in megacities of, 102; urban phenology in, 104–107
globalism and globalization: Aboriginal people and, 144; of slam poetry, 171
González, Grizelle, 6
Goodbody, Alex, 151–152
Gore, Al, 181
Gothic, Colorado, biological laboratory in, 90
Great Acceleration, 41, 69, 84–85, 91. *See also* repeat photography during Great Acceleration
Great Derangement, The (Ghosh), 119, 120
greed, culture of, 102
greenhouse gases, 141
Greenland, phenological mismatch in, 67–68
GreenSky, Hadassah, 221
Griffiths, Devin, 13
Grossman, Sara, 33, 38
Grover, Linda LeGarde, 247n92
Guardian, The: on climate change, 86; Wright op-ed in, 129
Guha, Ramachandra, 105
Gumbs, Alexis Pauline, 134
Gupta, Pamila, 109, 117

habituality of literary rhythms, 13
Haimbe, Mbozi, 23
Halberstam, Jack, 215
Hansen, James, 168
Harlem, New York, phenological observations in, 9–11
Harris, John, 64
harvesting: of acorns, 4; of flowers, 113. *See also* maple sugaring
Hasler, Arthur, 243n6
Hau'ofa, Epeli, 169
Hawitt, Rowan Bayliss, 7
Head, Bessie, 156
health, asthma changes as phenological trace, 12–13
heartbreak, in unseasonable literature, 205
Heglar, Mary Annaïse, 22
Heine, Dwight, 184
Heine, Hilda, 166
Heise, Ursula, 17, 19
Hensley, Nathan, 13
herbariums, 7
Herschel Island (Canadian Yukon), colonialism and, 76–77
Hesiod (Ancient Greek poet), 5
hibernation, 133–134, 137–138
Higginbothams Private Limited (Anglophone bookstore), 119
high (king) tides, 166
Hill of Summer, The (Baker), 247n92
hinges and fillers, 119–120, 124–125
Hobart, Hi'ilei Julia, 169
Hofmeyr, Isabel, 156
Hogue, Rebecca, 175
Holmström, Lakshmi, 121, 122, 124
homelessness (housing precarity, unhousing), 2, 205–206
homo sapiens, climate-related mistiming and, 94–95. *See also* human race
Hottest August, The (Story), 229–233
Houser, Heather, 52, 70, 79, 92

housing precarity (homelessness, unhousing), 2, 205–206
Howden, Mark, 138
Howe, Joshua, 181
Huang, Hsinya, 169
Hui-ch'ung (monk), 8
Hulme, Mike, 13, 56
Human Acts (Kang), 156–157
human race, Thoreau on destruction of, 52. *See also homo sapiens*
humidity, influence of, 45
hummingbirds, 90–91, 92
Hungry Tide, The (Ghosh), 155–156
hurricanes, 15, 86. *See also* cyclones
Hutcheon, Linda, 227–228

ice-geographies, 69
imagination, memory of, 5
imperialism, American, 70
improvement, Thoreau's use of term, 40–41
In a Queer Time and Place (Halberstam), 215
income inequality, 206
Indian Meteorology Department, 101
Indiana, Gary, 223
Indiana, Rita, 153
Indigenous peoples: in Canada, urban gentrification and, 223–224; capitalism's impact on, 138; land theft from, 38; oil theft from, 212. *See also* Aboriginal peoples
Indigenous writing, magical realism in, 136
infrastructure: Byrnes on, 127; energy-intensive, seasonal hegemony and, 148; seasonal infrastructure, 109; of *Water*, 124
Inkpen, Dani, 70, 73
intergovernmental gatherings, occasional poetry and, 27, 181. *See also* COP21

Intergovernmental Panel on Climate Change (IPCC), 56, 141
interlocutionary strategy, 189
interpretive gestures, 153–154
"Intervention, The" (Northern Territory National Emergency Response), 257–258n18
invaders, migrants versus, 143
Iraq, Kurds' acorn harvest, 4
"Island Haze" (Sarmiento), 176

Jagose, Annamarie, 215
Jakobshavn Glacier calving, 79–80
Jameson, Frederic, 120
Jamuna (character in *Water*), 104–107, 109–110, 114–115, 121–125
Japan and the Culture of the Four Seasons (Shirane), 15
Jayaraman, Nityanand, 26, 99–102, 252n1
Jetñil-Kijiner, Kathy: background, 169–170; "Butterfly Thief," 266n81; on climate justice movement, 189; "Dear Matafele Peinam," 163–164, 165f, 173, 186–187, 187–188, 191; the epistolary, use of, 185–186; Hobart on, 169; occasional poetry by, 181; poetry performances by, oral literature and, 172–173; on the spoken word, 172; "Tell Them," 177–178; at UN Climate Summit, 163–164, 165f, 167, 185, 186–188; as voice of climate change, 171
Johnson, Barbara, 189, 191
Johnson, Javon, 176
Johns-Putra, Adeline, 151–152
joinings, 172
Jones, Sara Elizabeth: on climatic impermanence, 54; "Dispersion and Average Dates," 57f; education of, 243n6; evanescence of, 42; importance, 33; on the land, 46; Leopold, correspondence with, 42, 44; mentioned, 25, 231; "A Phenological Record for Sauk and Dane Counties," 50; phenological records of, 41–42; phenology, view of, 51; Thoreaeu's phenological work, study of, 31–32, 38, 41–44
Jordan, June, 170
Journal (Thoreau), 36, 44–45, 53–54
Jue, Melody, 70, 77, 90
justice: economic, seasonal rights and, 210; environmental justice movements, impact of seasonal arrhythmias on, 221; seasonal, 219–223; transnational environmental justice, key challenges to achieving, 19–20. *See also* climate justice
Juvenal, *Satire VI*, 139–140

Kammen, Michael, 202–203
Kanaiyazhi (Tamil literary magazine), *Water* in, 103
Kang, Han, 156–157
Keali'i, D. MacKenzie, 169
Keeling Curve, 178, 182
keeping time, 199–228; adaptation, arts of, 223–228; anti-capitalist practices, 206–213; introduction to, 199–201; justice, seasonal, 219–223; seasonality, unsentimental, 201–206; trans life and seasonality, 214–219
Kelen, Alson, 183
Keller, Lynn, 23
King, Rachael Scarborough, 153
king (high) tides, 166
kinship time, 22–23
Klein, Naomi, 70, 94
knowledge, experiential and embodied knowledges, 174–175
Koch, Elizabeth, 213
Koch, Frederick, 212

Koch method, 212
Koehler, Arthur, 244n31
Koehler, Ethelyn (Mrs. Arthur), 42, 244n31
Kolbert, Elizabeth, 71, 82
Kollywood, 121, 124
ko<u>n</u>rai trees, 111–113
Krzywonos, Stephanie, 70, 73
Kumudimoolai, Tamil Nadu, water sources for, 126–127
Kurds, acorn harvest by, 4
Kwe (character in *Biidaaban*), 210
Kyoto, Japan, change in timing of cherry blossoms, 7

Land Back movement, 209
land theft, in Canada, 200
"Layers" (Siagatonu), 174–175
LeMenager, Stephanie, 37, 154, 208
Leonard, Christopher, 212
Leonard, Keith, 184–185
Leopold, Aldo: almanac form, use of, 49–50, 60; on anthropogenic climate changes, 55; on climatic impermanence, 54; "Dispersion and Average Dates," 57f; editorial pressure on, 48; fame of, 42; Jones and, 31, 42, 44, 243n6; on the land, 46; literary works, influences on, 47; mentioned, 25; "A Phenological Record for Sauk and Dane Counties," 50; phenological records of, 32–35, 41–42; phenology, view of, 51; Thoreau's influence on, 44
Levine, Caroline, 16, 50, 153, 241n29
Library of Ice, The (Campbell), 71
Lichtenstein, Jesse, 177
literature: climate, relationship to, 56, 58; criticism and, unseasonable, 20–28; of extremity, 167; literary adaptation, 227–228; literary almanacs, 59–60; literary craft, connection with environmental observation, 10; literary periodization, 182; literary phenology, actions of, 9; literary prosody, changing demands on, 14–15; literary realism, roles of, 104; literary seasonality, reinvigoration of, 23; oral literature, 172, 173, 189; phenological literature, narrative form of, 58; political ecology of, 18; seasonality and, in the age of climate change, 62; unseasonable criticism and, 20–28; of witness, 176–180. *See also* climate fiction; climate fiction and the unprecedented; poetry
Little Ice Age, 4, 52, 54
lived experience, poetry as confessions of, 176
long-exposure photography, 92–95, 93f, 94f
López, Esvin Rocael, 4
Luciano, Dana, 215
Lutz, David, 222
Lyell, Charles, 53

Macfarlane, R. Ashton, 6
Macfarlane, Robert, 63
Mach, Ernst, 80–81
machine-learning algorithms, 92
MacKenzie, Caitlin McDonough, 7, 172
Madras. *See* Chennai, India
magical realism, 121, 136
Mahindra Group, 125–126
making, urban gentrification and, 223–224
Mandaveli, Chennai, India, 108
Mann, Justin, 210
maple sugaring: anti-capitalist practices and, 206–213; limitations on, 199–200; in Rouge

Park, Detroit, 219–221; as seasonal practice, 27. *See also Biidaaban*; keeping time; *Natural History of Transition, A*
maple syrup: care taken by makers of, 201; hoarding of, 206–207; maple tapping season, changes in timing of, 200, 222
maple trees, 199–200, 214
"Markers of Time" (Seely), 67
Marsh, Selina Tusitala, 172
Marshall Islands, sea-level rise and, 163–164, 166
Marzec, Robert, 80
Massachusetts. *See* Walden Pond
Maurer, Anaïs, 175
McClintock, Anne, 71
McCormack, Michael, 137
McNeill, J.R., 84
"Meditations in Emergency" (Awkward-Rich), 205–206
Melbourne Writers Festival, 138–139
memory, of imagination, 5
Menely, Tobias, 22, 50
"Metra Simulti" (Seely), 92–93, 93f, 94f
metrical contracts, 60–61
migrants, invaders versus, 143
migrations, 138–145
Miles, Melissa, 74
milieu-specific analysis, 77
military: militarized repression, impact of seasonal arrhythmias on, 221; military imperialism in repeat photography, 78. *See also* U.S. Navy
Miller, Daegan, 40–41, 248n8
Miller, William, 246n73
Misek, Richard, 86
misogyny, 33–34, 139
Monk, Samuel, 185
monsoons: derivation of term, 116; impact of delays in, 101–102;
monsoon realism, 119–125; monsoonal rhythms, 116–118; 1969 failure of, 107; uncertainty over, 111. *See also* urban phenology and monsoon realism
Moondru Pillaigal (Narayan), 122
Moretti, Franco, 255n77
Morin, Edgar, 230
Mother Catastrophe (Mother Nature), 23, 130
motor city. *See* Chennai, India
La mucama de Omicunlé (Indiana), 153
Muir, John, 247n92
Muybridge, Eadweard, 249n21
My First Summer in the Sierra (Muir), 247n92
My Years With Boss (Ashokamitran), 122
Myers-Smith, Isla, 25, 69, 76–77
Mylapore, Chennai, India, 108

Narain, Sunita, 17
Narayan, R. K., 122
Narmada Bachao Andolan (Indian movement against megadams), 116
narrative adaptation, 227–228
National Academy of Letters (Sahitya Akademi, India), 116
National Geographic, Balog and, 83
National Petroleum Reserve-Alaska, 78
National Poetry Slam, 168, 170
Native slipstream, 202
Natural History of Transition, A (Angus), 24, 27, 201, 216–217
natural order, recognition of, 55–56
nature writing, relationship to phenological study, 25. *See also* phenological writing and composite year
New Indian Express, interviews with flower vendors, 113

New York Times, on drilling for fossil fuels, 226
New Yorker, environmental time-lapse films and, 82–83
Neyveli Lignite Corporation, 127
Nixon, Rob, 19–20, 187
normativity, environmental overtones in, 214
North with the Spring (Teale), 64
Northern Territory National Emergency Response ("The Intervention"), 257–258n18
Norwegian Refugee Council, 196
nuclear nomads, 183
Nuyorican Poets' Cafe, 168

Oblivia Ethyl(ene) (character in The Swan Book), 133–140, 142–143, 147–151, 158, 257n18
occasion, definitions of, 181
occasional poetry in stressed times, 163–198; decolonial occasional performances and anthropogenic time, 180–186; emergencies, rhythm of, 192–198; experiential witnesses, 174–180; introduction to, 163–173; United Nations, structures of address at, 186–192
oceanic literary community, 169
#OctaviaKnew, 158
Octavia's Parables (Reagon), 157
Offill, Jenny, 153
Ofosu-Bamfo, Bismark, 6
olini (Bay of Bengal current), 100
On Periodicity of Good and Bad Seasons (Russell), 146–147
one-point temporality, 75
Onigamiising: Seasons of an Ojibwe Year (Grover), 247n92
oral literature, 172, 173, 189
Oreskes, Naomi, 55
organic transgenderism, 217

Oxford English Dictionary, on urgency, 192

Pachauri, Rajendra, 181
Pacific literature, characteristics of, 172
"Pacific Salt" (Andrada), 193–194
Pacific Tongues, 169
pālai tradition in Tamil literature, 114
Palayam, S., 26, 99–102, 231, 252n1
Palit, Chittaroopa, 116
Pandian, Anand, 122
Papathanasiou, Peter, 137
paperback books, carbon footprint of, 95
Parable of the Sower (Butler), 157–158
Parantaja (Tuomainen), 153
Paris Agreement, 166, 183
Park, Lisa Sun-Hee, 2
Parks and Recreation (Leopold), 55
Pat-Borja, Melvin Won, 172
Peinam, Matafele, 163–164, 173, 194. See also "Dear Matafele Peinam"
Pellow, David Naguib, 2
Penrith, Australia, local temperatures in, 138
the performative, 181
periodicities, 38, 40, 50
peripeteia, anthropogenic, 63–66
permanent climate, belief in, 52–55
Peruvalluthi, V., 114
petroleum, literary arts and, 212–213. See also fossil fuels
petro-magic-realism, 136
Pfeffer, Wilhelm, 81
phenocams, 79
"Phenological Record for Sauk and Dane Counties, A" (Jones and Leopold), 50
phenological writing and composite year, 31–66; anthropogenic activity's impacts on seasonality and environmental time, 59–62;

anthropogenic peripeteia, 63–66; clockwork and thermometers, 44–47; composite year, discussion of, 55–58; introduction to, 31–36; permanent climate, belief in, 52–55; phenological writing, 47–52; Thoreau's phenological writings, attention to, 36–44
phenology: apocalypse versus, 53; in Australia, unpredicability of, 146–147; change in significance of, 65; emerging phenology of survival, 12; of gender transition, 216; introduction to, 5–12; literary, actions of, 9; literary conventions, resistance to, 65; narrativity of, 66; as national pastime, 38, 40; phenographs, 56; phenological activity, periodicities of, 38, 40; phenological changes, in Chennai, 101; phenological literature, narrative form of, 58; phenological mismatches, 67–68, 68f, 91; phenological records, 42, 63, 65, 101; phenological rhythms in *The Swan Book*, 130; phenological study, relationship to nature writing, 25
phenomena, Thoreau's definition of, 36
photography: anti-capitalist photographic craft, 213; frame rates in, 85, 87; long-exposure photography, 92–95, 93f, 94f; time in, 68–69; time-lapse photography, 79–88. *See also* repeat photography during Great Acceleration
Pillayar Kovali Kullum, search for, 125–128, 125f
Pillsbury, Arthur, 81–82
Pitawanakwat, David, 220
plants, ethylene in, 135

plastic litter, 99
"Plight" (Simpson), 27, 200, 204–205, 208–210, 227
Plum, Hilary, 213
poetry: of climatic witness, 176; ekphrastic, 8; occasional poems, 180–184; poetic address, 191; slam poetry, 164, 168–173, 177, 192; as source for phenology, 8. *See also* occasional poetry in stressed times; prosody
Poetry for the People, 170
Poetry Parnassus Festival, 170
points of view, in repeat photography, 75
polar amplification, 84–85
police: actions against Detroit Sugarbush Project participants, 221; police violence on Herschel Island, 77
politics of articulation, 185
politics of repetition, 223
pollen, 1, 10, 33, 41
postcolonial thought, 18, 142–143
poverty, 2, 175, 215
power: power inequalities, occasional poetry and, 185–186; of stories, 151
Power of Movement in Plants, The (Darwin and Darwin), 249n21
prescience, in climate fiction, 154–156
Primack, Richard, 35, 61, 62, 63
Princeton Encyclopedia of Poetry and Poetics, on prosody, 14–15
Producteurs Acéricoles du Québec, 206–207
progressive identity politics, 177
prophecy, Thoreau's form of, 53
prosody, 12–16, 61
proximities, introduction to, 16–20
Puchner, Martin, 153–154
pyrocumulonimbus clouds, 141

Quan Deyu, 8
queer temporalities, 215

Raboteau, Emily, 9–11, 18
racism, environmental, 180
Raghavan, Sekhar, 101
Raje, Suhaas, 118
Ramanujan, A. K., 99–100, 111–112
Ramaswami, Geetha, 112–113
rates, in climate science, 84
Ravenscroft, Alison, 136
Ravi, M., 125, 256n92
Reagon, Toshi, 157–158
realism: climate realism, of *Water*, 125; magical realism, 121, 136; monsoon realism, 119–125; realist fiction, hinges and fillers in, 119–120, 124; strict, 121. *See also* urban phenology and monsoon realism
recognition, in adaptations, 228
records (documents): on Indian Meteorology Department, 101; Jones's, 41, 65, 66; keeping of, 216; Leopold and Jones on keeping records, 51; phenological, 11, 42, 63, 64–66, 75; scientific, rhythm in, 16; search for, 34; Thoreau's, 31, 212; Thoreau's and Leopold's, 24–25, 33, 35, 44, 64, 66; of U.S. Weather Bureau, 42
"Registry of Periodical Phenomena" (Smithsonian Institution), 38, 40
reindeers, eye color of, 89–90
remembrance, in adaptations, 228
repeat photography during Great Acceleration, 67–95; benefits of, 74; colors and speculative futures, 88–92; fixing of viewpoint of, 76; introduction to, 67–73; limitations of, 75; long-exposure, 92–95; oil theft and, 212; repeat photography, discussion of, 73–79; time-lapse and acceleration, 79–88
repetitions, in a climatically altered world, 223
residential school systems, 210
resonance, in climate fiction, 156–157
Returning North with the Spring (Harris), 64
rhetorical pressure, 193
"Rhythmis: Auroral/Industrial," 93, 94f
"Rhythmis: Tidal/Industrial" (Seely), 93, 93f
rhythm(s): in adaptations, 227; in contemporary poetry, 198; of emergencies, 192–198; of human and nonhuman phenomena, 37; industrial, 93–94, 93f, 94f; in literary works, 13; in "Meditations in Emergency," 205–206; of monsoons in Chennai, 117–118; nature of, 2; in "Pacific Salt," 193; poetic, 194; rhythmic condensation, in time-lapse films, 87–88
Ribbens, Dennis, 49
Rip Van Winkle, 136
Rising: Dispatches from the New American Shore (Rush), 79
Rix, Harriet, 4
Robbins, Bruce, 152
Robin, Libby, 146, 153
Robinson, Angela, 174, 175
Rocky Mountain Biological Laboratory, 90, 91
Rooney, Brigid, 148
roro (Marshall Island oral literature), 173, 189
Rose, Deborah Bird, 131, 140
roses, 2
Rouch, Jean, 230
Rouge Park, Detroit, Michigan, 219–223

Roy, Arundhati, 126
Royal Canadian Mounted Police, 25, 77
Rumble Youth Slam, 170
Rush, Elizabeth, 79-80
Russell, H.C., 146-147

Sabe (character in *Biidaaban*), 202, 204-205, 206, 208, 211
Sacks, Susanna, 171
Sahitya Akademi (National Academy of Letters, India), 116
Saijiki (year-time almanac), 23
Salar (Raboteau's friend), 19
Sand County Almanac, A (Leopold), 32-33, 41, 50, 55
Sangam literature, 115
Sanitation First India, 127
sap season, 200
Saramago, Victoria, 127
Sarmiento, John "Meta," 167, 176
Satire VI (Juvenal), 139-140
Sattelmeyer, Robert, 48
Schulman, Sarah, 223
Schwartz, Charlie, 49
Schwartz, Jessica, 195
scientific authority, rhetorical rejection of, 178
seasonality: in arrhythmic times, 222-223; of carbon dioxide levels, 182; climate versus, 17; as literary/narrative form, 21-22, 47-48; literature and, in the age of climate change, 62; as prevalent form of environmental time, 50; seasonal form, environmental prosody and, 12-16; seasonal hegemony, 145-151; seasonal infrastructures, 107-110; seasonal injustices, tracking of, 11; seasonal justice, 219-223; seasonal literature, before anthropogenic climate change, 202-203; seasonal practices, in anthropogenic times (*See* keeping time); seasonal rhythms, 3-4; seasonal time, alterations to, 1; seasonal writing, 48-49; trans life and, 214-219; unsentimental, 201-206; varied rhythms of, 15. *See also* climate arrhythmias
seasoning, in slave trade, 22
seasons: in Australia, nature of, 130-131; as rhythms, 13; right to, 210. *See also* climate; seasonality
Seasons, The (Thomson), 22, 247n92
SeasonWatch, 112-113
Seely, Christina, 25, 67-68, 68f, 70-71, 92-95, 231
Seidl, Amy, 64
selective perspectivism, 72
Senate Select Committee on Indian Affairs, 212
settler atmospherics, 205
settler state violence, 211
Seymour, Nicole, 217
shadowtimes, 14
Shekhar, Anjana, 115-116
Shepheardes Calendar, The (Spenser), 247n92
Shirane, Haruo, 15
Shockley, Evie, 24
Siagatonu, Terisa, 167, 170, 174-175, 178, 264n32
Sierra Club of Detroit, 220
Silent Spring (Carson), 64
Silliman, Ron, 176
Simmons, Kristen, 205
Simpson, Clinton, 48
Simpson, Leanne Betasamosake: *Biidaaban* and, 200, 201, 204; "Caribou Ghosts & Untold Stories," 202, 205-206; "The Gift is in the Making," 202, 224; mentioned, 27; "Plight," 27, 200, 204-205, 208-210, 227

Sinangån-ta Poetry Slam, 169, 170, 171–172
Singh, Deepti, 118
Singh, Khushwant, 116–117
site-specific weather control, 147
situated witness, 179–180
skill and skilling up, 208
Sky of Our Manufacture, The (Taylor), 156
slam performance, 168, 175–180
slam poetry, 164, 168–173, 177, 192. See also occasional poetry in stressed times
sleeplessness, 24
Sloane, William, 48
Smith, Jen Rose, 69, 70, 72–73
Smith, Zadie: on the climate, 1; on climate arrhythmias, 2, 3, 4; on climate change, effects of, 2, 218; "Elegy for a Country's Seasons," 1, 229–230, 231; on rhythmic disruption, 14; on saying "abnormal," 214; on seasonal rhythms, 3–4; on White Christmases, 4
Smithsonian Institution, "Registry of Periodical Phenomena," 38, 40
social isolation, 232
Sólheimajökull Glacier (Iceland), 83
Somers-Willet, Susan, 177
Somervell, Tess, 21
Song, Min Hyoung, 10, 156–157, 240n22
sounds, of monsoons, 117
speculative futures, 88–92
Spenser, Edmund, 247n92
Spoken Word for the World (poetry competition), 166–167, 169, 170–171, 181
spoken word performances, stress in, 165
Stallings, A. E., 5

state power, impact on occasional poetry, 185
Steer, Philip, 13, 145, 146–147
Stoddard, Mary Caswell, 25, 69, 90–91
stop-motion animation, 225–226. See also *Biidaaban*
stories, power of, 151
Story, Brett, 230–233
Strategic Reserve (of maple syrup), 207
Streeby, Shelley, 151
stressed times. See occasional poetry in stressed times
stress(es), 164–166, 167, 197, 198
strict realism, 121
Strong, Amanda: *Biidaaban*, 27, 200, 201–205, 208–210, 213; *Biidaaban*, sources for, 224; on making *Biidaaban*, 225; mentioned, 27; as photographer, 213
structures of address, at climate summits, 186–192
Su Shih, 8
sugar maples, 199–200
survival, emerging phenology of, 12
Suzuki, Erin, 191
Swan Book, The (Wright): allusiveness of, 151; black swans in, 141–142; burned landscape in, 129–130; climate disorientation in, 147, 150; colonialism in, 144; heartbreak in, 205; mentioned, 26; migrations in, 142–143; narrative voice in, 23; temporal suspension in, 136
Swan Lake (location in *The Swan Book*), 139
Swan Lake (Tchaikovsky), 149–150

Taleb, Nassim, 140–141, 155
Tamil film industry, 121–122
Tamil literature, 99–100, 110–116

Tamil Nadu Progressive Writers and
   Artists Association, 116
Taro Islanders, 187–188
Taylor, Jesse Oak, 155–156
Tchaikovsky, Peter Ilich, 149–150
Teacher-Amma (character in *Water*),
   115, 123
Teale, Edwin Way and Nellie, 64
tear gas, results of inhalation of, 220
technomedia, 79
Tedford, Matthew Harrison, 225
"Tell Them" (Jetñil-Kijiner), 177–178
temperature, phenological rhythms
   and, 45. *See also* climate change
temporality. *See* time
tension, in monsoon rhythms, 118
Thanneer (*Water*, Ashokamitran),
   103–110, 113–116, 118, 121–125
thendi (Bay of Bengal current), 100
thermometers, clockwork and, 44–47
"This Is How We Live Now"
   (Raboteau), 10
Thomson, James, 22, 247n92
Thoreau, Henry David: as American
   Transcendentalist, 50–51;
   commonplace book of, 53; general
   phenomena for May, 39f; on
   human race, destruction of, 52;
   imagined return to Walden Pond,
   61–62; Leopold, influence on, 44;
   literary works, influences on, 47;
   mentioned, 25; on natural order,
   recognition of, 55–56; permanent
   climate, belief in, 52–54;
   phenological observation,
   meaning of, 40–41; phenological
   records of, 31–35, 36–38;
   phenomena, definition of, 36;
   temporal precision, 36–37
Thornber, Karen, 17
350.org, 171
Thyagarajan, Jagadisa. *See*
   Ashokamitran

Thyagarajan, Ramakrishnan, 108
Thyagarajan, Ravishankar, 127
time (temporality): aesthetic
   manipulation of, 83–84;
   anthropogenic, decolonial
   occasional performances and,
   180–186; color, correlation with,
   88–89; compression of, in
   time-lapse photography, 85;
   deep time, 69; environmental,
   influences on, 45; form,
   temporality of, 13; human
   manipulation of, 59; influence of
   temperature on, 45; kinship
   time, 22–23; Native slipstream,
   202; one-point temporality, 75;
   in photography, 68–69; queer
   time, 215; as relational, 45;
   seasonal, in glacial regions,
   72–73; temporal attentions,
   36–44; temporal injury versus
   temporal variation, 215;
   temporal optics, 69; temporal
   precision, Thoreau's, 36–37;
   Thoreau's cyclical model of
   temporality, 53; timescales of
   glaciers, 71. *See also* keeping time
Timefulness (Bjornerud), 71
time-lapse photography, 79–88
Times of India (newspaper), on failure
   of monsoons, 107
timing, in adaptations, 227
Tinker Bell (fairy), 136
Todd, Gary, 223–224
Todd, Zoe, 223–224
Toronto, Canada: rent strikes in, 209;
   trees in, 199
Trail of Tears, 22
trans people: trans life, seasonality
   and, 214–219; trans literature, 27;
   trans men, impact of tear gas on,
   201
transitions, Angus on, 219

transnational environmental justice, 19–20
"Tree Cricket Chirping Record" (Alexander), 42, 43f
trees: arrhythmias of, 111–113; maple trees, 199–200, 214
Trexler, Alex, 151
Triangle Motion Picture Company, 87
Tsing, Anna Lowenhaupt, 13
Tung, Charles, 86
Tuomainen, Antti, 153
Typhoon Haiyan, 193, 196

Under the Sea Wind (Carson), 247n92
unhousing (homelessness, housing precarity), 2, 205–206
United Kingdom (UK), nuclear testing by, 183
United Nations (UN): Pacific Islander testimony before, 183; structures of address at, 186–192; UN Non-Governmental Liaison Service, 170; UN Trust Territory, 168; United Nations Climate Summit (2014), 163–164, 165f; United Nations Conference of the Parties (COP21, 2014, 2015), poetry performances at, 166–167, 175, 176, 178, 181–182, 185–192
United States: Borgeson's witnessing of, 179–180; fossil fuels, drilling for, 226; imperialism of, 70; maple tapping season in, changes to, 222; nuclear testing by, 183–184; Senate Select Committee on Indian Affairs, 212
the unprecedented: in *The Swan Book*, 137; as term, use of, 131–132; unprecedented seasons, mentioned, 26. *See also* climate fiction and the unprecedented
the unseasonable. *See* global literatures, climate change in

unseasonable literature (unseasonable writing): heartbreak in, 205; seasonality in, 24; temporal ruptures in, 24
urban phenologists, Jamuna as, 104–105
urban phenology and monsoon realism, 99–128; climate change and Tamil literature, 110–116; Global South, urban phenology in, 104–107; introduction to, 99–104; monsoon realism, 119–125; monsoonal rhythms, 116–118; Pillayar Kovali Kullum, search for, 125–128; seasonal infrastructures, 107–110
urgency: in activist writing, 192–193; distress and, 197
Urur Kuppam, Chennai, India, urban phenological practices in, 99–100
U.S. Navy: historical photographs taken by, 25; oil prospecting by, 78
utilitarian almanacs, 59
Uttarakhand, India, automatic photography in, 79

Vaadai naal (Bay of Bengal winds and currents), 100
Van Winkle, Rip, 136
vanni (Bay of Bengal current), 99
vecinos fantasmas (ghost neighbors), 4
Venkatachalapathy, A. R., 116, 121
ventriloquism, in poetic address, 191
Verghese, Jacob, 113
vertebrates, assisted colonization of, 258n20
videopoems. *See* "Pacific Salt"; "Yolanda Winds"
Ville-Marie, Canada, 216
Vinothkumar, M., 114
Vishu celebrations, 112–113
Vizenor, Gerald, 258n27
Vlamingh, Willem Hesselsz de, 140

vulpes lagopus (arctic fox), 67–68, 68f, 70–71

Walcott, Derek, 4–5
Walden (Thoreau), 42, 45–48
Walden Pond, 46–47
Walls, Laura Dassow, 65
Water (Thanneer, Ashokamitran), 26, 103–110, 113–116, 118, 121–125
water pipes, tail-ends of, 108–109
water scarcity. See *Water*
waterlines, 105–106
weather: cyclones, 155, 156; extreme, acceleration of, 86; hurricanes, 86. See also climate; climate change; seasons
Weather (Offill), 153
"weather or not" (Shockley), 24
Web of Science database, 6
Well-Wrought Urn, The (Brooks), 51
Wendt, Albert, 172
Wenzel, Jennifer, 18, 136, 213
West Mambalam, Chennai, India, water shortages in, 108–109
western swamp tortoises, 258n20
White, Hayden, 65
White Christmases, 4
Whyte, Kyle Powys, 22–23, 132
Wikwemikong First Nations Reserve, 220
Willow Project, 78
Wilson, Rob, 169
Wilson, Stephen, 185
"Winter of Men" (historical fiction), 216–217

Wisconsin. *See* Jones, Sara Elizabeth; Leopold, Aldo
Wolff, Tristram, 47
Wolkovich, Elizabeth, 59
women, as slam poets, 170–171
Works and Days (Hesiod), 5
world literature, Wright on, 151
World Poetry Slam, 168
Wright, Alexis: on black swans, 158; on compositional quandaries, 158–159; *Guardian* op-ed by, 129; on "The Intervention," 258n18; at Melbourne Writers Festival, 138–139; mentioned, 26; narrative voice of, 23; on seasons, 131; the unprecedented, use of term, 131; on winter dioramas in the Christmas house, 149; on world literature, 151. See also *The Swan Book*

Yaftabad (Tehran neighborhood), 19
Yamamoto, Namiko, 23
year-time almanac (*Saijiki*), 23
"Yolanda Winds" (Borgeson), 179, 196–198
Yosemite National Park, time-lapse photography and, 81–82
Yousafzai, Malala, 171
Youth Speaks Hawai'i, 169
Yusoff, Kathryn, 70, 72

Zalamea, Marcela, 6
ziigwan (early spring), 201–202
Zimmerman, Jim, 54

Printed in the USA
CPSIA information can be obtained
at www.ICGtesting.com
JSHW020053231124
74143JS00018B/291